Wines and Spirits

Foods of the World

Wines and Spirits

by

Alec Waugh

and the Editors of

TIME-LIFE BOOKS

photographed by Arie deZanger

TIME-LIFE BOOKS, NEW YORK

THE AUTHOR: Alec Waugh *(far left)* was 19 when his first novel, *The Loom of Youth,* was published in 1917, and he has been writing ever since—more than 50 books including *My Brother Evelyn and Other Reminiscences* and *In Praise of Wine.* He divides his time between the U.S., Morocco, the Riviera and his native England, and never stops expanding his knowledge of food and drink.

THE CONSULTANTS: Sam Aaron *(left)* is the guiding spirit at Sherry-Lehmann, Inc., the wine merchants on Madison Avenue in New York. He has written extensively on wines and spirits and has lectured at universities in America and England. The technical consultant was Alexis Bespaloff *(far left).* He spent two years in Bordeaux representing an American importing firm, has written about wines for American and British magazines and, as a professional, tastes and evaluates a thousand different wines each year. André Gros-Daillon *(left),* a native of Paris, has retired to Northport, Long Island, after a career spent "behind the bars" at many distinguished establishments including the Carlton in Cannes, the Paris Ritz, Ciro's in Monte Carlo and—for 26 years—Le Pavillon in New York. He supervised the testing of all drink recipes in the Recipe Booklet.

THE CONSULTING EDITOR: Michael Field, once a concert pianist, is a foremost American food expert, teacher of cooking and author-critic on the culinary arts. His current best-selling book is *Michael Field's Culinary Classics and Improvisations.*

THE PHOTOGRAPHER: Arie deZanger went to major wine areas of the world, and then spent a month in the test kitchen, taking pictures for this volume. He has photographed many other books including Bil Baird's *The Art of the Puppet.*

THE COVER: A glass of Zinfandel wine from California and a glass of whisky from Scotland stand together as symbols of the subject matter of this book.

TIME-LIFE BOOKS

EDITOR
Maitland A. Edey
EXECUTIVE EDITOR
Jerry Korn
TEXT DIRECTOR
Martin Mann
ART DIRECTOR
Sheldon Cotler
CHIEF OF RESEARCH
Beatrice T. Dobie
PICTURE EDITOR
Robert G. Mason
Assistant Text Directors: Harold C. Field, Ogden Tanner
Assistant Art Director: Arnold C. Holeywell
Assistant Chief of Research: Martha Turner

PUBLISHER
Rhett Austell
Associate Publisher: Walter C. Rohrer
General Manager: Joseph C. Hazen Jr.
Planning Director: John P. Sousa III
Circulation Director: Joan D. Manley
Marketing Director: Carter Smith
Business Manager: John D. McSweeney
Publishing Board: Nicholas Benton, Louis Bronzo, James Wendell Forbes

FOODS OF THE WORLD

SERIES EDITOR: Richard L. Williams
EDITORIAL STAFF FOR WINES AND SPIRITS:
Associate Editor: James Wyckoff
Picture Editor: Iris S. Freidlander
Designer: Albert Sherman
Staff Writers: George Constable, Geraldine Schremp, Ethel Strainchamps, Carolyn Tasker, Peter Yerkes
Chief Researcher: Helen Fennell
Researchers: Sarah Bennett, Linda Ferrer, Penny Grist, Helen M. Hinkle, Helen Isaacs, Julia Johnson, Barbara Leach, Ann McLeod, Audry Weintrob, Arlene Zuckerman
Art Assistants: Elise Hilpert, Gloria du Bouchet
Test Kitchen Chef: John W. Clancy
Test Kitchen Staff: Fifi Bergman, Sally Darr, Leola Spencer

EDITORIAL PRODUCTION
Color Director: Robert L. Young
Assistant: James J. Cox
Copy Staff: Marian Gordon Goldman, Eleanore Karsten, Florence Keith
Picture Department: Dolores A. Littles, Joan T. Lynch

The text for the chapters of this book was written by Alec Waugh; the recipe instructions by Michael Field and Helen Isaacs; the picture essays and appendix material by members of the staff. Valuable assistance was provided by the following individuals and departments of Time Inc.: Editorial Production, Robert W. Boyd, Jr.; Editorial Reference, Peter Draz; Picture Collection, Doris O'Neil; Photographic Laboratory, George Karas; TIME-LIFE News Service, Richard M. Clurman; Correspondents Maria Vincenza Aloisi *(Paris),* Jean Bratton *(Madrid),* Margot Hapgood *(London),* Ann Natanson *(Rome).*

Contents

The Recipe Booklet that accompanies this volume was designed for use in the kitchen or home bar. It contains recipes for mixed drinks, for hors d'oeuvre and canapés. It also has a wipe-clean cover and a spiral binding so that it can either stand up or lie flat when open.

Learning the Joys of Wine, the Pleasures of Spirits

The wine lover need not know and usually does not care that a peeled ripe peach, pricked 99 times with a fork, revolves slowly in a bubbling glass of cold champagne. Nor does it matter to him that this is a delectable summer drink called *Stachelschwein*, "the porcupine," in the Rhineland, where it is popular. Such knowledge is reserved for the bookworm. As for the neophyte among wine lovers, there are thousands of other pieces of information (of great or little importance) that lie ahead of him. As he gets into the subject, he will find greater enjoyment in the beers and wines and spirits of his choice when he knows something of the history and characteristics of each type and its place of origin.

Everyone has his own point of departure in such an exploration. For the author of this book it was his family home in England. For me, it was far from home in Belgium. I still remember that I first enjoyed the experience of tasting wine in Brussels, at a little restaurant on the Quai du Bois à Bruler. It was right after World War I, in January 1920, and I had painfully learned, as an American student in a Belgian school, how little the postwar American relief effort in Europe was appreciated by its beneficiaries. But one Sunday my mother took me to lunch and let me have a small glass of an excellent young and fruity Moulin-à-Vent. My homesickness for New York was drowned right then in this one first glass of a light French wine. It launched me on a life that has been filled by love of the unlimited variety of the vintages of the world.

Much later, spending most of World War II in Spain and Portugal, both great wine-producing countries, I had many opportunities to enjoy local vintages from north to south, from the Atlantic to the Mediterranean. (French and German wines were completely unavailable in this area at the time.) I had a small *quinta*, or vineyard, at Colares, near Lisbon, where the Ramisco grape grows deep in the sand dunes of the coastal plain—so deep, in fact, that these vines never suffered from the killing phylloxera plague of the 19th Century. The wines of Colares are unusual in being virtually the only European vintages that are still made from the ancient vines of Europe, vines that do not need to be grafted onto phylloxera-resistant American roots. I got to know other Portuguese table wines very well. As a student in Spain I had gained a rather thorough knowledge of the wines of that country; now I had the opportunity of tasting most of these wines in the course of thousands of miles of travel. Including port, to be sure. In *The Romance of Wine*, the noted English author H. Warner Allen describes port as "the wine of philosophy." This may well be true; the great wines of the Douro are perfect for after-dinner conversation, for they create the mellow mood that encourages the exchange of ideas.

It does not matter much whether the first wines we savor are those of Australia or South Africa, whether the table wines of a family come from Italy or Chile or California. The important thing is that we take the time to read and learn as well as drink. Knowledge, along with constant tasting, can bring an appreciation of why and where and how we should enjoy our wines and spirits. There are many interesting differences to learn about. A brandy from Cognac and one made in Armagnac, for example, are both brandies—but being distilled in different ways and aged in different kinds of casks, they are quite different in taste. A whisky made in Scotland is very different from the product of Ireland or our own American ryes and bourbons. It is perhaps not surprising that table wines differ when made from different grapes; but it is remarkable that the dry white Blanc-Fumé wines of the Loire Valley are very different from the sweet white Château d'Yquem and other wines made from the *same* grape in the Gironde Valley just to the south. . . .

For the person who envies the evident joys his friends derive from choosing and drinking the right wine in the right place at the right time, this book will be a valuable guide. In its civilized text and its glorious photographs, it can lead the wine lover, in the guise of taking him through an elaborate dinner, to learn about the vineyards of the world in an easily understandable way, making of it what our elders called a *vade mecum*, a "go with me" to the cellar, to the table and into the glass.

The fluid style of the book and the attractiveness of its presentation must not lead anyone to the erroneous idea that wines and liquors can be enjoyed just by reading. Read on, of course, and sip on; and above all else, learn by sampling and the interchange of opinions that what is offered you locally or from the most vaunted vineyard may be but the introduction to a richly rewarding experience of life.

H. Gregory Thomas
Grand Sénéchal, Confrérie des
Chevaliers du Tastevin
Grand Maître, Commanderie de Bordeaux

I

Of Grape and Grain

Man has been accorded by a kindly nature four stout companions to sustain and console him on his terrestrial pilgrimage. They are wine, spirits (such as whiskey and gin), fortified wines (such as sherry, which contains added alcohol) and beer.

These drinks provide the solace, relaxation and stimulus that a man needs if he is to complete with equanimity his arduous and often arid journey. The golfer standing on the 18th tee gathers his strength at the prospect of the cooling gin and tonic or beer that awaits him in 10 minutes' time whether or not that final putt has won him the game; the businessman exhausted at the end of the day by the noise of the telephone and the typewriter anticipates the first cold sip of the Martini when he reaches home. How many marriages have been saved by the quiet 40 minutes that husband and wife spend with their predinner cocktails talking over the day's events; these are the recompense for the daily stint.

The highball, the cocktail and the glass of beer have helped so many of us to unwind, to make the transition from one kind of moment to another, totally different one. Wine, on the other hand, fills a somewhat different aspect of our need. It is for a different time, a different place from the stronger beverages. Wine may safely be said to be more subtle.

For wine enormously enhances the pleasures of the table. "A meal without wine is a day without sunshine," is a popular French saying. A meal accompanied by wine is taken slowly; it has to be, since wine must be sipped. It cannot be quaffed. And there should be a long pause between sips, so that the bouquet can linger on the palate and the wine can

The ancient arts of the vintner, and all his labors, are dedicated to the moment when the wine is opened and poured, to be sipped and enjoyed. Here, in the window of an Alsatian restaurant *(opposite)*, two freshly poured glasses of a fine, dry Riesling (1964 Reserve Hugel) stand ready to drink, shimmering through the tinted panes.

8

spread its beneficent warmth through every vein and nerve cell; you are in no hurry to take the next mouthful; you let the magic of that last sip remain. And as you are in no hurry to eat or drink, you have time to talk. The conversation mellows. You have a genial fellow feeling toward mankind in general and your present company in particular. And wine aids the digestive processes, from the very fact that it prevents hurried eating.

Although there are many reasons why a man could wish to have lived in another century rather than in our own, none of them concerns wines and spirits. There has never been a time such as the present when those who wish for alcoholic beverages have had such a variety of choice. The best of everything is available. We have only to decide how to make good use of it, and the purpose of this book is to give as much elementary information as can be contained within its limits, to offer some guidance and to deliver one or two cautionary words, it being always remembered that there are no rules of taste, that the preference for one libation over another is individual.

At the same time, there is such a thing as an educated palate. By tasting one wine against another you come to realize why the connoisseurs will rate the wines of one year and district above those of another, why one whiskey is preferred over another. If you do not agree with the connoisseurs, that cannot be helped. The great thing is to find out what you like yourself, in the same way that you read the books you yourself like, not just those that appear at the top of the bestseller list or get the highest rating from the critics. Moreover, preferences change with time. I am now in my 70th year, and I find that I like champagne more than I used to; it does something for me now that it did not do when I was 25. I did not drink Scotch whisky before I was 35, but now I like to have a Scotch and soda in the evening before I go upstairs to have my bath and change for dinner. I used to drink vintage port every night after dinner and very often after lunch. Now I prefer the smoother tawny port—provided it is very good tawny.

Tastes differ and tastes change, but there are certain rules about the care and serving of wines and spirits that have been drawn up as the result of long and widespread experience. They should be memorized, for they add greatly to the drinker's enjoyment. They are part of the rich mixture of custom, legend and technical fact that make the subject of spirituous potables so pleasant to read about.

Ancient and Ubiquitous.   Wine is the most natural article in the world. It can be made from fruits, grains, flower petals and other substances, but we shall concern ourselves here with wine made from grapes. The process can be absurdly easy. If bunches of grapes are put in a bowl, the weight of the top grapes will break the skins of the bottom grapes, and in a short time the resultant juice will start to ferment into wine.

The chemistry of fermentation is basic to the making of all alcoholic beverages, but for our purposes only a few of its details need to be understood. It is a process by which yeast acts on sugar, converting it first into alcohol and carbon dioxide gas and then, unless it is protected from the air, into vinegar. In the making of beer, it is malted barley and other starchy cereals such as corn or rice that are fermented, after being fla-

vored with hops; the resulting drink contains both alcohol and carbon dioxide (the fizz). In the making of wine, sugar ferments and becomes alcohol, and the carbon dioxide is usually allowed to escape, leaving what is known as still wine. Most wines that accompany food are still wines.

It is possible to ferment any liquid containing sugar by adding yeast, but wine makes itself; it has no need for human intervention. Innumerable yeast molds hover in the air above the vineyards and settle upon the grapes. The sugar that is already in the grape juice provides the alcohol. The sweeter the grapes, the higher the alcoholic content of the wine. When fermentation is complete, the wine is left in casks to mature; that is to say, its flavor and special quality are allowed to develop with time. It is seemingly quite simple.

And yet the making of really good wine is an infinitely complicated procedure, for it depends not only on the chemistry of fermentation but also on the kinds of grapes that are used and precisely where they are grown. The type of vine from which wine can best be made—the *Vitis vinifera*—flourishes in what might be described as two broad belts, one north and the other south of the equator. The one above the equator includes the vineyards of France, Germany, Italy and the United States, as well as Algeria and many other countries that produce wine but are not especially noted for it. The belt that stretches below the equator includes South Africa, Australia, Chile and Argentina.

Wine grapes grow best in the world's temperate zones, between latitudes that are shown on this map as broad belts of yellow. Only a few regions with important vineyards (*indicated in red*) lie outside these belts.

Continued on page 14

11

A Gallery of Wine Grapes

The flavor of wine starts on the vine—and though any of the 8,000 or so known varieties of grapes can be fermented, only about 50 produce first-rate wines. All these grapes belong to the species *Vitis vinifera*, cultivated for thousands of years in the Old World and transplanted a few centuries ago to California. Pictured here are the most honored and widely grown. They range in color from yellow to green (white grapes) and from red to blue-black (black grapes). Red wines and rosés are made from black grapes; their skins color the fermenting juice or "must." White wine may be made from either black or white grapes; the trick is to take the skins out before the juices can begin to ferment. Both white and black grapes may be sweet or tart, and many change flavor when fermented—which makes selecting great grapes a great art.

PALOMINO: Developed around Jerez de la Frontera, Spain, this grape is the basis for almost all sherry made there and in California.

GAMAY: Prized for red wines in Beaujolais, the fickle Gamay yields only ordinary wine in the rest of France and in California.

CARIGNAN: Thriving in the south of France and California, this hot-climate grape makes robust table wine and heady dessert wine.

CHARDONNAY (OR PINOT CHARDONNAY): The only grape that French law permits to be used in Chablis, it is also grown for champagne.

SÉMILLON (POURRITURE NOBLE): In its overripe state of *pourriture noble*, or noble rot, this grape produces the classic Sauternes dessert wine.

SÉMILLON: In its normally ripened state, this grape yields dry white wines. It is grown in the Graves district and in California.

ZINFANDEL: Most widely planted of all red-wine grapes in California, this mystery vine, its origin unknown, produces a zesty wine.

SAUVIGNON BLANC: Cultivated in Bordeaux, this grape is used in the dry white wine of Graves and the sweet wine of Sauternes.

PINOT BLANC: Grown widely in France, Germany and Italy, it produces dry white wines and is used in some champagnes.

SYLVANER: Cultivated from Alsace to Austria, from Chile to California, this abundant and fast-ripening grape makes fine light white wines.

TRAMINER: Favored in the Rhine, Alsace and the Italian Tyrol, it has a pronounced spicy aroma both as a grape and as a wine.

RIESLING: Esteemed for white wines, it is the choice grape of the Rhine. In the U.S. the authentic varieties are white and Johannisberg.

CABERNET SAUVIGNON: Celebrated as the vine of the great clarets of Bordeaux, it also makes some of the best California red wine.

CHENIN BLANC: Source of the Vouvray white wine of the Loire Valley, this is the only grape permitted in the Anjou whites.

PINOT NOIR: Famed as the grape from which red Burgundy is made, this "noblest vine of all" is also used in the best champagnes.

GRENACHE: Unexcelled in the *vin rosé* of the Rhône Valley, such as Tavel, this grape is used in California for rosé and some port.

13

It might be supposed that the vine that produces so rich and tasteful a potation requires especially fertile soil, but this is not the case. The ground that produces champagne at Épernay, in France, is chalky; in the Moselle Valley in Germany the vines sprout from slate; the great wines of Bordeaux are nurtured in gravel, sand and clay. On the whole it would seem that the best wines are grown on slopes, but it is one of the mysteries of wine that you cannot tell for certain what wine will be produced from a certain soil. One vineyard will produce great vintages, while the wine of another, only a few yards away, will be good enough only for a *vin compris table d'hôte:* a simple table wine. Wine has always held a mystery for man, and maybe that is one of its attractions.

Archeologists maintain that grape wine was made 10,000 years ago. It has been suggested that honey was fermented even earlier. Honey wine—fermented honey and water, flavored with herbs—is the drink called mead, which is often erroneously said to be an early kind of beer. Some authorities also hold that palm and date wine preceded grape wine. At any rate, wine is mentioned many times in the Bible. One of the first things Noah did after leaving the ark was to plant a vineyard. And, of course, wine is spoken of in the New Testament.

We know also that the Egyptians had beer as well as wine, and made them both much as we do today; their wall paintings show this to be so. Then, as now, the grape vines were arranged on pergolas, or arched trellises, although the Egyptians made their supports higher than do vintners in most countries today. It is necessary that the grapes receive by day the sun's rays reflected by the earth, and by night the warm exhalations of the sun-soaked earth. If the heat is very great, as it is in Egypt, then the grapes must be set higher.

The Greeks, like their more ancient neighbors to the east, cultivated grapes carefully and honored the wine they yielded. We know through literature a great deal about the drinking customs of the Greeks. We know for instance that they nearly always mixed their wine with water, reserving till the end of the meal a few mouthfuls of pure wine to be sipped. This custom has led many people to believe that the wine drunk by the ancient Greeks would be unpalatable by modern standards. However, H. Warner Allen, one of wine's noted scholars, is convinced that the Greeks put water in their wine only because they were a highly temperate people, with their motto of "nothing in excess," and also because they enjoyed the taste of water. They were proud of their springs and would compare the water of one spring with that of another in the same way that a modern gourmet will compare two vintages.

Aging and Distillation.   The Greeks kept their wine in a clay cylinder called an amphora. Because these amphorae were not porous, the wine inside them could mature undisturbed without being affected by the air. The Romans, who followed the Greeks, at first had inferior amphorae; they were porous and the wine evaporated. But the Romans then developed the art of pitching, or coating the inside of the amphora with tar to prevent evaporation, and they, too, matured their wine. They set store by their ability to distinguish between one vintage and another. Although, like the Egyptians and Greeks before them, they knew nothing of the chem-

Fermenting Grapes into Wine

Nearing harvest time, a cluster of Cabernet Sauvignon grapes ripens at the Château Mouton-Rothschild vineyard in the Médoc area of Bordeaux. At the center of this closeup, the grapes have been wiped free of the waxy film that collects from the air the natural yeasts essential to the fermentation process.

Checking grapes before the harvest, a cellar master determines their acid content with field testing equipment. The amount of acid present is one of the factors controlling the rate at which the yeasts on the surface of the grapes convert the sugar within them into alcohol, carbon dioxide and a variety of other compounds.

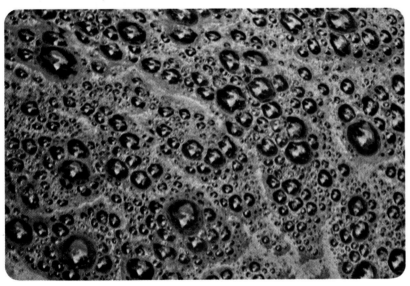

After the grapes are crushed, their pulp and juice ferment in a vat, producing the wine and giving off bubbles of carbon dioxide gas. The fermentation time depends on the type of grape being used and the wine being made. The process may be stopped after a few days or continued for more than three months.

15

istry of fermentation, they understood that good wine improves with age.

The Romans marked their amphorae with the name and date of the reign of the consul in office at the time of bottling. Opimian wine—bottled when Opimius was consul, in 121 B.C.—was the most prized. A century later, in the days of Augustus Caesar, Opimian was no longer for sale in the open market and was to be found only in private cellars. In the *Satyricon* it is Opimian that Trimalchio, a vulgar *nouveau riche*, serves to his guests:

"Presently came in two long-haired blacks, with small leather bottles such as are used for the sprinkling of sand on the stage, and gave us wine to wash our hands in, but no one offered us water. . . . Thereupon large double-eared vessels of glass close plastered over were brought up, with labels round their necks, upon which was this inscription: 'Opimian muscadine of a hundred years old.'

"While we were reading the titles, Trimalchio clapped his hands, 'Alas, alas,' said he, 'that wine should live longer than man.' Wine is life and we'll try it if it has held good since the consulship of Lucius Opimius or not; 'tis right Opimian and therefore make ready. I bought not so good yesterday, yet there were persons of better quality supped with me."

The Dark Ages supervened: dark not only in terms of culture and scholarship, but dark—stygianly dark—for the wine lover, because he was deprived of mature wine. The amphora had vanished; the French had not mastered—perhaps had not bothered to master—the art of pottery making, and the wooden cask took the place of the airtight cylinder. The cask was porous, there was evaporation, and air got at the wine, admitting bacteria that soon turned it into vinegar. This does not mean that there was not a great deal of highly palatable wine available. One of the fallacies concerning wine is the belief that it inevitably matures in bottle. This is not the case. No spirits do, and the only fortified wines that do are Madeira and vintage port. Champagne may, but often does not. The really great wines of the Médoc and the Côte d'Or, however, do not reach their peak for several years. Until comparatively recent times, that is to say, no great wine existed, because it occurred to no one to look for an equivalent for the amphora.

The wines and liquors that did exist found a receptive public. In Elizabethan times, nobody drank water. It was not fit to drink. Beer and ale were drunk at breakfast and at midday, wine in the evening. Wine was abundant and cheap. It was young wine, shipped in wood and drawn from the wood. Bottles existed then, but corks did not. Corks did not appear till James I's day, in the early 17th Century. Bottles were used only to carry wine from the cellar to the table. They were carafes more than bottles. Nobody wanted old wine. Young wine, a year old and freshly broached, was highly prized. The emptying of a cask did not take long: although the population of England was a tenth of what it is today, more wine was imported into England then. It was wine to be quaffed, not sipped. There was, however, a wine that was sipped—sherris-sack from Jerez in Spain, which Falstaff so eloquently loved. Sack was different because it had been fortified with spirits, that is, distilled alcohol had been added to the wine. Its arrival in England shortly before Shakespeare's day marks a high moment in the chronicle of the amenities of the table.

The dosage of alcohol that converted Jerez wine into sherry had to be made by distillation. We cannot be sure exactly when the secret of this technique was first discovered. But it is usually conceded that we of the West owe it to the Arabs. The principle of the process is very simple. Alcohol becomes a gas at a lower temperature than water does; its boiling point is 176° F. whereas the boiling point of water is 212° F. If an alcohol-water mixture is heated to 200°, its alcohol boils off while the water remains behind, then by means of an apparatus that gathers and cools, the alcoholic vapors can be recondensed into liquid alcohol. What had been a mixture of water and alcohol has now been separated into pure water and pure alcohol.

The ancient world was vaguely aware of distillation. Pliny describes a method of distilling spirits of turpentine from resin by cooking it in a pot covered with a fleece of wool, the spirits being squeezed out of the wool afterward. Aristotle stated in his *Meteorology* that "sea water can be made potable by distillation, wine and other liquids can be submitted to the same process." But it did not occur to the Greeks and Romans to subject their own wines to this experiment; they were content with what they had, and in that maybe showed reason, for spirits were not needed in the hot Mediterranean littoral. The Chinese, however, had produced a distilled spirit from rice beer; the East Indians had made arak from rice and sugar, while the Celts in Eire and the Highlands were producing a crude kind of whiskey that they called *uisgebaugh*—water of life. A curious appellation for a concoction that many have maintained imperils man's prospects not only in this world but the next. But from this raw, distilled liquid came malt whisky and the other great whiskeys we know today.

The Arabs, who knew about distillation, were forbidden alcohol for religious reasons, and they did not distill alcoholic beverages. But they relished the perfumes that they distilled from flowers, and it was almost certainly from them that the Spaniards of Andalusia learned the technique of distillation. Jerez marked the frontier between the Moors and Christians; that is why it is called Jerez de la Frontera, and it is here that the first fortified wine, sherry, was made.

Sherry reached England in the early 16th Century and immediately proved immensely popular. The addition of alcohol had stabilized it for travel. It did so even when the wine was stored in casks, and there was still no incentive to find an equivalent for the classical amphora. Not until the close of the 18th Century was it discovered that a bottle, firmly corked and laid on its side so that the cork would be kept in contact with the wine, would fulfill the functions of the amphora.

Surprisingly enough it was the Portuguese, not the French, who made this discovery, and the story of how it came about is an example of the adage that good sometimes comes out of evil. In 1688 when William of Orange staged "the glorious Revolution," captured the English Crown and drove James II to exile in the court of Louis XIV of France, he brought with him to his new responsibilities a firm resolve to damage the French economy as far as lay within his power. How could he better achieve this purpose than by hindering one of its most important exports, wine? He placed such a heavy duty on French wines and spirits that it put them out of reach of all except the richest of his subjects; then so that his sub-

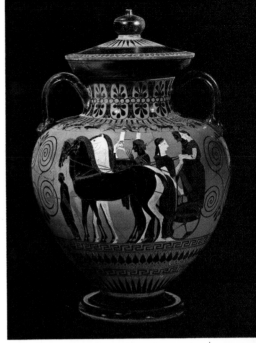

The ancient Greeks, and later the Romans, prized wine of good vintage, and used special containers like this one from Sixth Century Greece to age it. Called amphorae, these tall, two-handled covered jars were made of a nonporous terra cotta, which kept out air that would turn the wine to vinegar before it could mature. Later the secret of the amphora was lost, and it was almost 1,500 years before the technique of protecting wine from air by corking bottles was found—enabling wine lovers again to choose vintages mellowed with age.

Continued on page 24

The Unhurried Techniques and Unstinting Care That Make Great Wines

While present-day vintners might be happy to adopt modern laborsaving devices and machinery, the wine-making process in most instances refuses to be hastened. Some age-old devices, like this *lagar*, or press *(opposite)*, long used in the making of sherry in southern Spain, are virtually extinct. In times past, workmen would pile the white Palomino grapes grown in the vicinity of Jerez into a wooden trough, trample juice out of them with their boots, pile the final pulp under the press, wrap it with woven coils of esparto grass, and then laboriously squeeze out the remaining juices by hand. Today this *lagar* has been replaced by mechanical presses, but before the pressing the grapes are still slowly dried in the warm Spanish sun, and before the sherry is finally bottled, many wine makers remove impurities from it by a process called "fining," in which a mixture of wine and egg whites, beaten with a brush of sticks *(below)*, is poured into wine casks to carry sediments to the bottom—a method in use since Roman times.

Overleaf: Picked by hand, clusters of sherry-producing Palomino grapes are spread to dry on esparto mats.

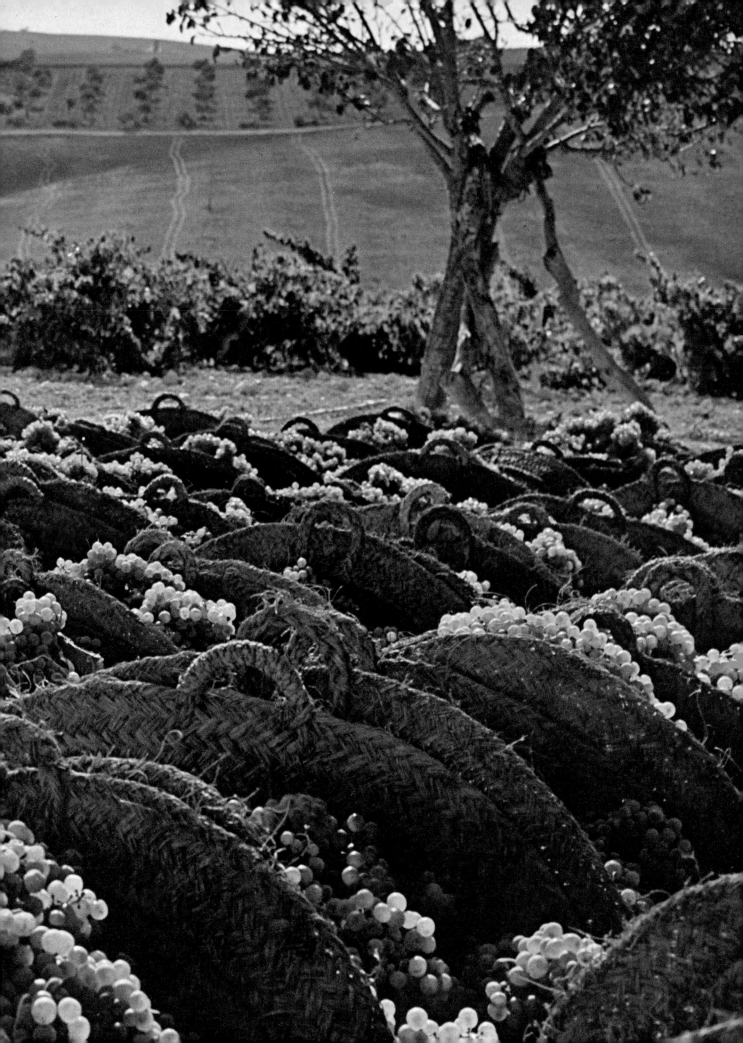

Traditional Tests for
Taste, Color and Clarity

Like many wines, sherry is aged in oak barrels in dim, cool cellars—and like all wines, it is periodically tested and sampled for quality, often by centuries-old techniques that modern technology manages only to supplement. The color and clarity of sherry are checked even today by placing a glass of the wine before a candle's flame, although the candle is now seldom housed in a wooden box like the antique shown at left. Still in use in the sherry country of Spain is a device called a *venencia* (opposite)—a flexible shaft of whalebone fitted with a silver cup at its tip. To take samples, the taster inserts the instrument in the bunghole of a cask, thrusts it down past the *flor*, or yeast, on the surface of the still-fermenting wine to fill the cup, withdraws the *venencia* and then, with great verve and skill, holds it high in the air to fill the traditionally tulip-shaped sherry glasses.

jects should not be deprived of wine altogether, he made a deal with Portugal known as the Methuen Treaty, which admitted Portuguese wines into the country at a minimal cost. It seemed to William a brilliant scheme; unfortunately he had not realized that a public that had acquired a palate for the pure clean wines of France simply could not swallow the harsh and bitter wines from Lisbon and Oporto. In 1693 a sad piece of verse was published in London called *Farewell to Wine:*

"Some claret boy!"—"Indeed, sir, we have none.
Claret, sir!—Lord! there's not a drop in town.
But we have the best red Port."—"What's that you call
red Port?"—"A wine, sir, comes from Portugal:
I'll fetch a pint, sir."

The wine is brought. It was very different from the noble liquid that graced 19th Century tables. The customer complains:

"Mark how it smells. Methinks, a real pain
Is by its odor thrown upon my brain.
I've tasted it—'tis spiritless and flat,
And it has as many different tastes,
As can be found in compound pastes . . ."

The 18th Century was a dark period for those who reverenced the cult of Dionysius. "Our ancestors," wrote Raymond Postgate, "who spent whole days fox hunting, were three-bottle men, no doubt, but we don't live their lives. Also, they died young, purple or yellow, gouty, savage-tempered and inflamed; the memoirs of the 18th Century are full of the results of port drinking." But the hour before the dawn can be the darkest, and one of the indirect results of the Methuen Treaty is the long catalogue of superb vintages that we enjoy today. It was because of it that the West learned that wine matures in a stoutly stoppered bottle.

A Change in Tastes.   Port wines were shipped to England from both Lisbon and Oporto. But the Portuguese wine merchants soon noticed a curious fact. The wines from Lisbon, indifferent though they were, proved more profitable than those from Oporto, because they had more flavor. It puzzled the winegrowers in Oporto, because their grapes were richer in sugar at the time of vintage. It was eventually realized that they had little flavor because of an *excess* of sugar; the must (grape juice) fermented too fast in a hot climate; the consequent wine had no sweetness left in it. There was a way, the vintners knew, to check the fermentation before all the sweetness was gone: the wine had to be fortified with alcohol. But after such drastic measures, a wine has to be allowed to mature. Sherry matures in a porous cask, vintage port will not. The port vintners were forced to develop an equivalent of the ancient amphora: a glass bottle firmly stoppered so that it could lie on its side, to keep the cork moist and prevent its shrinking. In 1780 just such a bottle was developed, and the path was clear not only for vintage port, but for vintage nonfortified wines like claret, Burgundy, and Sauternes. The days of darkness had reached their close at last.

Surprisingly enough, it was a little while before the French appreciated the significance of this discovery. The French had, of course, a great deal on their minds. They had a revolution, then they had wars, but they were producing charming wines, for which there was a ready market. Why be concerned with innovations? But once the idea had caught on, it was recognized that a revolution in taste had started.

A big wine, when it is young, is less palatable than a light and casual one. I would suggest to the reader of these pages the following experiment, though it will be a rather costly one. Let him buy a Château Margaux that is 10 years old, a current Beaujolais, and a Château Margaux that has just been bottled. Let him open them at 6 o'clock in the evening, and give them two hours to breathe. Then let him sip them one by one, with a dry cracker and a slice of sharp Cheddar cheese to clean his palate between each sip. Let him start with the young Margaux. It will have a considerable aroma, "good on the nose" will be his verdict; he will sip it; then he will wince, its flavor will be harsh and hard. He will be tempted to spit it out, then he should remember that this was the kind of Château Margaux that his ancestors drank at the end of the 18th Century, and he will not be surprised to learn that the winegrowers of the day doctored their wines, adding honey, fruit juice, anything that would give them sweetness. Then having cleaned his palate with a mouthful of cheese, let him sip the Beaujolais; it will be clean, youthful, fresh, with no great character or body, but a sound preparative for the big wines that should follow it. (This was the kind of wine that Shakespeare drank, a year or so old and from a cask newly broached.) After he has once again cleaned his palate, let him try the 10-year-old Margaux, having first held it to the light so that he can appreciate its color, then held it under his nose so that he can breathe in its rich aroma. Let him take a small slow sip, holding the wine in his mouth until every taste bud is aware of it; then let him swallow it, and as he surrenders to the peace of spirit that steals slowly over him, let him reflect that he is enjoying a pleasure that was denied humanity for 1,500 years while there was no equivalent in the world for the classical stoppered amphora.

I have tried in these pages to give a very brief survey, and I wish now to approach our subject in more detail. This book will try to present the subject of wines and spirits in the modern household in a practical, straightforward way, and I thought that the most effective would be to give a round-by-round, or rather sip-by-sip, account of what six people might consume at a Saturday evening dinner party. In this way the narrative can follow a curve, working from preliminary appetizers to the peak of a great vintage wine, then tapering off with the sweet dessert wines that accompany the fruit preceding the coffee and liqueurs. If it seems that the host and his friends imbibe a heavy load of alcohol, it should be remembered that they do not have to get up early or go to work the next day.

Making the Oak Casks for Wine

Essential to the production of sherry is the aging process, and essential to that process are the 150-gallon casks, or "butts," that make up the aging-and-blending units known as Soleras (*Chapter 7*) in which the wine spends its life from the moment when fermentation begins to the moment when it is finally bottled for shipment and sale. The butts have long been made only of American white oak; other woods have been tried and found wanting—they contain less of the tannic acid that helps to impart flavor and coloring to the finished product. While machines are being used today to manufacture parts of the butts, many of the bodegas, or winehouses,

of the sherry region still construct them entirely by hand, even to the point of maintaining their own blacksmith shops to forge the butts' iron hoops *(opposite, top)*. The hoops themselves are hammered down around the staves of the butts by a squad of coopers who circle around them, banging away rhythmically *(opposite, bottom)*. A fire burns continuously in the butt *(below)*, and water is regularly splashed on the outside to produce quantities of steam, without which the stout oak staves could not be bent into appropriate shape. When the butt is finally completed, a proud cooper burns the brand of his bodega into the top of the cask *(right)*.

Cork: Guardian of Wine

From sun-washed groves the length of Portugal comes half of the world's supply of cork, a material obtained from the bark of *Quercus suber*, the cork oak *(left, top)*. The bark of all trees contains some cork, but only the cork oak produces it in sufficient quality and thickness to warrant harvesting for bottle corks and other uses. Treated with respect—strict Portuguese laws permit the careful hand stripping of the bark *(left, bottom)* only once every nine years— a good cork oak may attain an age of 200 years. The cork is used for such varied purposes as heat and sound insulation and the making of plastics, but it plays a major role in wine making. Properly cut into shapes *(opposite)* appropriate to the necks of different wine bottles by laborers in Portuguese factories, a cork permits only a minuscule amount of air to enter the bottle and allows the wine to age slowly to perfection. Without the cork, kept constantly moistened by the wine itself in the tilted bottle, air would swiftly turn the liquid to vinegar.

II

Beer, Spirits and the Cocktail

We are now ready to begin the odyssey of our fictional dinner with the host's return in the late afternoon after a round of golf. He will have raised a thirst and he will want to quench it. (He might decide on a soft drink or iced tea or coffee; but this is a book on alcoholic beverages.) He may be tempted by a gin and tonic, a Bloody Mary or a highball. But he has a good deal of drinking ahead of him during the evening. I suggest that, allowing for the cocktail prelude to dinner, he would be wise to settle for a glass of beer.

There are several kinds of malt beverages that are classified as beer. They include lager, ale, stout, porter and bock. For all these the first stages of brewing are similar. The grain usually used is barley. It is first of all malted. That is, the barley is steeped in water until it begins to germinate and ripen and the starches in the grain become soluble sugar, which later can be fermented with the addition of yeast. The malted barley, or malt, is mixed with other cereals and cooked with water. At a certain stage the liquid, called wort, is strained off into the brew kettle, and hops (tiny blossoms of the hop vine) are added for flavor. After a few hours of brewing with the wort, the hops are removed, the wort is cooled, cultured yeast is added and fermentation begins.

It is the yeast that makes the difference between beers. There are two kinds of fermentation, and the type of yeast strain used determines which kind—bottom fermentation or top fermentation—takes place. Most beer is the result of bottom fermentation; in this process the yeast settles to the bottom of the fermenting vat after it has completed its work. Such beer is lager, from the German word for storing, or resting; the beer is aged several months to mellow it and clear it of sediment.

Ale is a top-fermented beverage. The yeast used in the process of making ale rises to the top after fermentation instead of settling on the bottom. Ale has a sharper taste than beer and a stronger flavor of hops. Stout and porter are variations of ale. Stout has a strong malt flavor. It has a heavy hop content and is made from roasted malt, which is why its color is dark. Porter is also a dark and creamy brew like stout. It is stronger in alcoholic content than stout but milder in hop flavor. It got its name many years ago from London's Covent Garden porters, a tribe that fancied it.

In the United States there is also a sweet potation called bock beer. It is made by using the sediment collected from fermenting vats when they are cleaned in the spring of each year. Bock beer is available only at this time, for about six weeks; and it was a good moment in New York in April, 1934 after the repeal of Prohibition to see the newly reopened bars placarded with the slogan "Bock is back."

Beer Countries.   Beer has always been a favorite drink in regions that do not produce wine, and wine-producing areas on the whole do not make attractive beer. Even in Germany, which makes some excellent wines, the regions that produce beer do not produce wine.

The Scandinavians produce great beers that are drunk all over the world —Denmark's Tuborg and Carlsberg, Sweden's Three Crowns are excellent. Mexico has the fine Carta Blanca, and Japan has Kirin. The Russian kvass, made from rye or barley, is an attractive brew; there is the noble Heineken from Holland, and of course Pilsner beer from Czechoslovakia. (The original Pilsner Urquell comes from Pilsen in Czechoslovakia, where the purity of the water gives it a clear, fresh, light-bodied flavor, but the term Pilsner is sometimes used by brewers everywhere to describe light lager beers.)

Britain is a great brewing and beer-consuming country. English draught beer is flat and cool, though there are times when it seems almost warm, and American soldiers were warned before they set foot in England during World War II that they must be prepared for a beer very different from their own. I wish they had also been warned that the beer they would be served in wartime would have much less body than the prewar brew. I myself spent the last four years of the war in the Middle East. During parched summer months in Baghdad, when I was limited to a ration of two bottles of beer a week, I used to think longingly of the day when I would return to England and lift to my lips a heavy tankard of British beer. The shock when I did was one of the greatest gastronomic disappointments of my life. Tepid, weak and sour! I could scarcely swallow it. To think of American G.I.s coping with that! I imagine that many of them laced it with gin or whiskey.

But though the G.I.s may not have liked the beer they were served in England, they enjoyed, so I have been assured, what went with beer: the friendly family atmosphere of the pub, with its darts and dominoes and miniaturized shuffleboard called shove-ha'penny, where a man would sit for a whole evening over a single pint, talking to his friends, with no one telling him to hurry up his drink, until the landlord issued the mandatory closing summons, "Time, Gentlemen, time."

In the United States, beer drinking may be less of a ritual, but the brew is no less enjoyable. Beer arrived here with the earliest settlers, but it was the German immigrants who, around 1840, made St. Louis, Milwaukee and Cincinnati world-renowned brewing centers. Today many superb beers are produced in various parts of the country to slake the thirst of a public that consumes almost 107 million barrels a year. Our fictional dinner host will probably limit himself to one glass of that gigantic total, for soon it will be cocktail time.

The Cocktail Hour.   When I started to go to dinner parties in 1919, the cocktail habit had not reached London. You were invited for 8 o'clock; you were welcomed by your host and hostess, you were introduced to the lady whom you were to "take in" to dinner, and you stood around. It was *le mauvais quart d'heure*—and very bad it could be on occasions, particularly for a young man of 21, as I was, not too sure of himself and anxious to make a good impression. The young of today are lucky to have been spared that experience. And even after the cocktail had made its first appearance in the more avant-garde circles, it was only one cocktail, and you had to drink it quickly if you arrived seven minutes late; if you were invited for 8, at a quarter past you went in to dinner. The cocktail dissolved *le mauvais quart d'heure* and that was all it did. Today, almost 50 years later, the preprandial session may last an hour or more and is considered by some to be almost as important as the meal itself.

Nobody knows for certain the origin of the cocktail. But there is a delightful story that has it originating during the Revolutionary War in a New England tavern run by Miss Betsy Flanagan. American officers frequented the place, and they often complained to Betsy about a prosperous Tory who lived royally nearby while they practically starved. One night Betsy served them a special drink of rum mixed with fruit juice. Each drink was decorated with a tail feather from the Tory's rooster. Amid the shouts that greeted the new drink the revelers heard the cry of a young French officer, "Vive le coq's tail." Whether that bilingual toast christened the before-dinner drink is unknown—the etymologists do not agree on the origin of the word—but the sentiment it expressed has won wide acceptance in the Western world.

I am more fond of some cocktails than I am of others, and in my view one of the noblest potations is the champagne cocktail, which some people say is not a cocktail at all. It is pleasant to taste, it looks marvelous, it sparkles, it does not impair the palate and it is not very strong. The recipe I like goes as follows: A lump of sugar is put at the bottom of a glass, a drop—but no more—of Angostura bitters is allowed to fall on it; rather more than a drop of brandy is allowed to slide over the rim of the glass, enough so that the lump of sugar is afloat; a lump of ice may be added, but eventually it will weaken the wine, which is not very strong to begin with, and in my opinion the ice is better omitted; a slice of fruit may be inserted, peach or lemon or orange—it does not really matter since the fruit is merely for decoration. Then the champagne is poured:

It should be very cold; it should be young and effervescent. (Another version is in the Recipe Booklet.)

The champagne cocktail is less commonly served now than it once was, for fashions change fast in cocktails. When I was young the Bronx (gin with sweet and dry vermouth) was popular; so was the orange blossom (gin and orange juice). You seldom hear them ordered now. Today the Martini is the most sophisticated of cocktails. It is also the purest: dry vermouth and gin or vodka stirred together with ice and poured into a chilled glass. Over the years it has grown drier, the proportion of spirits to vermouth becoming ever higher—a trend that owes much to James Bond, the fictional adventurer who greatly enhanced the prestige of the driest of dry Martinis. It is often served on the rocks, presumably because a cocktail needs to be cold and the contents of a cocktail glass get warm within 10 minutes. Some people like the flavor added by a dunked olive (or a small onion, which makes it a Gibson); others prefer the oil that clings to the inside of a lemon rind, which should be twisted to create a glaze upon the surface of the drink.

The best Martinis I have ever tasted are made in the most unlikely place, Porte's teashop in Tangier. The best cakes and sweets in the town are made there, and there is a raised platform where women and children drink tea, coffee and chocolate, and sip through straws at long frosty glasses. To cater to the taste of the occasional customer who likes a stronger drink, there is also a bar whose excellent barman has so little to do that he can devote his entire time to the mixing of his cocktails. He serves his Martini in a tall stemmed glass; it is a lagoon-sized potion, and inside the glass curves a thin sliver of lemon peel. By some miracle the drink maintains its coolness for nearly half an hour.

There was a time when across the road was a boutique called La Maison de France run by an American lady, a dear friend of mine. If a couple happened to come into her shop shortly before noon, she would say, "Now, Frank, you know how women like to gabble about clothes. You don't want to be bothered with us, and we don't want to be bothered with you. You go across to Porte's and order a Martini. We'll send for you when we're ready."

Twenty-five minutes later a messenger would seek out the husband. "Madame would like you to decide which of two dresses you prefer." Invariably the husband would say, "Have them both."

At this instant of writing I have just returned from a luncheon party in Tangier that was preceded by a Martini session at Porte's. My chief guest, a Scotsman, enjoyed the drinks as much as I did. But he said to his wife, "I wonder if they put into this the two drops of rose water that you recommend." I have no idea what effect rose water would have on a cocktail, but I relate this anecdote as a proof of my contention that each individual is convinced that he makes better Martinis than anybody else, not excluding famous bartenders.

The Martini is made with gin or vodka, but every cocktail has some kind of spirituous base—by spirituous I mean one of the distilled spirits. The main bases are rum, gin, vodka and whiskey. It seems convenient to deal with each of these ingredients in turn (brandy, though sometimes used as a base for cocktails, will be discussed in a later chapter).

Opposite: At the Oktoberfest in Munich, Germany, a foamy frolic held every autumn since 1810 to celebrate the Bavarian city's famous beers, a blond waitress smilingly serves up a number of steins of Munich's best: several *Dunkle* (dark) and one *Helles* (light).

The Pirates' Drink.   Rum is the drink of romantics, for it always
has been favored by adventurers. It was the pirates' drink:

> Fifteen men on Dead Man's Chest
> Yo, ho, ho, and a bottle of rum.
> Drink and the devil have done with the rest.

It is the soldier's drink. A tot of rum was served to British soldiers in
the line in winter. It is the sailor's drink, the base for the Royal Navy's famous grog. The word grog is derived from the nickname of Admiral
Edward Vernon, the English naval officer after whom George Washington's
estate was named. The Admiral was known as "Old Grog" because he
wore a shabby coat made out of grogram, a course fabric woven from
silk and wool. He insisted that his men take a daily dose of rum and
water as a precaution against scurvy. The diluted tipple eventually became known as "grog," and if it did nothing to prevent scurvy, it surely
lightened the dreariness of navy life.

Rum is made from sugar cane and is a clean, pure, wholesome drink.
The cane is crushed and mangled between rollers. The resultant cane
juice is then concentrated into a syrup by boiling. Most of the sugar is
then extracted from the syrup; about 5 per cent sugar remains in a residue called molasses, and it is from this that most rums are fermented
and distilled.

Rum can be made anywhere that sugar is grown. It is made in Mau-
ritius and in Indonesia, but rums other than West Indian are usually for
local consumption. They could not enter the competition of the market
dominated by the rums from the Caribbean. Rum-making began there almost as soon as Spanish colonists arrived, for sugar was one of the first
crops they introduced. Today the larger islands all produce their own
rums with distinct variations.

There are two main kinds of rum: light-bodied and heavy. The drier
light-bodied ones originally came from the islands with a Spanish background, Cuba and Puerto Rico. Virgin Islands rum is also light. Light
rums are more popular in the United States than they are in Europe because they are better suited to the cocktails and cold, long drinks in
which North Americans specialize. One of the most refreshing of these is
the tart Daiquiri—rum and lime juice—often served "frozen," that is,
mixed with finely crushed ice. The dark, heavier-flavored rums of Jamaica,
Haiti and Barbados (darker because of additional caramel coloring) make
a comforting drink in a cold climate such as England has. Such a climate
calls for hot rum drinks like the modern version of grog—hot dark rum
sweetened with sugar and flavored with nutmeg. But the similar rum
from the French-ruled island of Martinique makes a traditional cooling
drink—and still one of the best.

This is rum punch, and if you order one in Martinique, they will set in
front of you a slice of lime, a small bottle of syrup, a bottle of rum, an
earthenware jug in which water has been cooling, perhaps some ice, and
leave you to mix it for yourself. If you are wise, you will follow the classic formula—"one of sour, two of sweet, three of strong and four of
weak." The lime is the sour, the syrup the sweet, the rum itself is the
strong and the water that dilutes it is the weak.

The Ups and Downs of Gin.   Rum has never lost its prestige, but gin, which is now the basis of a large proportion of the best tall, cold drinks, has taken a long time to live down the bad reputation that it acquired in the 18th Century. As late as 1920 George Saintsbury was writing that he had always been sorry for gin, "that humble and much reviled liquid which is the most specially English of all spirits." One of Anthony Trollope's heroines was shocked when her uncle for reasons of economy adopted it. The essayist William Henry Hazlitt was upbraided for his addiction to it. After a period of rehabilitation, the reputation of gin declined again. One recalls all the contemptuous references during Prohibition to "bathtub gin." The trouble was that, though it was easy to make and was cheap, it was often bad.

Gin was introduced into England in the 17th Century by William of Orange. It had been created as a medicine by a Dutch chemist, Professor Sylvius, who had distilled from grain a spirit that he flavored with juniper berries and called *jenever* after the French word for juniper, *genièvre*. Since it was thought to have medicinal properties, it was sold only in apothecaries' shops. But it proved so popular that many apothecaries set up distilleries on their own. English soldiers in the Low Countries tasted it and liked it, and William of Orange decided that it would make a tolerable substitute for the brandy that his enemy the French produced. When he placed prohibitive taxes on French wines and brandy coming into England, he at the same time allowed anyone who applied to the excise bureau to set up a distillery. Within a short time, the English had created a drink something like *jenever* and shortened its name to gin. Deprived of French spirits, the less affluent Englishmen had no alternative to the new, cheap and fiery potion. Within 40 years gin production in England rose from half a million gallons a year to 20 million gallons. The slums were littered with gin-sodden crones, and gin earned the sobriquet of "mother's ruin." Hogarth's pictures show the degradation into which the lower classes sank through their addiction to gin. The situation is implicit in the notice that a Southwark publican hung outside his tavern: "Drunk for 1d. Dead drunk for 2d. Clean straw for nothing."

The type of liquor that the London distillers eventually developed is very different from the Hollands gin that is still made in the Netherlands. In Hollands the final spirits, which are distilled at low strength, retain a very clean but pronounced malty aroma, so pronounced that this gin cannot be mixed to make cocktails; its own flavor would predominate. It needs to be drunk straight, slightly chilled. I have myself drunk it only when I have been traveling in Dutch ships or in the Netherlands itself. I have enjoyed it but not enough to keep a bottle in my cocktail cabinet. The name is the only thing Hollands gin has in common with the London dry gin that is distilled in England and America and that is nothing more than diluted pure alcohol that has been flavored with what are known as botanicals, such as juniper and coriander. Each distiller guards the secret of his own botanicals, since they provide the only characteristic distinguishing one brand from another.

Gin is not something one ages; it can be drunk within a half hour of being made. London, or dry, gin when taken by itself is highly unpalatable; you have to mix it with something that mitigates the harsh taste. Gin

Continued on page 42

Frosty rum drinks for summer time are *(from left)* a peach Daiquiri, Mai-Tai, Daiquiri, planter's punch and Bacardi.

Rum: It Cools on Its Own or with Fruit

It's no news—but always good news—that rum makes a cooling hot-weather drink wherever in the world the weather gets hot. Purists savor the bittersweet taste of rum alone, poured over ice cubes or in a highball with water or soda. *Opposite:* Chilled glasses of white and dark rum stand invitingly on a stack of sugar-cane stalks like those from which rum is distilled. For those who prefer mixed drinks, rums blend smoothly with all kinds of fruit. The five favorite rum-and-fruit potations above use everything from sweet peaches to tart limes. The peach Daiquiri starts with whole peeled fruit; in Hawaii the Mai-Tai cocktail is flavored with lime juice, apricot brandy and orange liqueur, and garnished with a pineapple spear; the classic Daiquiri cocktail is basically rum and lime juice; on Caribbean islands the planter's punch requires sliced lime and a cherry; the Bacardi cocktail mixes rum with lime juice and grenadine (pomegranate syrup).

Holiday Cheer: Some Like It Cold, Some Like It Hot

Rum is a spirit for all seasons, hot and cold; and besides its leading role in
chilled summer drinks it is a traditional ingredient of wintertime holiday cheer.
Three of the four drinks shown here could not do without rum. The ice-cold,
colorfully garnished eggnog opposite brings back memories of Dickensian
holiday seasons past; it is an old-time drink that never goes out of style, and
there are family recipes for eggnog that have been treasured for many generations.
This one, made with rum and blended whiskey, is popular throughout the
United States. The three classic hot drinks shown below are *(from right) Glühwein*,
a spiced and sweetened mulled red wine; hot buttered rum; and Tom and Jerry,
a blend of rum, brandy and milk, enriched with butter and beaten eggs.

and water, and gin and soda, are unpleasant. Pink gin, for a long time highly popular with the Royal Navy, is simply a little Angostura bitters swilled round inside a small glass with gin and some water. And, of course, gin and tonic is an extremely popular drink these days. Gin, without doubt, is a favorite in many cocktails and long drinks, particularly in the ever-popular Martini.

Vodka's Rise.   Challenging gin, vodka has also become popular in recent years as a base for cocktails. There are many who ask for vodka Martinis and others who prefer Bloody Marys—vodka with tomato juice, to which are added various flavorings such as lemon, salt and pepper, Worcestershire sauce and a dash of Tabasco.

The vodka we drink in the West has very little taste or smell. A businessman can have two Bloody Marys before his lunch, and his secretary will be ready to believe that he has had a club sandwich and a cup of coffee in a cafeteria. Vodka does not spoil the taste of anything you put in it. There are one or two soft drinks like Fresca and Bitter Lemon whose charming flavors are diminished by the addition of gin; this does not happen with vodka. The only drawback to present-day vodka is that it is insidious. Often you do not realize that you are imbibing alcohol until your reflexes tell you.

One tends to think of vodka as a uniquely Russian beverage; yet such is not in fact the case. Vodka did originate in imperial Russia, but there is American vodka, as well as German and English. Vodka made in the United States and in England is practically tasteless, but traditional Russian vodka was flavored with pungent herbs, such as mustard, almond, cinnamon or berries. Today the only vodka bottled in Russia for sale in the U.S., called Stolichnaya, has a faint grain flavor but no pungency. The Polish vodka, Zubrowka, is flavored with a wild buffalo grass. It used to be claimed that vodka was made from potatoes. It was, but not exclusively; anything that happened to be around would do. More often it was based on a grain, rye or wheat, as it is today.

Whisky and Whiskey.   Whiskey is an excellent prelude to any evening. There are several kinds—bourbon, rye, Canadian, Irish and Scotch, to name the principal ones. All are noble spirits, admirably equipped to prepare the mind and body for a gastronomic treat. And they all have this special quality, that they are indigenous to certain areas, even reflecting regional peculiarities in the spelling of the word whiskey—in Scotland and Canada whisky has no "e"; in Ireland and the U.S. it has the "e."

In the beginning, the Scots had difficulties with authority over their whisky. The story of those troubles has been admirably told in Sir Robert Bruce Lockhart's *Scotch*. It is his contention that the fate and future of this noble liquid was decided at the battle of Culloden in 1746, when the English finally conquered the Scots and opened the Highlands to the Lowlands; one fortunate result of this conquest was a road that made Highland whisky accessible to the rest of the world. Until then the Highlanders and their whisky had lived secure in the fastnesses of their glens, where there was a distillery to every family.

Civil wars are followed by injustice to the defeated, and as a British equivalent for the carpetbaggers who poured into the Southern states after the defeat of the Confederacy, the Highlanders after Culloden had excisemen extorting taxes on their whisky, taxes that discriminated unjustly against the Highland Scots. It is not surprising that they resisted stoutly, and for over 70 years they continued to distill whisky secretly in their valleys. They had natural advantages in their favor. The manufacture of whisky is not complicated, and the remoteness of the hidden glens provided perfect concealment for the illicit stills. Moreover the distillers had on their side the native population, for moonshining was "the secret half a county keeps." There were spies in plenty to give warning to their compatriots of the approach of the hated excisemen. It was not till 1823 that the Duke of Gordon made a deal with the government, in which he promised that if the taxes were equably adjusted, he and his friends would do their best to suppress the illegal stills.

The bargain held and Scotch became legitimate, but even so it did not for a while "catch on" as a profitable commodity. It was too strong; that was the trouble with it. The whiskies that the Highlanders distilled were entirely different from the blended Scotch of today. Malt whisky is made entirely from malted barley; no other grains such as corn, wheat, oats or rye are used as they are in other grain whiskies. The Scotch we drink today is still made from malted barley, but neutral spirits and unmalted grain whisky are blended with it to make it lighter and more palatable.

Not until the invention of the patent still would it be found possible to produce the modern blended Scotch whisky that would suit the palate and constitution of the city worker. The malt distiller favored the pot still because it allowed each whisky to assert its own character. The patent still produced whisky of lighter flavor, simplifying the blending of a standard whisky with a consistent flavor.

As a commercial property the patent still had everything to commend it. It was relatively inexpensive; it could be installed anywhere. Highland malt whisky could be distilled only in certain sacred places in the belt of land bounded on the west by the River Ness and on the east by the River Deveron, where the water—and Scots claim, even the air—affects the whisky flavor. But grain whisky can be distilled almost anywhere and a large grain whisky distillery can produce as much in a week as a malt distillery in a nine-month season.

The Lowlanders soon realized that they were on to a good thing with their patent still. But even so it was some while before the attractions of blended whisky were appreciated south of the border. It was not until the middle of the last century that whisky became known in England, and Winston Churchill wrote in his book, *A Roving Commission:* "My father could never have drunk whisky except when shooting on a moor or in some very dull chilly place."

The distillers of malt whisky looked on the new blended whisky with disfavor. They in fact long denied that the blended version was whisky at all. They objected to grain whisky being sold as Scotch, and in 1905 instigated a government council to take out summonses against a number of publicans for selling an "article not of the nature and substance demanded." The subsequent action was known as the "What is whisky" case, and the first hearing, after seven sittings, failed to reach a decision,

Overleaf: Surrounding a clear glass of vodka with a lemon peel in it is a sampling of varicolored vodka cocktails. Moving clockwise from the red Bloody Mary at the top, the drinks include: a Bull Shot, a Green Dragon, a gimlet, a screwdriver, a Black Russian and a vodka silver fizz.

Continued on page 46

A group portrait of vodka cocktails

the bench being divided. This presented a very real problem for the grain distillers. If they could not market their commodity as Scotch they were in a bad way. It was finally agreed that Parliament should appoint a Royal Commission to decide the issue. And it has to be confessed that the malt distillers had a strong case. In France no wine can be called champagne that does not come from the area around Épernay, nor can brandy be called cognac unless it comes from Cognac. And on that principle the malt distillers could argue that for generations "Scotch whisky" had been recognized as a spirit made from malted home-grown barley, specially distilled and matured, with its own particular flavor and quality. It had consequently a unique character that, because it could not be imitated, was of great benefit and value to Scotland. They had a case. But so had the grain distillers. They contended that grain whisky as made in Scotland was a true whisky, that it changed character by aging in wood, that it was made in terms of a scientific formula, that it was in fact purer than malt. They produced medical evidence to support this claim, and in the end they won their case.

Most of us can be thankful that they did. For Scotch as we know it today provides one of the most pleasant drinks that are to be found.

How one should drink Scotch is a matter of individual taste. Many of the misunderstandings about the proper way to drink Scotch arise out of a confusion between malt whisky and blended whisky. A great many of us have never tasted unblended malt whisky. I rarely have, and on those few occasions have recognized that it is a noble potation, but it is not for me, an elderly urbanite. It was distilled by Highlanders to be drunk by Highlanders, men of brawn and prowess, living in the open air, in a hard, stirring climate. When Scotsmen say that it is a crime to mix soda water with Scotch, they are referring to malt whisky, and there I would agree with them. The same contention holds true for bourbon. I would never think of mixing soda water with a fine, aged bourbon, but blended Scotch is another matter.

Personally I prefer it either with ice and soda or neat in a small glass with water as a chaser. But that is a personal preference. I do not think that it retains its flavor in any cocktail except Scotch mist (Scotch over cracked ice). The smoky peat flavor, which comes from drying the malt over peat fires, should be allowed to assert its individuality. Today 99 per cent of the Scotch that is drunk outside Scotland is blended. Scotch is one of Britain's most important exports; half of all the Scotch sold each year goes to the United States, and the blenders are careful to consider American tastes. In recent years the consumers have favored light, dry liquors; so whisky is made paler. This does not mean that the whisky is any lighter in character or alcoholic content, because the color is supplied by burned sugar or by the whisky's having been aged in sherry casks. Indeed to someone of my age, this lightness of color can cause confusion. When I was young, I judged the strength of a Scotch and soda by its color. I would say, "Oh, that looks rather dark; a little more soda please." Now when I am handed a glass that is quite pale, I still presume that it is fairly weak. One can make mistakes that way.

Scotch matures in the wooden casks in which it is stored. There is a real difference between a whisky that is eight years old and one that is 12 years old. Scotch does not change in the bottle, and a bottle that is opened will not lose its quality provided that the bottle or decanter is firmly stoppered. But malt whisky will. My younger son, who was once in the wine trade, made the experiment recently of pouring a quarter of a bottle of malt whisky into a carafe. Within three weeks its flavor and power had evaporated.

Bourbon.   Nothing could be more American than bourbon. James E. Pepper, whose grandfather Elijah settled in what came to be known as Old Pepper Spring, on the Frankfort Pike near Lexington, Kentucky, and who started a log-cabin distillery there in 1780, maintained the trademark "Old 1776" and the slogan "Born with the Republic." His boast was close to the truth.

In colonial days rum was the staple hard liquor, but the break with Britain and the ending of the slave trade changed that. There was a fortunate alternative. The Scotch-Irish settlers who poured down the Shenandoah Valley, over the Pennsylvania ridges and through the Cumberland Gap had brought with them the art of distillation; they were old hands with the pot still, that primitive but efficient instrument that was so easy to transport and assemble. They were grain distillers; whiskey was easier to transport to market than the grain itself, which was usually rye. They bartered it for salt, sugar, nails, bar iron, powder and shot, and pewter plates. Sound rye whiskey was a stable measure of value.

For a while the pioneer whiskey makers prospered. They were soon, however, to be exposed to governmental interference; in 1791 money was in short supply, and George Washington decided to levy an excise tax on whiskey. This caused great indignation, particularly among the Pennsylvanians, and what is known as the Whiskey Rebellion ensued. Tax collectors were tarred and feathered, and troops had to be sent to quell the riots. Peace was restored without bloodshed, but a number of the farmers moved out of range of the tax collector, into Kentucky, where the corn grew tall and immigrants could find relief from postwar depression, the weary confederation, high taxes and governmental interference. There they continued to make whiskey out of rye, until a year when the rye crop failed. Then they mixed corn with their rye mash and found the result excellent. Because they were living in Bourbon County, their whiskey became known as Bourbon County whiskey. Distillers have continued to use corn as the primary grain base in the making of bourbon, and today Federal law requires that all bourbon have at least 51 per cent corn. In addition to bourbon and rye there is corn whiskey, the mash for which must contain at least 80 per cent corn. It is raw and colorless and is sold mainly in rural districts.

So much in the history of wine and spirits has turned on chance. It was by chance that the Kentuckians discovered that whiskey improved with age. They did a good trade with New Orleans, sending the barrels down by boat. They had to wait for the spring rise of the rivers. They found that their whiskey tasted better in New Orleans. It had matured during the wait and the trip down the river.

Kentucky was soon dotted with private stills that were located in hollows where the clear cold water flowed, a water that made, so it was

Continued on page 54

47

Scotch: From Bonnie Braes and Burns, a Spirit beyond Compare

Often imitated (never successfully) by producers in other lands, Scotch whisky is inseparably wedded to the highlands and lowlands of its native heath. It is compounded of elements indigenous to Scotland: crystal-clear water obtained from the sparkling streams the Scots call burns, barley grown on the mountain slopes known as braes, the peat fuel that gives Scotch its characteristically smoky flavor, and even, say the Scots, the pure air of their land.

The original Scotch was an unblended spirit called malt whisky—so named because it was made exclusively from barley that was germinated, or malted, by steeping it in water before fermentation. Strong, and harsh on the palates of most drinkers other than the Scots, who profess to enjoy it, malt Scotch is still made in Scotland, and some is spared for export; what the rest of the world calls Scotch, however, is a blend of up to 60 per cent of this malt whisky with other spirits distilled from corn, rye or oats.

The exact proportions and origins of the ingredients of their products—up to 50 whiskies may go into a single Scotch—are closely guarded secrets of the distillers. About the only fact that manufacturers do not keep locked in their Scots hearts and vaults is the age of the product. British law stipulates that any Scotch must mature for at least three years, but most of it is four years of age or more when it is put on the market. The older Scotch is, the more it costs—though many experts feel that it does not improve after 12 years in cask.

In a test for quality in The Glenlivet Distillery on the River Spey in Scotland, the firm's owner, Captain W. Smith Grant (*at left*), sniffs a sample of Scotch in the company of his manager, Robert Arthur. Captain Smith Grant is a descendant of the founder of the distillery, which in 1823 became the first to be licensed by the British government, and which today makes a highly regarded, superior Scotch known as The Glenlivet. This is a malt whisky that is bottled for sale unblended and is also sold to other distillers to be used in making blended Scotches. The clear liquid in the glass on the captain's desk is newly distilled whisky (only after years of maturing, often in casks previously used to hold sherry, does Scotch take on the warm coloration familiar to its fanciers). The absolute clarity of the new whisky reflects the purity of the streams of the Spey region (*overleaf*), heavily drawn upon by the numerous distilleries that nestle in its glens.

Source of Scotch: A bright stream winds through a field near the River Spey.

1 After barley has been steeped in water, a workman at the Glenfarclas Distillery in the Spey region spreads it to allow it to germinate, or malt.

2 In the next step at Glenfarclas, the malted barley is dried over a fire of the peat *(foreground)* that gives Scotch its characteristically smoky flavor.

3 At The Glenlivet Distillery, which does not malt its own barley, the malt is mixed with hot water in an enormous "mash tun."

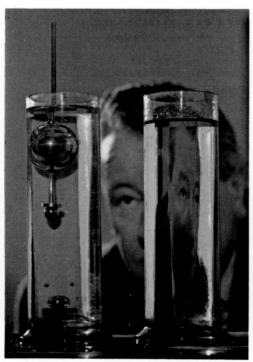

7 Through the "spirit safe" at Glenlivet, padlocked by British tax officials, flows low wine for redistillation into legal whisky.

8 Using a hydrometer, an instrument with which the alcohol content of liquids can be measured, a tax official checks the proof of the new whisky.

9 After its alcohol content has been reduced to about 55 per cent by the addition of water, the whisky is drawn into casks for maturing.

4 A workman stirs the mixture during its several hours' stay in the tun. At the end, the bulk of the barley's starch has been converted into sugar.

5 Its temperature watched, the drawn-off liquid ferments in vats after the addition of yeast, which shortly converts the sugar into alcohol.

6 The solution is distilled in great copper pot stills. A mild alcoholic beverage known as low wine is created in the first distillation.

10 As the whisky gradually nears maturity, samples are taken from the casks to be given still another rigorous check by a tax official.

11 Using an olfactory test known as nosing, Glenlivet's general manager, Robert Arthur, takes a final sniff of a sample of finished malt whisky.

12 At a blending house, a workman draws a few ounces of malt Scotch for a blender to test. Blended whiskies are in the white tanks above him.

The kind of difference of opinion that makes horse racing also makes Americans famous for inventing an almost limitless variety of mixed drinks. Local tastes differ so much that every drink has dozens of variations. Here are a dozen drinks popular in bars and living rooms across the country. In the front row on this page are an old-fashioned with lemon peel and another with an orange slice and cherry as well. In the middle row are three Martinis: the Gibson with pickled onion, the dry Martini with lemon peel, and the perfect Martini made with sweet and dry vermouths and garnished with orange peel. In back are a whiskey sour and an apricot sour. Opposite, in the stemmed glasses, are two Manhattans: a regular one served with a cherry and a perfect Manhattan blending sweet and dry vermouths with the whiskey and served with orange peel. In front are three classic Scotch drinks: Scotch and soda, Scotch on the rocks, and Scotch mist over shaved ice with lemon peel.

claimed, the grass blue, the horses frisky, the women beautiful! The character of the water used does have a great influence on the taste of whiskey. By experimenting, the distillers found that the best water came from springs that rose out of layers of limestone rock. The limestone region runs along western Pennsylvania, through southern Indiana into Kentucky. There is also a limestone region near Baltimore. These are still the chief whiskey areas.

The process of production is straightforward. The corn is cleaned and coarsely ground; the chopped kernels are mashed and mixed with limestone water and rye. In what is called the sweet-mash method, malted barley —like that used to make beer—is then added to the mash. This is stirred, heated and cooled; when the fresh yeast is added, the mixture is fermented in an open-topped vat. It is now "distiller's beer," ready to be distilled into whiskey.

In the sour-mash method the mash is scalded with fresh hot "slop," residue from a previous distillation. Sour mash got its name because the thin spirit "beer" left over in the still had a slightly acid taste, although the resultant whiskey was anything but sour. After the mash has been scalded, it is left until the next day to cool, or sour. Then the whiskey is distilled off.

Bourbon can be made both ways. The sour-mash method is more general, but sometimes the whiskey is not advertised as sour mash for fear the term would put off the customer.

Confusing Labels.   The nomenclature of American whiskey can be confusing. Rye and bourbon whiskey can be classified in three ways: straight, blended straight or blended. Straight whiskey is distilled at a proof not exceeding 160 (that is, 80 per cent alcohol). After distillation, the whiskey is diluted with water, aged in new charred oak kegs, and diluted again to the desired proof, usually between 80 and 100 proof. The

lower the proof at which it is originally distilled, the more full-bodied the taste and aroma will be. Some of the heavier-bodied bourbon is first distilled at 125 proof so that it will retain much of its natural flavor and is then reduced to the marketing proof.

Blended straight whiskey is made up of two or more straight whiskeys. The label may read, "bourbon—a blend of straights."

Blended whiskey is a mixture of whiskey *and* neutral spirits. Neutral spirits, sometimes called "silent spirits," are almost pure alcohol, obtained by distilling to 190 proof or higher. Spirits lose virtually all flavor when distilled to this point. Blended whiskey, therefore, is usually lighter than straight whiskey in taste and aroma. It is also less expensive and, because its ingredients are less distinctively flavorful, it is easier to prepare as a standardized product that will not vary in taste from year to year. About 25 per cent of all spirits sold in the United States are blended whiskey.

In the eastern part of the United States any blended whiskey is often mistakenly referred to as rye whiskey. If you order a rye old-fashioned in a New York City bar, for example, what you will get is an old-fashioned made with a blended whiskey, which may or may not—but probably does not—have a genuine rye whiskey base. Most blends are composed of corn whiskey and neutral spirits, but any grain or combination of grains may be used to produce them.

The green stamp over the stopper of some American whiskey bottles, authenticating the statement "bottled in bond," is not an indication of quality. However, it does assure the customer of getting straight whiskey, the product of a single distiller in a single season, bottled at 100 proof and stored in government warehouses for at least four years.

Of the many fine cocktails made from whiskey, the old-fashioned, the whiskey sour and the Manhattan are the most popular, yet in terms of legend the mint julep is the most famous. Verbal duels have been fought

Resplendent in the traditional silver mugs, a bourbon-laden bouquet of mint juleps stands ready for serving in Louisville, site of the annual running of the Kentucky Derby—where the julep is almost as important a part of the race as are the horses.

over the right way to serve it. And no one has questioned its supremacy. Perhaps the last word on the subject should be left with Judge Soule Smith, who in the late 19th Century proclaimed, "The Honey of Hymettus brought no such solace to the soul. The nectar of the Gods is tame beside it. . . . Bourbon and mint are lovers. . . in the same land they live, on the same food are fostered. . . . Like a woman's heart, mint gives its sweetest aroma when bruised."

But there are connoisseurs of whiskey who contend that rye and bourbon are too noble to be sophisticated into cocktails. I am far from being sure that I do not agree with them. When I order an old-fashioned I ask the barman to put in the minimum of Angostura and no water at all. What I relish most is the first sip of the bourbon before the ice and "garbage" have got to work. When I go to a cocktail party at any American consulate or embassy and am asked what I would like, I usually opt for bourbon on the rocks.

Irish and Canadian whiskeys have their own distinctive tastes. Many peo-

Mint juleps *(Recipe Booklet)* should always be served ice-cold—previously packed with ice and chilled in a refrigerator long enough for a frost to form on the outside of the silver mug or glass. A straw facilitates fighting one's way past mint and ice.

ple have found Irish whiskey their most satisfying drink—and this includes most of the Irish. Although the same grains are used as in blended Scotch (barley, malted barley, corn and rye), Irish whiskey is triple-distilled. It is produced exclusively from pot stills, but unlike Scotch it does not have a smoky peat flavor because, when the grain is dried before distillation, it does not come in contact with peat smoke. Taxes on whiskey are still so high in Ireland that a great deal of illegal whiskey, called poteen, is made for informal sale. More popular in the United States than Irish (and less expensive to import) is Canadian whisky. It is made from the better grades of cereal grains—corn, rye and barley—and like most blended American whiskeys is light in color and taste.

So much for the spirits that go to make the cocktail. But there is another kind of drink that our hypothetical host may wish to serve his guests before sitting down to dinner. This is the apéritif, and we shall deal with it in the following pages.

III

The Hour of the Apéritif

The French have always, and with justice, been regarded as the world's gastronomic authorities. They have maintained that some mildly alcoholic beverage is required to set the gastric juices in motion, and they have developed a succession of delightful predinner concoctions that they call apéritifs to perform this function. The Italians, in fact all the Mediterranean peoples—and even Americans—have joined them in their pursuit. For many of us one of the chief memories of our first trips to France and Italy is of those endless notices painted and plastered on the walls, signs advertising Byrrh, Lillet, St. Raphael and Cinzano. How my heart used to lift when the westbound train came out of the tunnel after Beaulieu and I read on the Villefranche waterfront the blue Dubonnet sign. How relieved I was when I saw it still there on my return after the war. It survived the German occupation, but it did not survive the march of progress. It has gone now, alas.

There are a number of apéritifs that would make an admirable introduction to a thoughtfully planned dinner, but the choice depends on the kind of dinner you are proposing to give. If it is to be a buffet-style meal accompanied by a suitable table wine, then you can devote an hour to the cocktail period, during which a certain amount of nourishment will be provided; but the dinner that we are preparing to discuss is an elaborate one, at which a number of different wines will be served, and for such a meal it is desirable that the guests should sit down to table with their appetites unimpaired and their gastric juices no more than set in motion. If you are going to serve good wines, then it is necessary to invite guests who will appreciate them and who can be trusted out of respect for the wines to arrive punctually, so that the period of waiting can be a genuine *"bon quart d'heure,"* for which one cocktail, highball or apéritif will be sufficient. It is quite another matter if the cocktail period is going to be the meal itself—as it is nowadays in many houses.

Most of the apéritifs we shall discuss are aromatic wines, the ones that have been fortified and then treated with herbs and special flavorings, such as roots, barks and flowers.

Of the various aromatic wines that have crossed the Atlantic, Dubonnet has proved the most popular. In fact, most of the Dubonnet that is drunk in the United States is now made in this country. It is at its best served on the rocks. It is made out of a sweetened red wine that is given the necessary astringency by adding bitter bark and quinine. A white variety is also made. Three other aromatic wines exported to the United States since World War II are Byrrh, St. Raphael and Lillet. Byrrh (pronounced beer) is a red wine that has been fortified with brandy and flavored with quinine. St. Raphael is very similar, containing the same ingredients but in different proportions. Lillet, on the other hand, is not flavored with quinine, though it is fortified with brandy. It is made with red or white wine and tastes rather sweet.

The popular apéritif vermouth is not, strictly speaking, a wine, though its base is red or white wine. It is one of the most "manufactured" of all alcoholic beverages, being soaked with as many as 40 aromatic herbs, fortified with spirits, pasteurized, refrigerated and thoroughly filtered, to give it a hardiness that can withstand just about anything except extreme heat. It has rather a different use from the other aromatic wines, since its chief contemporary function in America and many other places is to act as an ingredient in the cocktail. Not many Americans find French vermouth, which is dry, attractive in itself, but—however sparingly it is used—it makes the dry Martini. Italian vermouth, on the other hand, which is sweet, is quite popular served on the rocks.

A very popular apéritif in France, and one that is gaining popularity in the United States, is vermouth cassis. It is vermouth mixed with a few drops of crème de cassis, a French liqueur made from black currants. The French also drink cassis mixed with dry white wine; for obscure reasons of their own they call it *rince cochon*—pig rinse.

The Italians favor a rather bitter apéritif called Campari. Often they mix it with soda. It is quite refreshing. Campari is actually an Italian bitters and, like such other brands as Fernet Branca and Amer Picon, is often used in cocktails. Bitters is an extract of distilled spirits and herbs. One drink made with Campari is the Americano, which consists of Italian vermouth, Campari, a slice of lemon and a splash of soda. The Negroni is an Americano laced with gin or vodka. It costs half as much again, and I prefer the taste of the Americano.

Exotic Apéritifs.   There is another apéritif, of somewhat lethal character, that is rarely seen in England or the U.S.A.: Pernod, or *pastis*, as it is called on the Riviera, one of a number of licorice-flavored Mediterranean spirits such as ouzo and arak. All of these are almost colorless, cloud when you pour water on them and are highly potent. In Lebanon and

Syria arak is made from grapes; in Iraq and Egypt it is made from dates. In Turkey and the Balkans arak is called raki and is made from a variety of things—potatoes, plums, molasses, wine or grain. A similar-tasting apéritif is anis, which is flavored with seeds of the star anise plant. It is extremely popular in France and Spain and drunk as a liqueur as well as an apéritif. I do not really like the taste of these drinks, and I sometimes wonder why I take so many of them. When I first tasted ouzo, in 1926, I could not finish the glass.

If you drink arak in the Middle East, the Arabs will solicitously inform you that it is important to nibble something while you are sipping it. If you do not, they warn, you will suddenly find the room spinning around you, but two mouthfuls of food will restore your equilibrium. In Middle East cafés they always serve with your arak a plate of *maza*—little savories of radishes, cheese and hard-boiled eggs.

But of these licorice drinks it is Pernod that we know most in the West. Pernod is the successor to the drink that was so popular in Paris in the '90s—absinthe. There are not so many people alive who can remember absinthe, since because of its lethal effect it was prohibited at the beginning of the First World War by the French government, and most other countries followed suit. It used to be served in London, in the Domino Room at the Café Royal. It was a green liquid; you put a little in a tall glass across whose top was set a silver filter on which was laid one lump of sugar. Water was poured onto the sugar, and it dripped slowly through onto the liquid, which slowly clouded. I tried it once, and one sip was enough. Perhaps today I would like it.

Absinthe was so popular in the 1890s that the hour of the evening apéritif was known as *l'heure verte*. The drink contained the herb wormwood—which was said to drive one mad or to suicide—a fact that alone would have endeared it to the decadents. A special mystique grew around absinthe. Some people claimed that it doubled the intoxicating power of anything drunk after it. Certainly it was an admirable pick-me-up after a rough channel crossing. It was supposed to have hastened the demise of many poets and painters; and probably it did, not because of the wormwood but because of its potency—it contained 70 to 80 per cent alcohol. In Soho, in the 1920s, one would order a dry Martini with a "dash"—the dash being absinthe, not bitters. As the Martini in England was then composed of one half gin to one half French vermouth, it will be appreciated that the mixture did need enlivening. But absinthe itself is nearly extinct though it can be obtained now in Spain, where it is made in Tarragona. The Pernod that is shipped from France to the United States and to other countries in Europe contains less alcohol and no wormwood.

Northern Apéritifs.   We have already mentioned vodka as an ingredient of the Martini. But vodka found its first durable service to humanity as an apéritif. The vodka we drink in America and England today is different from the vodka that figured so prominently in prerevolution Russian novels, and that I myself drank in Moscow in 1933. One took this Russian vodka in a small glass. It was oily and had a taste I found somewhat sickly. One did not sip it, but tossed the glassful straight to the back of the throat, and took a mouthful of hors d'oeuvre, caviar if it

Continued on page 64

A Café Milieu Celebrated in Art

When absinthe was the toast of Paris, so were the bistros, the cafés that dotted the sidewalks of the city. To them flocked plain Parisians, musicians, novelists and above all the artists, who came both to savor the hour of the apéritif and to attempt to capture on canvas the special ambiance of their favorite haunts. *L'Absinthe*, the painting above, was executed in the late 1870s by Edgar Degas, and portrays Ellen Andrée, a well-known actress of the time. At the right is Auguste Renoir's *Moulin de la Galette*, a Montmartre café that the artist liked so much that he painted it twice. Today, while the powerful but deleterious absinthe is gone, outlawed by the government, the cafés continue to flourish— occupied from dawn, when workmen breakfast on *un vin blanc*, to long past midnight, when the gossip is done, the elections have been analyzed, the girls have been appraised, and the last good glass has been downed.

was available, or failing that, herring or anchovies. The general effect was rather pleasant: The hors d'oeuvre flavor was accentuated; a warm glow spread through one's veins. The vodka was not overly potent—80 proof.

There is another Northern apéritif that I have found particularly pleasant, and that is the schnapps of the Scandinavian countries. Sweden, Norway and North Germany all produce their own varieties, but Denmark's aquavit is the one best known abroad. It is very strong—90 proof. It is rumored that it is made from sawdust; actually it is distilled from grain or potatoes and often flavored with caraway seeds. It must be served ice-cold in a small iced glass. It is an admirable prelude to a meal, but it does not make a good cocktail-hour drink because it needs to be drunk, accompanied by food and beer, while you are seated at a table.

There is a ritual to the serving of aquavit: You never drink without raising your glass to one of the other guests and saying "skoal." (At one time it was the custom that no guest could drink till he had been toasted by his hostess, but this custom was abandoned when it was recognized how deleterious an effect this had on the hostess' composure.) You raise your glass, you look into the other's eyes above it. You tilt your head back and drain your glass. Then you look into the eyes a second time, raise your glass, nod, then lower it.

The food that accompanies the aquavit is usually salty: herring or anchovies; sometimes there is an open sandwich, and you may drink beer in between your sips. Usually you have two glasses of aquavit and a bottle of beer. Then a hot entrée is served. Wine may be served with the entrée, but wine is expensive in Scandinavia; you are more likely to be offered beer. Aquavit may be served throughout the meal, especially if the food is very rich. More often beer is drunk with the meal, but if a cheese course follows, there is a return to the aquavit. After the cheese, the table is cleared for the dessert and the coffee that the Danes in particular love so dearly and prepare so well.

If, in fact, you are going to serve aquavit, you need to make a Scandinavian meal of it. It is not therefore the proper "preparitif" to a meal whose primary objective is the serving of fine wines.

There is another local and fiery potation, tequila, which is distilled from the juice of a particular kind of maguey plant that is grown only in the Mexican state of Jalisco. The Mexicans take tequila straight; and its taking is attended with appropriate ritual. A sprinkle of salt on the back of one hand, thumb and forefinger holding a slice of lime—in the other hand, a shot glass of tequila. First you take a lick of the salt, then the tequila is shot into the mouth and swallowed fast, followed immediately by biting into the slice of lime.

Tequila is not a drink that is ever very likely to be popular among Northerners, whose palates have not been hardened by the unrestrained use of chili, but it has recently been used effectively as the basis for the Margarita. In this drink the force of an ounce of tequila is diminished with a dash of Triple Sec liqueur and the juice of half a lime or lemon; the mixture is shaken well with ice and strained into a glass whose rim has been lined with salt.

We must not overlook one of the noblest of preparatory drinks—and

Opposite: As the clock nears the pleasant hour of the apéritif it is good to remember that these drinks are simplicity itself to serve; most just need chilling. Pernod should be diluted with a little extra water— which turns it cloudy—and bitters like Campari are often mixed with soda. Here on a silver tray are nine popular apéritifs. In the front row, from left, are sweet and dry vermouth on the rocks, a semi-dry Lillet, and bittersweet Byrrh on the rocks. In the middle row are Pernod with ice, tasting of licorice; St. Raphael and Punt e Mes, both slightly tart, and Campari and soda, the bitterest of the lot. In the back row are champagne (the author's favorite of all) and Dubonnet Blonde on the rocks, lighter and drier than red Dubonnet. On the compote are four tempting hors d'oeuvre. On the top tier are steak tartare balls filled with black caviar and sprinkled with chives, and fresh mushroom caps with anchovy-cream-cheese stuffing. On the bottom tier are onion sandwich rounds rolled in parsley, and chicken salad rounds rolled in nuts.

that is sherry. Sherry is an ideal beverage with which to start an evening of good food, good drink and conviviality. Yet I would prefer not to deal with sherry now, but later at the end of the book, with those other two great fortified wines, port and Madeira. For sherry, like them, can be a dessert wine as well as an apéritif.

Champagne.   Any of these apéritifs helps to prepare the palate and set the mind and body at rest. But to this author the very best drink before dinner is a glass of vintage champagne.

Champagne has had a checkered career and has known many vicissitudes of fortune. It is, in the authentic version, a white sparkling wine, produced from grapes, mainly red, grown in a limited area around Rheims and Épernay in northern France. French champagne is a manufactured wine to the extent that the natural processes of fermentation have been interrupted. It receives more care and attention than any other wine in the world. It also has been associated with frivolity, vulgarity and the goings on in private rooms in restaurants. That is one of the reasons why it is highly taxed. Raymond Postgate, the English author, wrote, "Puritanism in decay no longer persecutes sinfulness, it makes money out of it; governments therefore have put a specially high tax on this wicked wine. Mill-girls (says the Treasury in effect to Sir Jasper the Bad Baronet) must, of course, continue to be ruined by you, twirling your moustache and offering them bottles of 'bubbly,' but to mark our disapproval you shall pay us an extra tax per foaming bowl."

But champagne is expensive for another reason—the time and difficulty that are involved in its manufacture. It is quite easy to make an effervescent wine: If you bottle it tightly stoppered, before the fermentation is complete, the carbon dioxide gas cannot escape until you open the bottle. The man credited with discovering this was Dom Pérignon, who was cellar master of the Benedictine Abbey at Hautvillers, near Rheims, for the last 47 years of his life, which ended in 1715. The French have long revered him in song and statuary as the man "who put the bubbles into champagne," which is not strictly true. Nature put them there; Dom Pérignon found a way to keep them there—by using a cork tightly tied down so that the action of the expanding gas could not force it out. Until that time, corks had not been used in the Champagne region. Bottles were simply plugged with tow, and olive oil was dripped on the top to keep out the vinegar bacteria.

Certain modern historians, however, insist that Dom Pérignon's chief claim to honor was his skill as a blender. He was blind, but he had a remarkable sense of smell, and he taught the winegrowers how they could improve the taste of their wines by judicious blending.

Champagne is blended chiefly from the juice of the Pinot noir, Pinot blanc and Pinot Chardonnay grapes. The juice of the Pinot noir is white, but the skins are a midnight blue, almost black, on the outside, red on the inside. If the juice stays with the skins more than the briefest time, it will take on unwanted color. One of the remarkable facts about champagne is that its pale golden liquid comes partly from the same black grapes that produce Chambertin and the other rich red Burgundies of the Côte d'Or. The northern area of Champagne, above the Marne River and

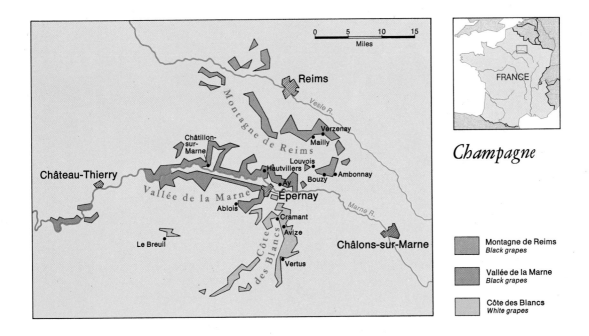

Champagne

Montagne de Reims
Black grapes

Vallée de la Marne
Black grapes

Côte des Blancs
White grapes

around the town of Rheims, is planted in black grapes. On the Côte des Blancs in the south, around and below the town of Épernay, the white grapes, Pinot Chardonnay and Pinot blanc, are planted.

At harvest time, the best grapes are carefully selected by a team of women, who go over each bunch and cut away those grapes that are broken or bruised or otherwise imperfect. This process is called *épluchage*. Only ripe, sound grapes are put into willow baskets, called *caques*, and carried to special presses that have been erected throughout the vineyards so that the grapes may be pressed as quickly as possible before the skins have broken. Everywhere else in France, grapes are transported from the vineyards to the wine maker for pressing.

The first pressing of the grapes, called the *tête de cuvée*, will be used for the best and most expensive wines. Several weeks after the pressing, when fermentation has died down and the wines can be tasted, expert tasters get to work in special blending rooms that are spotlessly clean and utterly free of any odor that might detract from the true taste of the wine. The wine is fairly acid at this point; to us it would be totally unrecognizable from the tingling, frothy beverage that bubbles into our glasses. But an expert taster can determine what proportion of wine from different lots is needed to obtain the particular style and personality that his firm strives to maintain year after year.

When it is blended, the wine is ready to be put into bottles. Just before it is sealed with its temporary cork, a "dose" of sugar is added. This sugar will induce a second fermentation in the bottle, producing the carbon dioxide gas that gives the champagne its sparkle. During secondary fermentation, the wine is stored on its side in underground cellars, to mature from two to four years.

The soil of Champagne is chalky and the major portion of the wine is stored in the deep, damp chalk cellars around Rheims that were constructed by the Romans; they were simply chalk mines in those days. The cellars

Three small areas within the Champagne region produce the two kinds of grapes used for French champagne. Nearly all champagne is made from a blend of juices from black grapes, traditionally grown in the north, and white grapes, traditionally grown in the south (the region's very name, Côte des Blancs, means hill of white grapes).

consist of long galleries broken every now and again by air shafts that taper upward to the ground above. It is extremely cold there, and if you scratch the walls you can see the clean white of the chalk.

As the wine undergoes its second fermentation, tremendous pressure builds up from the carbon dioxide that is formed in the process. In earlier days, before the sugar dosage could be precisely measured, the pressure often became too great for the hand-blown bottles of the time to withstand it, and so many bottles burst that it was actually dangerous to work in a champagne cellar. Today, breakage is down to 1 per cent, but since one million bottles is not an unusual stock for a major shipper, that can still mean a loss of 10,000 bottles.

The second fermentation "throws," or disperses, a sediment throughout the wine, and it is to get rid of this sediment—a natural but unavoidable by-product of the induced secondary fermentation—that rather complicated and expensive manipulations must be employed. The first of these is *remuage*. The bottles are set neck down in slanting racks called *pupitres*. Every day each bottle is given a slight twist to the right and a slighter twist to the left and is tilted very slightly downwards. Eventually the bottle points straight down with all the sediment collected on the cork. This process of *remuage* takes about four months; *le remueur*, a highly trained man, can turn as many as 30,000 bottles in a day.

The next problem is to extract the cork with the sediment attached to it without losing the carbon dioxide. This is done by a *dégorgement*, the cork being skillfully extracted and a second clean one substituted. It is an extremely difficult operation, for which a man needs a five-year apprenticeship. The change of cork is effected by freezing the wine in the neck of the bottle in chilled brine, so that, with the cork, a small lump of ice composed of wine and sediment can be extracted. A small empty space is left in the bottle, which is filled in with what is known as a dosage —sugar soaked in still wine and a trace of brandy. Some firms, feeling that the wine changes if frozen, simply uncork the bottle, removing the sediment with a bit of wine that is replaced when the sugar dosage is added. This operation must be performed with great deftness in order to lose as little wine as possible. The amount of sugar in the dosage determines what kind of champagne the wine will be: brut, which contains not more than 1 per cent sugar; extra sec, 1 to 2 per cent; sec, 3 to 6 per cent; and demi-sec, 5 to 10 per cent. The cheaper champagnes are the sweeter ones because the sugar can disguise a certain lack of quality.

There are two other ways of making a sparkling wine. One is by the tank method. Enameled tanks are used for the second fermentation and, when it has partially subsided, the temperature is lowered and the yeast cells settle. The wine is then filtered and transferred into another tank, where the dosage is added. The tank method provides a much cheaper way of producing an effervescent wine since a great deal less labor is required. The Germans adopted this technique, calling the product *Sekt;* it frequently can be a very pleasant beverage. Some American champagnes are also made by the tank method. The other method is called impregnation: Carbon dioxide gas is forced into a white wine of fairly high alcoholic content before it is bottled.

The Champagne district operates differently from other vineyard districts

Continued on page 74

For a Majestic Wine, Royal Care

Champagne is a queen among wines and is treated regally both in its manufacture and its service. As long ago as the early 18th Century, champagne was drunk from special glasses *(below, center)*, frosted to conceal the sediment then common to these wines. Later the other glasses shown evolved, still in the fluted shape to keep the sparkling bubbles. Displayed with them, in the Épernay cellars of Moët et Chandon, are antique bottles, a pipette *(center)* for drawing wine from the cask and a *pomponette (right)* for tasting wine. The stained glass shows Dom Pérignon, the monk who perfected champagne-making methods around 1700.

Épluchage: The Champagne Grape's Exacting Test

Just unloaded from the two-wheel wooden carts that are traditional in the vineyards of the Champagne country east of Paris, baskets and boxes of freshly picked Pinot noir grapes *(opposite)* wait near a press house to be culled. Before pressing, each bunch must pass the painstaking inspection called *épluchage*. Trained workers *(below)* examine every bunch, grape by grape, and cut away any that are green or overripe, or have been damaged by rain during the autumn harvest. Only perfect grapes pass the test and go into the making of fine champagne.

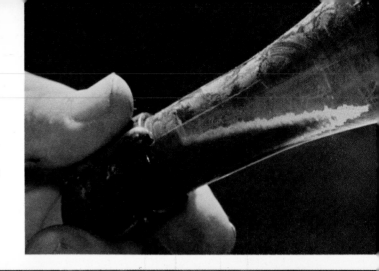

A Twist, a Pop to Clear Champagne

As it ages in its bottle, champagne develops sediment that makes it cloudy. To remove the sediment, wine makers use two techniques: *remuage* and *dégorgement*. In the *remuage* process, bottles are stored on a slant in a rack called a *pupitre* and are gently shaken and turned daily (*below*). The slant increases over three to four months until the bottle virtually stands on its head— and the sediment settles against the cork (*right*).

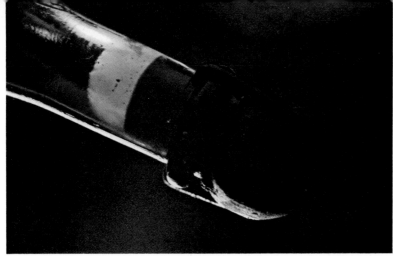

In *dégorgement*, the bottle's neck is dipped in a freezing brine solution, creating a small plug of ice that encases the sediment *(left)*. The *dégorgeur (below)* then cuts the wire holding the cork, and ice and sediment fly out in one swift, satisfying burst. The clear champagne is recorked shortly thereafter.

in France in that the farmers who grow most of the grapes for champagne sell them to manufacturers, called shippers, who make the wine and ship it under their firm names. This is largely because the process of making champagne takes longer and costs more than the making of most other wines. The shippers are located primarily in Rheims and Épernay, and all of the important ones own vineyards in the area, but they buy the bulk of their grapes from the owners of smaller vineyards. They pay according to how the soil of a particular vineyard has been officially rated. The top shippers try to buy as much of their raw product as possible from plots with the highest official rating, but most champagne is blended from grapes coming from a variety of soils.

There are 20 shippers who are world renowned and who are responsible for 75 per cent of the total production, but there are some 120 firms that supply champagne. Some of this wine is not up to the standard of the big 20, who are, alphabetically, the firms of Ayala, Bollinger, Charles Heidsieck, Heidsieck Dry Monopole, Henriot, Krug, Lanson, Laurent Perrier, Mercier, Moët et Chandon (makers of Dom Pérignon), Mumm, Perrier-Jouet, Piper-Heidsieck, Pol Roger, Pommery et Greno, Louis Roederer, Ruinart, Saint-Marceaux, Taittinger and Veuve Clicquot.

Each brand has a slightly different flavor, each shipper aiming at a consistency of taste. In consequence of the blending of champagne there is not the same importance attached to a vintage year that there is with Burgundy and Bordeaux; the nonvintage wines are intended to have the same taste every year. That is the business of the blender. The shippers draw a simile from music. They achieve a harmony through a succession of different notes. They retain a certain amount of the previous vintages for blending with the new.

Vintage and Nonvintage.   There is such a thing as vintage champagne, however. In an occasional year when the grapes have matured exceptionally well, a vintage is declared, the champagne is made from that year's crop alone, and a date is set upon the bottle. It is a more expensive wine, and you have the advantage of knowing the bottle's age. Nonvintage champagne should be drunk when young; so do not lay it down. It remains on a plateau of quality after the *dégorgement;* beyond its fourth or fifth year on the market it tends to go off, to become darker and to lose its taste. It will have taken on the color of Madeira and will taste flat and musty. Such wine is said to be maderized.

If you see a nonvintage champagne on a wine list you may get a wine older than you want. That is the advantage of buying vintage wine. Vintage champagne is richer, more full-bodied and may keep a dozen years or more. Occasionally a special year produces a very special wine; 1928 was such a year, and I do not expect to meet a wine to equal Krug's 1928. Yet during the winter of 1966-1967, I met a nonvintage Krug that was nearly as good, in of all unlikely places, Oklahoma City. I say unlikely because Oklahoma has ceased to be a dry state only in recent years, and it is not a state that has a tradition of wine drinking. I found this wine in the Cellar Restaurant, whose director, John Bennett, had acquired a substantial cache of it. Each time I tasted a bottle—and I tasted quite a number—I got the same sense of approaching a divinity. It is impossible to describe the taste of a wine. One has to find a simile. Alexander Dumas said of certain great Burgundies that whenever you encounter one, it deserves to be drunk while you kneel bareheaded in front of it. The Cellar's nonvintage Krug had that effect on me.

Some champagnes are labeled *blanc de blancs*. This means that they have been made exclusively from white grapes. They are lighter in body than other champagnes and very pale. Because of the current vogue for "lightness" they bring a higher price, but their quality is not necessarily superior to that of the blends. There is also a rosé, or pink champagne, which is light and dry and generally more expensive than regular nonvintage. The color may come from leaving the skins in the vat for a little longer, as is done with the best rosé, but quite often the color is produced simply by adding some local red wine.

Two other words that are easily confused may occasionally appear on a champagne label: Cramant and *crémant*. Cramant is the name of a town on the Côte des Blancs below Épernay. Some of the *blanc de blancs* come from here. *Crémant* is a type of champagne that is less effervescent. Made usually from both red and white grapes, it has a pleasing, subdued sparkle and a delicate taste.

Only wine made within a certain area can be sold as "French Champagne"; but other sparkling wines advertise themselves as having been made by "la méthode Champenoise." If this is in fact the case, then they are entitled to use "champagne" on the label as long as it is qualified by adding, for example, "American" or "California" or "New York State." Some of the best sparkling wines of America are made in California from the same kinds of grapes used for French champagne: the Pinot noir, Pinot blanc and Pinot Chardonnay varieties. The firms of Almadén, Korbel, Paul Masson, Hans Kornell, Weibel and Beaulieu, located in the cooler northern regions around San Francisco, produce very good champagne and in much of their production take the necessary pains and time that the champagne method requires. So do such Eastern firms as Taylor, Widmer, Gold Seal and Great Western. In New York State, the grapes used are often the Delaware and Catawba, blended with California wine, and the sparkling wines on the whole tend to be somewhat sweeter than those produced in California.

When, Where and How.   Champagne is the drink for an occasion: for a christening, for a wedding, for any kind of celebration. You can drink it at any time of the day, with any course during a long meal.

When I was young there were those of us who considered it smart to decline champagne when we were offered the choice of it, saying we would prefer "a real wine." There was a time when it was considered ostentatious, vulgar, *nouveau riche*. I remember reading in the 1920s a book on etiquette by a titled lady saying that it was "bad form" to serve champagne at lunch. I cannot think why it should have been, and I have noticed that it has become the mode in certain London clubs to serve champagne in silver tankards, so that one's fellow members' attention is not called to one's relative affluence. It was, in fact, almost reluctantly that I found myself forced to concede that the only wine I preferred to champagne was a really great Burgundy, and as that came my way so seldom, champagne became my favorite wine. My heart never fails to lift at the sight of a gold-foiled bottle and at the sound of the pop that reassures me that the wine is young and vital. I welcome it at any time, but I still consider that it fulfills its purpose best as an apéritif. When I give an ambitious party, whether it is lunch or dinner, I start with a glass of very dry champagne, accompanied by a dry biscuit or a plate of nuts. Champagne makes a party go as nothing else does. Because of the bubbles and acidity you do not feel inclined to drink it fast; a glass and a half will last you through the half hour before you take your seat at table. Your palate by then is well prepared for the wines and foods that are awaiting you; your taste buds are alert, your gastric juices moving.

The wine should be chilled but it should not be frozen. Wine is a living thing and should not be subjected to violent shocks. The proper way to open champagne is not by letting the cork fly across the room: Too much sparkle and wine are lost. The recommended way is to slant the bottle about 45°, with a napkin or towel placed between your hand and the cool neck of the bottle. Holding the cork in the other hand, slowly twist the bottle away from the cork. You will get a delicate pop and a wisp of vapor—but the champagne will not foam out onto the table—all the bubbles will be saved for your glass.

There is one thing about which you should be on guard, and that is the glass you drink from. A great many restaurants have adopted the habit of serving champagne in a low, wide saucer-shaped glass. This is doing a great disservice to the wine because it disperses the bubbles. The maker has been at great pains to get them there, and they should be retained as long as possible. The glass should be tulip-shaped, with the top rim bent slightly inwards. It should be not more than half filled, and it should have been chilled. When possible, a glass that contains champagne should be a thin, clear pretty one, because champagne is a pretty wine. But any glass that allows its holder to sniff the wine and that retains the bubbles is satisfactory. In Moët's Château de Saran, they told me that the best glass of all for retaining the bubbles is one with a hollow stem; however, health laws in some U.S. states prevent restaurants from using this type of glass because it is hard to clean. I cannot deprecate too strongly the use of a swizzle stick to take out the bubbles. If you do not want bubbles, why not order Chablis?

A sparkling drink for festive summer occasions, champagne cup *(Recipe Booklet)* is served ice-cold with strawberries.

IV

The White Wines of Germany and Alsace

One of the steepest vineyards in the world clings to a hillside above the Moselle River village of Bernkastel, home of Germany's famous Bernkasteler Doktor wine. The ground is covered with fragments of slate, partly to help retain the heat of the sun.

The first wine to be served at the kind of dinner this book sets out to present must be a white one. Light wines must always be served before heavy ones; and white wines, since they are lighter in taste than red wines, are more pleasant with the light foods that are usually served at the beginning of the meal.

Wine experts are universally agreed that the world's greatest table wines come from the vineyards of France and Germany, and as all the supreme German wines are white, it is convenient to devote this chapter to a discussion of the wines that are produced in southwestern Germany, on the banks of the Rhine River and its tributary, the Moselle, as well as some that are produced on the French side of the Rhine's upper reaches, in the region of Alsace.

The Rhine and Moselle Valleys are the northernmost wine area in Europe, and winegrowers there are faced with innumerable difficulties. There is a lack of sun, the summer is brief, the hills flanking the rivers are so steep that the vineyards have to be terraced. Carts cannot be taken along them, and the awkwardness of the terrain adds considerably to the cost of the wine. There is a likelihood of spring frost and the consequent danger of partial or complete loss of a crop. Sugar often has to be added to the freshly pressed juice in poor years to increase the alcoholic content and stability of the wine. If this is done, the wines are euphemistically known as "bettered" *(verbesserte)*. In good years, when it is not necessary to sugar the wine, you will see on the label the word *Naturrein* or *Naturwein*, which means that the wine is in its natural state.

Rhine Wines.   The wines of the Rhineland share a basic family resemblance—the best are all made from the same variety of grape—and
yet they may vary considerably in taste. They are dry and sweet, light
and powerful; some fragrant like a garden in spring, some overpoweringly
lush like a tropical garden redolent with jasmine. One of the difficulties
of ordering from a German wine list is that it is very hard to be certain
how the wine will taste. One knows how a French wine should taste.
One does not know with a German wine.

I remember returning to England from New York in January 1939 by a
North German Lloyd ship, the *Hansa.* I was convinced that war was im-
minent, and I was anxious to remind myself before the curtain fell of
how many delightful sides there were to "the German way of life." I also
thought it was an excellent opportunity to sample German wines. It was
an eight-day voyage, and I was in funds. I had with me a book on German wines, and I surrounded myself with a battery of bottles. During
eight lunches and eight dinners, you can experiment quite a lot. I had a
wonderful time, yet I was often astonished by the difference between
what I had expected and what I received. A wine that I had expected to
be dry proved to be sweet, and vice versa. I kept thinking to myself,
"Wouldn't it have been terrible if I had given a dinner party. If I had ordered grilled salmon as my main dish and had served this lush, scented
wine to go with it. Or if I had at the end of the dinner accompanied a
Grand Marnier soufflé with this dry rich wine, the sugar in the soufflé
would have killed it!" I would never run the risk of serving big German
wines at a lunch or dinner without asking the advice of an expert. But learning to understand the intricacies of German wine labels will put you on
surer ground, because Germans are quite precise in indicating the type of
wine the bottle contains.

The three main wine-producing regions along the Rhine are the Rheingau, the Rheinhessen and the Rheinpfalz, which is also called the Palatinate.
Although similar, the wines of each have a subtly different flavor.

The Rheingau lies along a 20-mile stretch on the east bank of the
Rhine between the towns of Wiesbaden and Rüdesheim. It includes such famous wine villages as Eltville, Rauenthal, Erbach and Hattenheim, and
the even more notable estates of Steinberg, Schloss Johannisberg and
Schloss Vollrads. Most of the Rheingau is planted in Riesling grapes,
which are always used for the best German wines, and in good vintage
years the great Rheingau vineyards produce the most extraordinary white
wines of the world. These wines have been characterized as having a certain austerity or crispness, even the richest of them.

The second of these regions, the Rheinhessen, is on the west bank of
the Rhine south of the Rheingau and the town of Mainz. Here, the Sylvaner grape is the most abundantly planted, though the best vineyards in
the villages of Nackenheim, Nierstein and Oppenheim are planted pre-
dominantly in the more highly regarded Riesling. Wines of the Rheinhessen
are richer and softer than those of the Rheingau. Liebfraumilch, which is
so well known in America, originated along the Rheinhessen. Many people think Liebfraumilch is the name of a certain wine; actually, the name
can refer to any wine that comes from the Rhine vineyards. It is available
at all prices and its quality varies considerably; it is often a blend of less-

er wines. But the reputable shippers do offer sound and attractive Liebfraumilch under their respective brand names—to name a few, Sichel's Blue Nun, Langenbach's Crown of Crowns and Hallgarten's Blackfriars.

The third Rhine wine area, the Rheinpfalz, is also on the west bank of the Rhine. It is protected from icy northern winds and snow by the Haardt Mountains, and consequently there is more sunshine there; the summers are hotter, and some of the wines are so rich that they are best served with dessert. Others are not so sweet as they are spicy, which makes them particularly good with rich meats such as game, which is plentiful in most parts of Germany. Another sweet potation from the Rhine, May wine, is popular in the United States. It is flavored with woodruff, a European herb, and is usually served chilled in a large bowl with strawberries or other fresh spring fruit floating in it.

In addition to these three main regions there are two minor ones: the Mittelrhein between Rüdesheim and Koblenz, and the scattered vineyards in the foothills of the Black Forest, around Baden. Reference must also be made to two tributaries of the Rhine, the Nahe and the Main, whose

Europe's northernmost wine-producing areas are among those shown on this map. Germany's Rhine and Moselle River Valleys and the French district of Alsace—often held by Germany in the past—produce some of the world's finest white wines. Spellings of place names conform to usage in each country; thus it is the Mosel River in Germany and the Moselle in France.

Germany
and Alsace, France

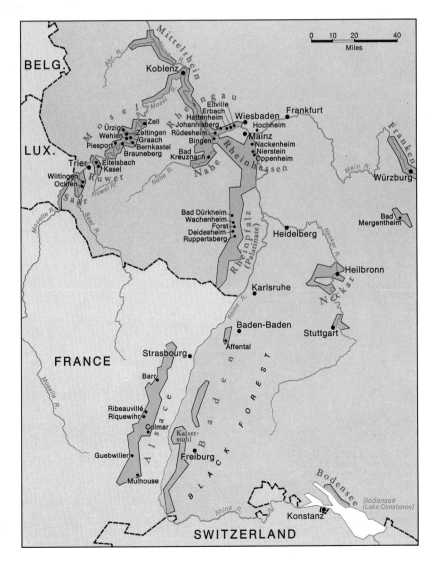

vineyards produce much excellent wine. The Main flows through Franken (Franconia), and the wines from Würzberg, which are known as Frankenweine, or Steinwein, are shipped in a stumpy flagon called a *Bocksbeutel*. Steinwein is dry, more closely resembling French white wines than the slightly sweeter Rhines and Moselles.

Moselle Wines. The Moselle Valley lies to the west of the Rhine. Moselle wines are lighter, gayer, drier than those of the Rhine. A Moselle is the perfect wine with which to begin a lunch or dinner, for it prepares the palate for all the excellent sensations to follow. These are the world's lightest wines in alcoholic content; rarely is it more than 10 per cent.

The terrain where grapes for the Moselle wines are raised is even more dif-

The finest German wines come from overripe grapes *(top basket)* covered with mold. Grape pickers carry two piggyback baskets to separate these prized specimens from ordinary ripe grapes. The mold on the overripe ones eats away the skin, causing the water to evaporate. The remaining drop of juice is rich in sugar; it makes a wine of superb bouquet and quality.

ficult than that of the Rhineland. The Moselle is a winding river: The straight-line distance between Koblenz and Trier, near the French border, is about 65 miles, but by boat you would be forced to cover twice that distance. The windings of the river are very short and the impression from the air is of a succession of peninsulas. The banks are considerably steeper than those flanking the Rhine—so steep that those facing north get no sun at all. The sunny slopes are too valuable to use as anything but vineyards, and some inhabitants of the region are forced to have their vineyards on one side of the river and their houses on the other.

Along the Moselle the winegrower has one task that no other has. The vineyards are lined with slate, which during the winter he has to cut out from the rock in slabs and break up into small pieces. These slates fulfill sev-

The color and shape of the bottle is the hallmark identifying different types of German wines. The slender green bottle on the left contains a fresh young Moselle wine; the taller brown bottle at right holds a mellow golden Rhine wine. The squat flagon in the center—known as a *Bocksbeutel* —contains a light, dry Steinwein, from the Würzburg area.

eral functions. They keep the soil moist and, during hot summer days, they also store up the heat of the sun, which at night is radiated back. The slates disintegrate and act as fertilizing agents; consequently they must be renewed periodically.

In one sense it is easier to deal with Moselle than with Rhine wines; there is less fundamental difference between one Moselle wine and another than there is between any two of the Rhine. One wine writer suggests that the secret of Moselle can be told in two simple words: slate and Riesling. They produce the variety that makes each wine slightly different even from its nearest neighbor and the light, delicate quality, full of incomparable bouquet that proclaims it inimitably Moselle.

The best-known wine-producing villages along the Moselle are Zeltingen, Bernkastel, Wehlen, Brauneberg, Ürzig, Graach and Piesport. The valleys of two tributaries of the Moselle, the Saar and the Ruwer, also produce some exceptional wines. Along the Ruwer are the two villages of Eitelsbach and Kasel, and along the Saar the towns of Ockfen and Wiltingen, the latter containing the world-famous Scharzhofberg vineyard. All over this region, vineyards produce Moselblümchen (little Moselle flower), which is more or less the Moselle's equivalent of Liebfraumilch from the Rhine. In poor years, when this wine is too acid, sugar is added. Sometimes, but rarely, Moselblümchen can be pleasant to drink.

Moselles are shipped in green bottles, Rhine wines in brown, and this suggests, perhaps, the difference between them: the fresh, green-gold, elegant, delicate wines of the Moselle and its tributaries, and the somewhat richer, more golden, fuller wines of the Rhine. Moselle wines mature quickly and are best drunk young, after four years or so.

The most famous of Moselle wines is Bernkasteler Doktor. Six hundred years ago the archbishop of Trier was struck with fever when he was visiting the village of Bernkastel. Every known remedy was unavailing. The holy man's end seemed near. But an old friend, a soldier, reminded of a cure that he had practiced on himself, brought round to the sickbed a flagon of his best Bernkasteler. He poured out a brimming glass. "Drink this," he said. "This will cure you." The archbishop looked at it askance, but at any rate he drank. His friend refilled the glass; the archbishop emptied it, then fell asleep. When he awoke next day, the fever had subsided. He was delighted. "I have been cured," he exclaimed, "by this great wine, this excellent doctor.' Ever since, the wine has been known as Bernkasteler Doktor. And you will see that name on the label of the bottle.

German Wine Labels.   Labels are important where any wine is concerned, but they are especially interesting in respect to German wines. To ascertain exactly what you are drinking, you have to study the entries on the label, and when you are dealing with an important wine there are many entries. This can confuse the neophyte, but once he has mastered the nomenclature he will find that he is given more precise information as to the contents of a German bottle than he gets from the label of a French, Spanish, American or Italian bottle. He is told not only the exact site from which the grapes were picked, the year and the grower or owner, but also something of the vintage conditions and even of the method used to make the wine.

On most German wine labels, the first word indicates the village from which the wine comes: Bernkasteler (from Bernkastel), Piesporter (from Piesport), etc. The second word indicates the site, or vineyard, and the word is usually a picturesque one: Altbaum (old tree), or Sonnenberg (sunny hill), for example. To this extent the German wine names resemble those of Burgundy—a village designation plus a vineyard name— except that a village wine from Burgundy can be fairly high up on the scale of quality, whereas a simple village appellation in German (Bernkasteler, Piesporter, Niersteiner) unaccompanied by a vineyard name will have little to recommend it besides price. Occasionally, however, you may find one of these little wines to be quite delightful. But wines without a vineyard listing are very likely to be blended wines.

There is an exception to this rule of label information: Certain individual vineyards are so outstanding that their designations will appear on their labels without any identification of the villages in which they are located. Schloss Johannisberger, Schloss Vollrads and Steinberger are three such wines from the Rheingau; Scharzhofberger is one from the Saar.

After the village and vineyard appellations there may follow the grape name, almost invariably Riesling, as it is the finest wine grape of Germany, and a grower would be unlikely to draw attention to his use of the lesser Sylvaner or Muller-Thurgau. Oddly, however, the finest vineyards producing the best of German wines do not necessarily indicate the grape on their labels; it is taken for granted that these great vineyards are planted exclusively in Riesling. There may follow a word indicating the ripeness, and hence the sweetness, of the grapes when they were picked. The four designations most commonly used, in the order of increasing ripeness and sweetness are: *Spätlese, Auslese, Beerenauslese* and *Trockenbeerenauslese*, meaning respectively, late-gathered (after the normal harvest days), selected gathering (specially ripe bunches), selected overripe berries, and selected dried or raisinlike berries. German producers make several wines in sunny years, and the later pickings produce richer, fuller, more powerful wines, which must be more expensive; not only because the vineyards have been harvested several times but also because the producer is by then risking frost that would destroy the remaining grapes with which he had hoped to make his finest wine, the *Trockenbeerenauslese*.

A curious wine from late-picked grapes is designated *Eiswein*. It is the result of a rare combination of circumstances by which ripened grapes have been partially frozen while still on the vine, and from them the sweetened juice has been carefully pressed. But this wine is fairly expensive, and very little is produced.

The effort behind the label entry *Trockenbeerenauslese* (selected overripe or dried berries) is worthy of description. The grape pickers carry, in addition to their regular baskets, small ones into which they put individual grapes that have been shriveled by the sun. They are partially covered with mold. This is known as *Edelfäule*, the equivalent of *la pourriture noble* in France. Only one drop of syrup can be extracted from each of them. These grapes are pressed separately; the wine from them will be very rich and sweet and will be of a deep golden color. They merit on the label the designation *Trockenbeerenauslese*.

If you find none of the words indicating the use of overripe grapes,

you can assume that the wine has resulted from the normal harvest and will therefore be fairly dry.

The next thing to appear on the label is the vintage year, and it is important to remember that the good wine years in Germany do not always correspond to those in France. Because of the northern, less sunny location of the German vineyards, there are fewer really fine years in Germany than in France.

German vineyards are often split up among several owners, and one must look for the name of the producer on the label, as one does for estate-bottled Burgundies. Individual holdings in German vineyards can be quite extensive, and one producer may have vines in several villages and several vineyards. The German government is in fact the largest owner of top vineyards in certain districts, and other large holdings are those of charitable institutions, schools and old titled families.

As the best German wines are bottled straight out of a cask without being blended, the number of the cask appears on the label as *Fass* or *Fuder* (such as *Fuder* No. 127). Often the adjective *bestes* (best) will be included, which means the wine is from the owner's best barrel—the word means what it says and these wines will always be more expensive.

A somewhat similar ranking by the grower of his product often appears before the word *Spätlese, Auslese, Beerenauslese* or *Trockenbeerenauslese,* where you may find *feine* (fine), *feinste* (finest) or *hochfeine* (very finest). *Wachstum, Gewächs* or *Kresenz* means "growth of," and the word will be followed by the name of the owner of the vineyard. *Kellerabfüllung* or *Kellerabzug* mean cellar bottling; these are equivalent to *Original-Abfüllung* (sometimes abbreviated into *Orig.-Abf.),* which is an indication that the wine was bottled by the man who made it, similar to "château-bottled" for Bordeaux wines. Such wines have the owner's seal and the vineyard's name branded on the cork: *Korkbrand* (branded cork) may then appear on the label.

Inside my copy of H. R. Rudd's contribution to the *Constable Wine Library* are pasted two pre-World War II labels. One is a Marcobrunner 1920. It bears in its center the coat of arms of the owner of the Marcobrunn vineyard, Freiherr Langwerth von Simmern. In the bottom left-hand corner it has *Edelbeeren* (a less frequently seen term meaning berries of superior quality), and in the right-hand corner it has *Auslese* (selected picking of overripe grapes). At the top is the word *Cabinet,* which means special reserve, from the owner's best wines. I have forgotten the circumstances under which I acquired this label, but I can tell from the vineyard name and the designation *Auslese* that it was a medium-sweet dessert wine. The other label reads Rheingau 1934 Mittelheimer Edelman, Riesling, *Spätlese, Original-Abfüllung;* the grapes were late-picked *(Spätlese)* in the Mittelheim vineyard and the wine was bottled in the cellars *(Original-Abfüllung)* of the man who made it (Edelman). As it was a *Spätlese* Rheingau wine, I would assume that it was big and full-bodied, not oversweet—the kind of wine that if the main course was to be fish, salmon or lobster, could be the meal's main wine. But you can serve such a wine equally well with meat or game. There are some who maintain that you cannot serve white wine with meat. But that is a fallacy. Red wine does not go with fish, but a dry white wine goes with anything. Of course, it

Opposite: Happy harvesters stop to sing on their way home from a day of grape picking near Zellenberg, in Alsace. The vineyard they work belongs to a man named Wachter *(far left).* His holdings are less than four acres, too small for him to make his own wine, and so his relatives help him pick the grapes and take them to a cooperative to be pressed with others of the same variety.

is with dessert that you must serve a full, rich *Trockenbeerenauslese*.

I have not drunk nearly as many great German wines as I would have liked. There was the intervention of the Second World War, when they were practically unobtainable, and I have spent a large part of the last 20 years in the West Indies, Morocco and the South of France, where I have had to rely on what was to be had in local stores; but I have drunk enough great German wines to recognize that they have something no other wines possess. It is impossible to describe what that something is. But it seems to me that there is a sequence of sensations on the palate that cannot be explained but has to be experienced.

The greatest German wines, *Beerenauslese* and *Trockenbeerenauslese*, are not easy to find; there are very few of them and they are inevitably expensive. So much labor goes into their creation. The number of shriveled grapes is small and each one can yield only one drop of nectar.

At the same time, there are many light and pleasant table wines produced both on the Rhine and on the Moselle that are not expensive and should be drunk when they are young.

Alsatian Wines.

The wines of Alsace bear a close kinship with those of the Moselle; they have the same lightness and freshness, and are made from the same grapes. They have not acquired the reputation of Moselle wines, but then they have had an interrupted history. Alsace was part of the German Empire for 47 decisive years (1871-1918), the years in which the wine trade of the world was reforming itself after the ravages of phylloxera, the infestation that destroyed vines all over Europe. During this period the Germans, influenced possibly, if only subconsciously, by the uncertainty of their tenure, denied an identity to Alsatian wines, refusing to build up reputations that might later prove a challenge to themselves; they planted the vineyards with cheaper vines and used the wines for blending. When the French regained possession of Alsace in 1918, after World War I, they recognized that if the best value was to be obtained out of the recovered territories, the vineyards would have to be replanted. This was done, but it took time and money, and it was not till the early 1930s that Alsatian wines again appeared upon the market. They quickly proved popular, but no sooner had they become established than the Germans resumed possession—by conquest—in 1940. In 1945, after World War II, Alsace was restored to France, and the French had to start again from scratch, since the Germans had lowered the quality of the wine in favor of quantity. The Alsatians are at present doing exceptionally well. We shall probably find during the next 10 years that their wines are even better than we suspect.

Presented in tapering green bottles, Alsatian wines are marketed by the variety of grape, such as Riesling, Sylvaner, Traminer or Gewürztraminer. The name of the village is occasionally added; for example, Ribeauvillé, Riquewihr, Ammerschwir, Guebwiller. The Riesling and Traminer wines are generally considered superior to the Sylvaner ones. *Gewürz* means spicy; this name is given to the Traminer wines that develop a rich, fruity flavor. Gewürztraminers are more expensive than the Riesling and Traminer wines, but their sweetness sometimes makes them more suitable for the end of a meal, with fruit or a dessert.

Slender bottles of Riesling and Gewürztraminer are displayed with a pheasant and desserts outside a café in Alsace.

V

The Great Wines of France

A candlelit glass of Mouton-Rothschild, one of the great Bordeaux red wines, stands surrounded by spider-web-encrusted magnums of the 1923 vintage. The wine shown here is from the cellars of Baron Philippe de Rothschild, whose family has owned the Médoc district's famous Château Mouton-Rothschild for 100 years. In the dim recesses of the cellar, candlelight is still used to check the color of the aging wines.

The truth is that there are only a very few great wines. That is the miracle and the mystery of wine, that the vine—the *Vitis vinifera*—has traveled right around the world, and yet in only a few fate-favored places is *great* wine produced. What do I mean by "great" wine? Simply this: Certain spots in some magical way combine the right soil, the right amount of sun, the right amount of rain, the right angle of slope—all these things for the right kind of grape to produce wines that in their balance, their bouquet, their subtlety of flavor, and often their longevity, are unmatched by any others. They are all different from one another, having in common only their nobility, which they express in endless, enthralling ways; and it is a good thing that your palate will prefer this one and mine prefer that one, so that there will be no end to the delightful debates over their respective virtues.

But in this select company all are superb, and all unique. Each is a creation that could not be duplicated chemically, or even naturally in another spot—not even by using the same grapes and importing the same soil and the same workmen with the same methods of cultivation and harvest. Move the vine and the wine will be different. There are vineyards in Burgundy where the vines at the top of the hill yield a far finer wine than do those a few hundred yards farther down. Half a mile away the situation may be reversed; the lower slope may be the favored one. Why one vineyard should produce an ordinary wine and another across the valley should produce a supreme one, no one knows; but that is the way it is, and we should be grateful that in a standardized, machine-

made world there is one article that cannot be turned out to pattern.

We have already talked about the champagne from Épernay and Rheims, the white wines of the Rhine and Moselle, and the white Alsatians—and now we cannot delay longer dealing with the world's greatest wines, the ones ideally suited to accompany the main meat course of our imaginary dinner: the fabulous French wines of Bordeaux and Burgundy. Both of these regions produce red and white wine—and in each the best is generally conceded to rank with the best in the world. Bordeaux comes in tall, slender bottles and has been called the queen of red wines. It is subtle, inclined to be on the light, dry side, with an aftertaste that is indescribable. Its appeal is discreet and aristocratic. By contrast, Burgundy is the king. Its bottle is stouter in shape, with sloping shoulders, and the wine is stouter too. It is heavier, "chewier"; it hurls its imperial brilliance at you with a shout.

Getting to know the Bordeaux and the Burgundies, with their apparent infinity of place names and complicated labels, seems a hopelessly confusing task. Actually it is simpler than it seems, for the French government has established regulations to aid the wine lover. These are the famous *appellation contrôlée* laws, put into operation in the 1930s. Their aim is not only to prevent such sharp practices as the adulteration of good wines with

At the stately Château Bouscaut, students and townsfolk from the nearby city of Bordeaux pick ripened grapes. This vineyard, comprising less than 100 acres, takes about 10 days to harvest. Like all fine Bordeaux wines, the reds and whites produced here are bottled at the château, rather than at a shipper's winehouse.

bad ones and the use of misleading labels, but also to try to force each district to produce the very best wines that it is capable of. To that end, the laws specify the exact boundaries of each district, the kinds of grapes that may be grown in those districts, and even the amount of wine that can be produced per acre in each district. In the Médoc district of Bordeaux, for example, the general quality of the wine is very high, and *appellation contrôlée* laws are aimed at keeping it that way—the Médoc is subject to stricter standards of quality than the other wine-producing districts in both Bordeaux and Burgundy.

Bordeaux.   Let us take up Bordeaux first. With no exception, without even a rival, this all-important area stands supreme for the extent, quality and variety of its wines. Every type of unfortified wine is made there: delicate and full-bodied reds, dry and sweet white wines, even a little rosé. The wines of Bordeaux run the full gamut of quality and price, from obscure local pressings that sell for a few cents a bottle and are drunk on the spot (they are not worth shipping), to the great château names like Lafite and Haut-Brion, which ring like bells in the imagination of the wine lover, and which, for a good vintage, command upwards of $10 a bottle on the New York market—when they are available.

93

To find good wines from the modest vineyards that supply all but a twentieth of Bordeaux's famous clarets, shippers' representatives like buyer Olivier Penigaud *(above, in blue smock)* and wine broker Maurice Touton sample freshly pressed grapes on a Médoc farm, one of many they will visit during the autumn. Later they continue their evaluation by inspecting a vineyard *(center)* with farmer René Renon. Penigaud, the chief buyer and *maître de chais*, or cellar master, for Bordeaux's largest shipper, the house of Calvet, is a familiar figure in the region and is widely respected for his judgment; his word can make or break a wine.

The boundaries of the Bordeaux region are defined by the *appellation contrôlée* laws. Any wine grown there, so long as it conforms to other provisions of the laws, may be labeled Bordeaux—Bordeaux red, Bordeaux white. Primarily, that designation guarantees the place of origin. It says nothing about the quality. However, a dealer in wines, or a shipper, may add his name to the label. He goes around to different vineyards, selects the wines he thinks are best, blends them and markets them under his own name. From year to year "his" wine, if he is a reliable man, will approach a dependable standard. It will be good but not exceptional, because it is an average, both of individual vineyards and also often of good and not-so-good years.

To find a somewhat better grade of wine, one does not buy a mere Bordeaux; one should select a bottle from a certain part of the Bordeaux region, which is divided, again by the laws, into two dozen separate districts. Many of these produce rather undistinguished wines, but five of them produce some of the greatest wines in the world, and the quality within those five districts is so superior that there is an obvious advantage for the grower in any one of the five in labeling his wine as coming from there. The five are: Médoc, Graves, St.-Émilion and Pomerol, renowned for their reds, and Sauternes, for its supreme dessert wines, which are white.

The Médoc.   Therefore, if you find a bottle labeled Médoc, with a good shipper's name added, this will be a good wine—and it will have a certain characteristic that will clearly distinguish it from the wines of Pomerol or Graves.

Are all the wines of the Médoc of similar quality? By no means. The district is divided into two areas, the Haut-Médoc (High Médoc), and the Médoc. The latter used to be called the Low Médoc, but that term somehow sounded derogatory, the vignerons who had holdings there objected strongly, and they succeeded in getting the "Low" eliminated. They had a right to feel sensitive, for their wines are good too; yet the best wines of the Médoc are indeed made in the Haut-Médoc section.

So, narrowing down still farther, we find ourselves in the Haut-Médoc, which in turn is divided into 28 municipalities called communes. Four of the best known of these are Margaux, Pauillac, St.-Estèphe and St.-Julien. Thus, a bottle label saying *appellation contrôlée,* and St.-Julien, pinpoints the wine as coming from one small commune in Bordeaux where red wines of almost uniformly outstanding quality are produced. There remains only the question of what specific vineyard in St.-Julien grew the vine. And for the greatest wines of all, that is all-important. It is traditional in Bordeaux to refer to individual vineyards as châteaux. These

Like all connoisseurs, Olivier Penigaud considers cheese the perfect complement of a good wine. On his way home from a vineyard, he often stops at an outdoor stall *(above)* to buy cheese to go with the evening's wine. Penigaud's judgment is crucial not only to the vineyard owner but to consumers as well. He is in charge of all of Calvet's wine stocks. When the name of a house such as his appears on a bottle of Bordeaux, it is a familiar reassurance to the buyer. Other houses with the same kind of renown: Barton et Guestier; Cordier; Cruse; Delor; Eschenauer; Ginestet; N. Johnston; Kressmann; Alexis Lichine et Cie.; de Luze; and Sichel.

châteaux, incidentally, are not the imposing castles that you will find on the Loire River; they are generally spacious country houses, although some are little more than storage buildings in the vineyards. But whether the building be imposing or modest, the wine that many of the Médoc châteaux put out is glorious. The owners guard the reputation of their labels jealously—some of them to the point of refusing to put their name on any wine at all if the year should be a bad one; then they sell their whole crop anonymously to a shipper to be blended. This happens rarely.

There are a great many châteaux in Médoc alone, and to settle some of the confusion, a committee of Bordeaux wine brokers sat down in 1855 to divide them into five classes. The system is a simple numerical one. The top grade, for example, is *premier cru*, which translates literally as "first growth" but really means "vineyard of the top class." When someone refers to Château Calon-Ségur as a third-growth Médoc, which it is, he means that the château produces wines of the third class; they are not quite as superb as those of the first or second growths. Yet even a fifth-growth Médoc is far from a poor wine. On the contrary, it is something special, for out of the hundreds of châteaux that were rated in 1855, only 62 were deemed worthy of classification. Three were put in the first division: Lafite-Rothschild, Latour and Margaux; and a fourth, Haut-Brion, was added, although it is not a Médoc at all but a Graves. All the names in the five categories are listed in the Appendix.

So, in addition to the warranty of quality supplied by the words *appellation contrôlée* on a Bordeaux bottle, one also has, for the finest wines, the name of the château itself, and such words as *mis en bouteilles au château* (bottled at the château), which give the buyer the assurance that the wine in the bottle was grown in a certain vineyard, by a certain man, and bottled right there.

In making the great classification of 1855 the wine brokers did not simply trust their palates. They drew up their list in terms of the prices that the various vineyards had received over the years. "The higher the price the better the wine," is how the wine trade puts it, and they might have chosen a worse yardstick. Some vineyards in the original classification are no longer producing wine, and others deserve to be moved up a notch or two; by now Mouton-Rothschild would certainly qualify as a first growth. But the list has stood up reasonably well against the changes and chances of more than 100 years; the classification still represents the *grands seigneurs* of the Médoc. And when you order any one of these château-bottled Bordeaux, you know you are buying a superior wine.

I am not suggesting that anyone should memorize the five divisions of the Médoc classification, but I would suggest that every student of what is after all a fascinating subject should run his eye fairly often over the list. He will not remember the wines one by one, but his mind will retain a visual memory of the list, so that he will be on his guard when he sees a totally unfamiliar name.

The famous Médoc châteaux, along with many others in Bordeaux, owe their fame not only to the excellence of their wines, but also to their large size. Most of the great vineyards of Burgundy, the Rhine and the Moselle are divided among a number of proprietors, some of whom may own only an acre or two in a choice location, and each of whom makes a

Opposite: The greatest red wines of Bordeaux are displayed in the cellar of Delmonico's Hotel in New York. In the front row are Château Lafite-Rothschild 1952, Château Latour 1953, Château Margaux 1947, all from the Médoc, and Château Haut-Brion 1918, from Graves. These four châteaux were rated as finest in the 1855 classification. In the back row are Château Mouton-Rothschild 1955, also from the Médoc district; Château Pétrus 1953, from Pomerol; Château Cheval-Blanc 1952, and Château Ausone 1964, both from St.-Émilion.

slightly different wine, following his own counsel. In Bordeaux, properties of 100 and 200 acres in single ownership are not unusual. Château Lafite, for example, contains 150 acres under vine and produces up to 15,000 cases of red wine a year. The wine in all the Lafite bottles of a given year is identical. This adds immeasurably to the ease with which a Bordeaux lover can pinpoint his favorites. Because of the large production, he will have less difficulty in procuring the wine. Having once sampled it and filed the name of the vineyard away in his mind, he can always return to it with the assurance of getting the same thing again. This would not be the case in Burgundy. Le Montrachet for example is a tiny vineyard of only 18½ acres, and it has (when last I heard) eight owners, the best wine being produced from a plot of less than four acres.

Graves. It was only the red wines of the Médoc that were graded by the committee of Bordeaux brokers in 1855, but there are three other districts where superb red wines are made—Graves, St.-Émilion and Pomerol. These have since been classified by other experts. Red Graves have not got the reputation they deserve, chiefly because the name has become identified with a rather ordinary sweetish white wine that is put upon the market in great quantities and labeled "Graves." The red Graves are something else again. They include (in addition to the magnificent Haut-Brion) Pape-Clement, Haut-Bailly, Smith-Haut-Lafitte, La Tour Haut-Brion, Domaine de Chevalier and La Mission-Haut-Brion, all of which are as great as most of the second-growth Médocs. Excellent white wines come from Graves too.

St.-Émilion. St.-Émilion actually produces more wine than the Médoc, and a great deal of it finds its way to the market under the name St.-Émilion alone, without the identification of a specific vineyard. But there are some famous châteaux in St.-Émilion: Châteaux Cheval-Blanc and Ausone are considered the finest; slightly below them are Figeac, Canon, Clos Fourtet, Magdelaine and La Gaffelière Naudes. St.-Émilion has always been popular in England, providing a welcome antidote to the damp clammy climate. In my view, its wines are the fullest and richest of all the Bordeaux.

The medieval town of St.-Émilion is one of the loveliest in France: The steep streets are paved with ancient cobblestones, and the view of the hillside vineyards from the town's summit is magnificent. It has very close links with the world of Roman letters: In the Fourth Century that graceful poet Ausonius, who was born at Bordeaux, the son of a Roman senator, became the tutor of the future Emperor Gratian, and his pupil rewarded him by making him prefect of Gaul, Italy and Africa. After a successful career as a lawyer and colonial administrator, Ausonius retired to a villa outside the walls of St.-Émilion to write verses in tribute to the local wines. The wine that is today called Ausone comes from a château that stands, according to legend, on the ruins of his villa.

Pomerol. The smallest of the fine-wine districts of Bordeaux is Pomerol, and its wines have long been linked with those of its neighbor, St.-Émilion. Actually the wines of Pomerol have a distinctive taste of their own, rich and with a special undertaste described by experts as a "truffle taste." The properties are small, so their production is limited, and for that reason the wines are relatively expensive and hard to find. Château Pétrus is the finest wine of Pomerol and is ranked on a par with the first growths of the Médoc.

These four districts—the Médoc, Graves, St.-Émilion, and Pomerol—contain the finest vineyards of Bordeaux, and their 50 or 60 leading châteaux have long produced the bulk of the fine red wines available in New York, London or Paris. Today, however, they are becoming increasingly expensive. Production is limited by the *appellation contrôlée* laws, which, as we have already said, define not only the legal geographical limits of the terrain, but also the number of gallons permitted per acre of vines. And as demand increasingly outstrips supply, there has been, in the last few years, greater interest in the *cru bourgeois* of Bordeaux. These wines from less well-known châteaux are not classified by "growth," but they are attractive and agreeably priced and have found a ready market with those many of us who can only on occasion afford to buy the best. Some of these châteaux have made respectable reputations for themselves: Château Loudenne, for instance, Château Citran, Château Timberlay and Château Greysac.

Sauternes. I have written perhaps without enough enthusiasm for the white Graves, but I find it hard not to be ecstatic when I write of the white wines of the fifth famous Bordeaux district, the great Sauternes, of which Château d'Yquem is the undisputed monarch. They are rich and sweet in flavor, golden in color; they are to be sipped and brooded over. Many are so rich that you cannot take much more than one glass at a meal, and that glass should be taken at the end of the meal, with the wine sharply chilled. There is a strong resemblance between the way in which Sauternes and the German *Trockenbeerenauslese* wines are made. The vintage is late; I have even seen the leaves stripped from the vines so that the grapes could catch every last shaft of sunlight. The laborers go over the vines six or seven times, judging which grapes need an extra day of sunshine before the essential degree of overripeness, the *pourriture noble,* has been achieved.

There is a legend concerning the discovery of *pourriture noble* at Yquem. Generations ago, the owner of the château had to leave his estate before the grapes were picked. He left instructions that nothing was to be done about the harvest until his return. He was delayed on his journey, and when at last he got back he was horrified to find that his instructions had been carried out literally, and his vines were covered with shriveled grapes. He decided, however, to make the best of a bad job and ordered his laborers to proceed. To his astonishment and delight the resulting wine gave him a series of sensations that he had not suspected the world had for giving. "Never again," he vowed, "will the grapes be picked before they are completely rotted."

This happened before chemistry could explain how this miracle was brought about. The owner of the Château d'Yquem, like the ancients who two millennia before matured their wine by storing it in amphorae, had stumbled on the solution of a mystery, without recognizing that there was a mystery to solve. Wisely, he too accepted the gods' gift to man. We know now that the superbly smooth sweetness of his wine was caused by a mold called *Botrytis,* whose filaments can penetrate the skin of the grape and draw off the water from inside without damaging the ultimate taste of the wine. The juice that remains is 40 per cent sugar.

If dry wines are desired from grapes, *Botrytis* is the grower's greatest enemy, and usually the grapes are picked before it can get to work on them. But it is the fairy godmother of the great dessert wines, which is why the growers refer to it as *la pourriture noble*—the noble rot.

The wines of Sauternes are divided by classification as the wines of the Médoc are. Yquem stands in a class by itself. In addition there are 11 first growths, all of them magnificent. I cannot claim to have a favorite, though I seem to have drunk more Rayne-Vigneau than any other. And with Rayne-Vigneau I have sentimental associations. During the second year of World War II, I was posted as staff-captain to an organization called the Petroleum Warfare Department, which concerned itself with the malevolent uses to which petrol could be put in the event of an enemy invasion—flame throwers and the like. I worked and also had my flat in London. There was also living in my building a lady of considerable attractions with whom I was much concerned. We used to meet in the evening, when our respective offices had closed, for a glass or two of sherry. When the noise of the bombing—that was the season of the first London Blitz—set our nerves on edge, we would cross the Strand and go to Boulestin's, that famous underground restaurant that was so impervious to bombing that one of its rooms had been converted into an air-raid shelter. Not too many Londoners were dining out at that particular period, and the full effect of rationing was not yet felt; Boulestin's excellent cellar was still intact. It had a cache of Rayne-Vigneau—I forget the year—in half bottles. We would always finish our dinner with a half bottle instead of a liqueur or port; we sipped it slowly, appreciatively, not knowing what manner of disaster awaited us in the street above.

Clos Haut-Peyraguey is another magnificent first-growth Sauternes, and it too brings to mind personal associations. In my brother Evelyn's novel *Brideshead Revisited,* Sebastian Marchmain and Charles Ryder take a bottle of Haut-Peyraguey on their picnic on the occasion of Charles' first visit to Brideshead. I have wondered how they managed to get it cool; but even as I wonder, I remember that a reluctance to cool wines other than champagne was one of Evelyn's eccentricities. Readers of *Brideshead* will recall that in another scene, during the Atlantic crossing, Charles Ryder is presented with iced soda water to mix with his Scotch—and asks for some hot water to take the chill off it. In Evelyn's home, Coombe Florey, he did have cool larders for his meat and game, but I saw no signs of ice. His elder son-in-law—an American professor—was disconcerted on his first visit to Coombe Florey to be offered on a hot August night a warm Scotch and soda. And I remember that the last time I saw Evelyn—I was spending the night at his home—he served a very fine Sauternes (I fancy it was a Coutet) at room temperature. Well, that was the way he liked it, and a host is entitled to have things the way he likes. But 99 per cent of wine drinkers are agreed that a Sauternes should be served cold.

It is difficult wine to serve. There is a prejudice, I cannot think why, against it. People seem ashamed of saying that they enjoy a sweet wine, probably because there was a Victorian tradition that "the Ladies, God bless them, liked a glass of something sweet." The Victorians used to serve Sauternes with the fish course. It is generally agreed now that this was a mistake; it was so strong that it killed the light red wine that prepared the way for the robust red wine that was the evening's centerpiece. Sauternes must come at the end of a meal; but if you serve a bottle to a dinner party of eight, you are quite likely to have half your guests refusing it. After a big red wine they are ready to wait for their coffee and liqueur. That means you have half a bottle of one of the world's greatest wines upon your hands. One glass really is enough for anyone—unless you are in a sentimental mood, which you are unlikely to be in at a dinner party for eight. It is best, perhaps, to have two dinner parties on consecutive evenings—or more practically, to buy half bottles.

Burgundy. The author of *La Vie de Bohème* said, those many years ago, that the first duty of a wine was to be red; as a young man I used to add "and its second is to be a Burgundy." During 50 years I have lost faith in much, but not in that. As a younger man, I also used to say that life had little better to offer to a Londoner than curling up in a corner seat of a French train headed south. Perhaps it has been windy and wet in Paris, and when the traveler wakes and draws the curtains he will see the red-tiled roofs of Provence, the villages clustered on their mountaintops, the palms, the sunlight and the south. Where else could you find such a contrast; you go to sleep in one world, you wake in another. You are reborn; you are another person. Where else in the world could that miracle be performed?

Today in a jet-haunted world, I still prefer to go south from Paris by train; I take the *Mistral* that leaves shortly after 1 and reaches Nice at midnight. I prefer it to the *Blue Train,* because it carries me by daylight past that strip of hillside that holds what is for me the dearest treasure upon earth, the Côte d'Or, the golden slopes of Burgundy. Three hours out of Paris the *Mistral* reaches Dijon, and for the next half hour on the way to Beaune it passes near vineyard after vineyard whose glories have been celebrated for centuries. The late Camille Rodier, High Chancellor of the Confrérie des Chevaliers du Tastevin (Brotherhood of the Knights of the Winetaster's Cup) described their red wines as "rough and hard in their youth, divesting themselves, softening with age and when years have ripened them, shining bright, pure, soft, perfumed and delicious in all the splendor of a magnificent glory."

Riding past the homes of these wines, I am reminded of all sorts of Burgundian lore. Burgundy has a regal quality and power that no other wine possesses. There are those who consider that it has too much power, that it is a heavy wine. Perhaps it has, perhaps it is, for those who live in a southern climate. And it is and has been always most popular in the northern countries, in England, Holland and Belgium.

Burgundy has always been an expensive wine, too, not always easy to come by. Parisians themselves had few opportunities of appreciating it until the 16th Century, when Charles V of Spain and the Holy Roman Empire handed over the Duchy of Burgundy to the crown of France. I question if Shakespeare had drunk much of it; if he had, would he, in *King Lear,* have talked of "waterish Burgundy"? I question if much of it reached the Thirteen Colonies. In the 18th Century the Crown imposed prohibitive duties on French wines. What little reached England and the Colonies was almost entirely smuggled in, and it was much easier to conduct a smuggling operation with Bordeaux from the coast of Aquitaine than with Burgundy from a valley south of the Massif Central. But the main problem about Burgundy then as now is that there is so little of it. In comparison with Bordeaux's annual 100 million gallons of wine of *appellation contrôlée* quality, there are only six million gallons of fine red Burgundy and about 1.5 million of the white from the Côte d'Or.

Burgundies reach their prime earlier than Bordeaux do. When I was young, we used to give a big Burgundy eight years to reach maturity. After 12 it started to go off. But now Burgundy is usually ready to drink after five years and begins to go off after eight. This is because nowadays wine makers—in Burgundy as well as Bordeaux—aim at allowing less tannin to enter the wine. Tannin, an acidic substance that comes from the pips, skins and stems of the grapes, gives Burgundy its strength and staying power, but it also gives the immature wine that harsh flavor to which Camille Rodier referred. Louis Latour, a leading grower and shipper in Burgundy, told me that his father had recognized the need for a faster-maturing wine after World War I. He foresaw that the days of cellars and big country houses were at an end and that a new generation living in a restless, turbulent and uncertain world would not want to lay down in 1921 wines that could not be drunk till 1931. How prescient he was. And it seems to me that the fine Burgundies that I am drinking now are every bit as good as those I was drinking in the '20s.

Burgundy *(map, page 113)* is divided into two parts—the Côte d'Or and southern Burgundy. The best, the supreme Burgundy, comes from the Côte; it in turn is divided into two sections: the Côte de Nuits and the Côte de Beaune. The Côte de Nuits immediately south of Dijon contains the great red vineyards—among them Chambertin, Romanée-Conti, Musigny and Clos de Vougeot—to the latter of which one of Napoleon's colonels ordered his men to present arms as they marched past: "My children, it is to protect these beauties that you go to fight." Clos de Vougeot is now the headquarters of the Tastevin brotherhood, where its banquets are held. The train threads its way toward Nice through these hills, and I feel that I should rise and bow to them. I very often do.

South of the Côte de Nuits and the famous township of Nuits St.-Georges begins the Côte de Beaune, home of the supreme white Burgundies. Three of them—Montrachet, Corton-Charlemagne and Meursault—are renowned for their combination of rich fruitiness with unmistakable dryness. We could even say that there are *no* greater dry white wines than these—along with Chablis, which is ranked as a burgundy though it lies a number of miles northwest of the main Burgundy area.

The riches of the Côte de Nuits and Côte de Beaune are almost an embarrassment, for they exist in so many variations as to mislead the unwary. Larmat's *Atlas de La France Vinicole* explains why: "In Burgundy, particularly on the Côte d'Or, the dividing up of vineyards, the differences of soil and climate have prevented the establishment of large estates with wines of fixed and settled nature. There are instead a number of *lieux-dits* [sections], each of whose vines may be divided among several different owners. These sections make up *climats* [vineyards], many of them very small, producing famous wines.''

What this means is that you may find three bottles legitimately labeled "Chambertin 1959" that come from different parts of the Chambertin vineyard and have been made by three different growers. The best wines of Chambertin come from the middle slopes, yet wines produced from grapes grown at the top or the bottom of the hill are equally entitled to call themselves Chambertin. Thus you cannot accept a Burgundian label in the way that you can one from Bordeaux—or more properly, you have to bring more knowledge into play when reading Burgundy labels or scanning a list of Burgundy wines. I suspect that this is one of the reasons why many experts do not feel as confident with Burgundy as they do with Bordeaux. They have to trust their own noses and palates, whereas any two bottles of Bordeaux Lafite-Rothschild 1959 will taste the same, provided they have been properly cared for.

Today recognizing an outstanding Burgundy is much simpler than it was when I drank my first bottles. Despite the widespread feeling that the multiple ownership of the vineyards—dividing each into many individual plots, or *domaines*—would make any kind of classification impossible, a number of dedicated men did manage in the 1930s to institute clearly defined *appellation contrôlée* laws for Burgundy. Wines from the Côte d'Or are divided into three categories. One is *village wine,* from any vineyard within the particular village; it is identified only by the name of that village, for example, Nuits St.-Georges, Pommard, Volnay or Chambolle-Musigny. A *premier cru,* or "first growth," is usually labeled with the name of the village followed by the name of the vineyard, for example, Nuits St.-Georges/Les Vaucrains; Pommard/Épenots; Volnay/Champans; or Chambolle-Musigny/Les Amoureuses. At the very top are the *grands crus,* or "great growths"; these wines are so consistently outstanding that the vineyard name appears alone on the label. There are 30 such vineyards, among several hundred in Burgundy *(Appendix).* Obviously, one must do a little more homework to read a Burgundy wine label, but reference to the map will clarify a great deal. Once you have the names of the dozen or so villages firmly in mind, you know that any wine so labeled is a village wine, and can be quite good. If another name follows that of the village, you have got hold of something that will be better, a big step up, with the personality and character that come from a particular vineyard. And if you come across a *grand cru,* then you know you have arrived at the pinnacle of quality.

This system still leaves unsolved the problem of multiple ownership of these vineyards. A 10-acre vineyard may have five owners, and the largest of all, Clos Vougeot, with 125 acres, now has about 80 owners, each tending the soil, pruning, harvesting, pressing and caring for the wines on his own plot in his own way. Thus, there are practically 80 different kinds of Clos Vougeot produced in any given year. Actually, they are all somewhat alike. They share the magnificence of bouquet that sets Clos Vougeot aside from all other wines. But some are markedly better than others, and they cost more. Finding a good one is becoming less and less of a problem since more and more of the finer wines are being estate-bottled, the equivalent of Bordeaux château bottling; the name of the man who made the wine and bottled it can be found on the label along with such indications of estate bottling as the words *mis en bouteille au domaine* (bottled at the winery) or *mis en bouteille à la propriété* (bottled at the estate). Anyone who has visited with these proprietors, tasting of the different barrels in their small cellars, will appreciate even more the pleasure of being able to drink the unblended product of a particular vineyard, its individuality and distinction guarded by one man jealous of his own reputation.

A word of warning is appropriate here, particularly for those purchasers who might scan a Burgundian label quickly, looking only for the name of one of the great vineyards.

Unless one is careful it is all too easy to mistake a mere village wine for a *grand cru,* since it is the custom in the Côte d'Or, particularly in the Côte de Nuits section, to attach the name of a *grand cru* vineyard to the name of the commune, or township. For instance, Corton is a *grand cru* vineyard; it is situated in the commune of Aloxe, and so all the general village wines of the commune are called, justifiably or not, Aloxe-Corton. The wines of the commune of Gevrey similarly become Gevrey-Chambertin. These village wines, although not *grand* or *premier cru,* can be very good. In some other cases the name of the commune is very like the name of some of the vineyards it contains. Vosne-Romanée contains the three great vineyards of Romanée-Conti, La Romanée and Romanée-St. Vivant. But a wine labeled Vosne-Romanée is not at all the same as one that is labeled, with grand simplicity, La Romanée.

Chablis.   To the northwest and some miles away from the Côte d'Or is the town of Chablis—whose white Burgundy is always held to be the best accompaniment to oysters. That I cannot myself judge, because I have an allergy to oysters, but I have enjoyed Chablis immensely with hors d'oeuvre and fish. In spite of being very dry it is full of richness. It is very pale in color. They say it has a "flinty" quality, and the French describe its taste as that of *pierre-à-fusil* (flint). That seems to be the kind of simile that irritates the neophyte. "How ridiculous," he may exclaim. "Who has ever tasted flint?"

The *appellation contrôlée* laws permit Chablis to be sold under four different categories: *grand cru* Chablis, *premier cru* Chablis, Chablis and, finally, *petit* Chablis. There are seven *grand cru* vineyards around Chablis and they consistently produce the finest wines; there are a couple of dozen *premier cru* vineyards, with somewhat different soil and a different exposure, on the hillsides surrounding the town, and they too are excellent. Without bothering to learn the various vineyard names, you can be pretty sure that a *grand cru* or *premier cru* Chablis will give you a good bottle of wine. The third category of Chablis is good, but should be less expensive than the first two, and *petit* Chablis, from the area around the best vineyards, can be very good value, but it will not retain its charm and freshness as long as will a *premier cru;* it should be drunk within three years of the vintage.

Chablis, when it is real Chablis, stands alone; but a great many more bottles bear the word Chablis on their label than were ever filled in that

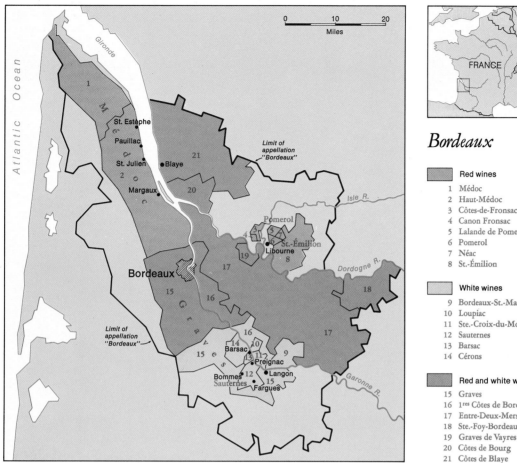

FRANCE

Bordeaux

	Red wines
1	Médoc
2	Haut-Médoc
3	Côtes-de-Fronsac
4	Canon Fronsac
5	Lalande de Pomerol
6	Pomerol
7	Néac
8	St.-Émilion

	White wines
9	Bordeaux-St.-Macaire
10	Loupíac
11	Ste.-Croix-du-Mont
12	Sauternes
13	Barsac
14	Cérons

	Red and white wines
15	Graves
16	1ʳᵉˢ Côtes de Bordeaux
17	Entre-Deux-Mers
18	Ste.-Foy-Bordeaux
19	Graves de Vayres
20	Côtes de Bourg
21	Côtes de Blaye

small parish. Chablis is, unfortunately, the most imitated wine in the world. Its name has been appropriated outside France to designate a generic type of dry white wine that is made in many different parts of the world. You may buy Spanish chablis, California chablis, Chilean chablis and Australian chablis—but none of them can approach the richness and finesse of a genuine Chablis from one of the *grand cru* vineyards in France. One sniff of its austere bouquet, one sip of its exquisite nectar will convince you of its inimitable character.

Chalonnais, Mâconnais and Beaujolais.   Chablis is only one of

the important Burgundies that come from sections outside the world-famous Côte d'Or. South of Chagny, where the Côte d'Or ends, lie the districts of Chalonnais, Mâconnais and Beaujolais. The wines of Chalonnais, though good, are not so well known as they deserve to be, but Mâconnais is the home of Pouilly-Fuissé, which has become very popular in the U.S. A pale golden wine with a greenish tinge, it can be drunk when it is young. It is excellent with fish or white meat and with hors d'oeuvre. The wines of nearby Pouilly-Vinzelles are very similar to Pouilly-Fuissé and often just as good.

The third of these districts is Beaujolais, a vast region that is the source of tremendous quantities of wine in a wide range of qualities. The

This map of the Bordeaux region shows 21 districts (keyed by numbers) where grapes for some of the world's finest wines are grown. Five of the most famous districts are identified by name, as are the localities whose wines connoisseurs of Bordeaux might seek out.

Continued on page 112

Buyers wait in line *(above)* in the Hospices de Beaune cellars for winetasting. Later, in a tapestried hall *(below)*, the auction proceeds. Tradition specifies that when the second candle burns out, the bidding ends, but auctioneers do not follow this custom strictly.

A Famous Burgundian Hospital That Cares for Wine

In the heart of Burgundy stands a hospital known to wine lovers all over the world. Called the Hospices de Beaune, after the town where it is located, it is a charity hospital that has served the poor of the community for more than 500 years. Its good works are possible because its founders and patrons endowed it through the years with fine vineyards. Every year on the third Sunday in November the wines from these vineyards are sold at public auction. The occasion is the climax of a weekend known as Les Trois Glorieuses—Three Glorious Days. Church bells ring and people swarm through the streets. Before the auction the public is admitted to the hospital's low-ceilinged cellars for a fee of five francs to sample the new vintage. The professional tasters come in later with their *tastevins*— silver tasting cups. Then on Sunday merchants from France, the United States, England and other countries bid for the wine, and the prices they offer are an indication of the quality and probable success of the year's new Burgundy vintage.

Two Hospices de Beaune Burgundies bear the names of a founder, Nicolas Rolin, and his wife, Guigonne de Salins.

Begun in 1443, the Hospices de Beaune is a fine example of medieval Gothic and Romanesque architecture, embellished with a brightly colored tile roof. This hospital building was financed by Nicolas Rolin, Louis XI's tax collector. "He has ruined the people with his taxes," said the King; "it is fitting that he should provide them with an almshouse." The hospital includes medical, surgical and maternity departments, a school for nurses and facilities for old people. It also maintains a wine museum with an extensive viticulture library, a fine collection of wine glasses, bottles, carafes, old wine labels and silver winetasting cups.

109

Brotherhood of Burgundy Lovers

In the depression years of the early 1930s three successive Burgundy vintages failed. Thousands of small vineyard owners were all but wiped out, and only the renowned Hospices de Beaune wines sold well. In 1934, to put the wine industry back on its feet and to achieve for all Burgundies the kind of attention that only Hospices de Beaune wines had been attracting, a new association was formed. Called the Confrérie des Chevaliers du Tastevin—The Brotherhood of the Knights of the Winetaster's Cup— it was an association of wine connoisseurs whose membership has now swelled to 17,000. To promote their favorite wines the association holds a succession of banquets throughout the year. The liveliest of these comes the night before the Hospices de Beaune auction in the Chevaliers' headquarters, the 600-year-old Château du Clos de Vougeot in Burgundy. On this occasion the Brotherhood gathers in a joyous mood to welcome new members into its order, hear its musicians, the Cadets de Bourgogne, sing Burgundy's praises *(left)* and sample the new vintage *(below)*.

Officers of the Brotherhood try out a bottle of Burgundy.

111

southern part of the district produces ordinary Beaujolais, the middle area produces somewhat better wines entitled to be called Beaujolais-Villages, and the northernmost section contains nine wine communes whose wines are the *grands crus* of Beaujolais: Moulin-à-Vent, Brouilly, Morgon and Chénas, to name a few. Wines in Beaujolais are made from the Gamay grape instead of the Pinot that the *appellation contrôlée* regulations specify for other Burgundies. Elsewhere the Gamay is held in low repute; it stands for quantity, not quality. But in Beaujolais where the soil is granitic, it produces excellent wines. These wines of southern Burgundy are much lighter than those of the Côte d'Or. There are many who believe that they should be served slightly chilled, particularly if you are drinking them in a warm climate. They can be drunk very young; they seldom improve after three years. At a recent gastronomic dinner in the Casino at Nice we were served a Beaujolais straight from the wood; it was delightful.

Some sparkling wines, both red and white, are made in Burgundy. The whites among these *vins mousseux* have no particular quality, but red sparkling Burgundy, because it looks so pretty, has its adherents. It was in

Near the village of Denice in Beaujolais, farmer Jean-Louis Giraudon pours a splash of wine for his eight-year-old daughter Christine. Many French children drink wine— often simply added to water—as readily as American children drink milk. Both Christine and her sister Evelyne, six, sitting at left, help their father harvest the grapes.

Edwardian days very popular with ladies of the chorus. But it can never be very good—because there is so little fine Burgundy that the winegrowers would never devote their best wines to it.

The Loire Valley.

To the west of Burgundy is the Loire Valley, famous not only for its great châteaux but also for its delightful white wines. The greatest of them, Pouilly-Fumé, is naturally confused with Pouilly-Fuissé and there is a resemblance between them even though Pouilly-Fumé is made from the Sauvignon grape instead of the Pinot Chardonnay used for Pouilly-Fuissé. Pouilly-Fumé is sometimes called Blanc-Fumé (White Smoke) because of the misty blue dust that the grapes give off at harvest time. It is a beautiful sight to see the mist hanging over the vineyards in the cool autumn air. Not a great deal of this wine is produced and it seems to be better known outside than inside France, even though it was Marie Antoinette's favorite.

When I ordered a Pouilly-Fumé a few years ago in a New York restaurant, the wine waiter told me that his stock was exhausted for the moment. "Have a Sancerre," he said, "it's practically the same wine, but cheaper." He proved right. Sancerre lies just across the Loire River from Pouilly and the vineyard is twice as large. It is a delightful wine. Ernest Hemingway drank it whenever he drove through France. He would pick up a case and keep it chilled so that whenever he wanted a bottle he could drink it "crackling cold," the way he liked it.

There are other well-known wines produced in the Loire Valley: Muscadet, Vouvray, Saumur, and the rosés of Anjou. Muscadet is a pleasant dry white wine that goes well with oysters. Its popularity has increased in recent years as the price of Chablis has mounted. Of the many sparkling white wines made on the Loire, Vouvray and Saumur are the best known; they also come as still wine.

The Rhône Valley and Provence.

One other region of France is justifiably famous for the substantial wines that suit a dinner's main course. This is the Rhône Valley, which produces more than 20,000,000 gallons of wine a year, mostly *ordinaire,* but also including some superior types that are particularly well known and liked in the U.S.: the hearty red Châteauneuf-du-Pape, the refreshing rosé called Tavel, and the big reds and whites of Hermitage.

All these wines come from the southern part of the valley, near Avignon. This historic walled city was the headquarters of the Roman Catholic Church in the 14th Century, and the presence there for 70 years of the lively papal court is commemorated in the name of the Châteauneuf-du-Pape district, a small area about 20 miles northeast of Avignon containing several villages and vineyards. Its wine is unusual because, unlike fine Burgundies and Bordeaux, which are each pressed from a single variety of grape, it is made from a blend of grapes. For the best Châteauneuf-du-Pape, 12 or even 13 varieties are used, including the Syrah, a grape presumed to have originated in Persia and to have been first planted in the Rhône Valley by the Greeks in about 500 A.D., when Pliny the Younger described it; and it was noted again in the 1780s, when that indefatigable agronomist and wine lover, Thomas Jefferson, visited the re-

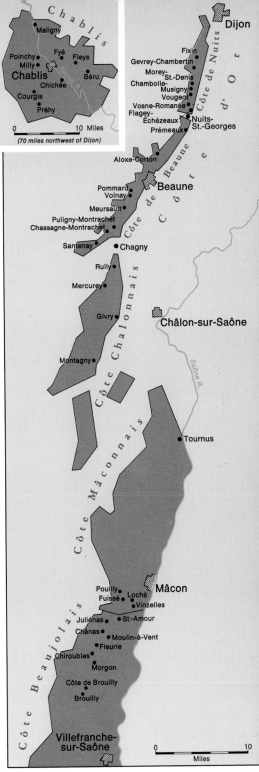

Burgundy

A long, narrow strip of land in eastern France is the source of Burgundy wines.

gion. Jefferson's characterization of Rhône wine—"keeps well, bears transportation and cannot be drunk under four years"—applies to Châteauneuf-du-Pape. The red (there is also a less well-known white) is rich in flavor, so deep in color that it appears purple, and strong (the alcoholic content is at least 12 per cent). The experts recommend that it be given no less than four or five years to mature.

Rosé. Just five miles from Châteauneuf-du-Pape, west of Avignon in arid country away from the river, is the village of Tavel, home of France's best rosé. A rosé is what its name implies—pink wine. It is fresh, it looks pretty, and it suits a variety of occasions, a nice, casual wine for a picnic. But it also serves well as the accompaniment to the main course at dinner, particularly if that happens to be ham or a cold buffet.

Some rosés are made by mixing red wine with white, but in Tavel and its neighboring village of Lirac a more difficult—and effective—process is employed. Red-wine grapes are pressed and the skins are removed from the juice as soon as it reaches the prescribed shade of pink. The result is a sharp, full-bodied wine that has delighted connoisseurs around the world.

Often when I think about the big wines that mean so much to an eventful meal, I recall a dinner that I gave for nine friends in April 1957—my most ambitious gastronomical undertaking.

I was at work on a book that was published 18 months later under the title *In Praise of Wine,* and I thought it would be a good idea to conclude the book with a description of the best dinner that could be given in London at that time, without considering the cost but without indulging in extravagance. My purpose was historical. Wine books are quickly dated, because they describe wines that are either no longer available or have faded, and they soon go out of print. But they linger on library shelves, and it is of interest now and then to see what was being eaten and drunk 50 or 100 years ago and what it cost. I have re-read many times de Maupassant's account in *Bel-Ami* of the dinner that Madame de Marelle offered to three of her friends in the private room of a Paris restaurant and for which the entire bill was only 120 francs (today, about $25). And I thought that a future writer, if he should read *In Praise of Wine,* might well be grateful for my information.

I sought the advice of an old friend, that well-loved *doyen* of wine writers, André Simon, and I put myself unreservedly in his hands. I made only two stipulations: that the main wine should be a red Burgundy and that we should finish with a Sauternes—but not a Château d'Yquem. André, with supreme and characteristic generosity, crowned my project by presenting to the feast as the main wine two bottles of Château Gris/Nuits St.-Georges 1928, estate-bottled. "I have," he said, "been waiting for the proper occasion to drink these."

The dinner was held at the Belfry—a lunch and dining club in West Halkin Street, a quaint building architecturally that was originally designed as a chapel for the furtherance of an eccentric spiritualist cult, the Society of Progressive Souls. The upper room, which had been reserved for my dinner, had once been the organ loft. The roof was curved into a point. It was all exceedingly ornate.

Both the foods and the wines were designed to lead up to the Nuits St.-Georges. The dishes read as follows:

Canapés de Foie Gras

Barquettes de Caviare
(Caviar-filled Pastries)

Profiteroles de Cervelle Mignonette
Sauce Moutardée
(Minced Calf's Brains in Pastry Puffs with Mustard Sauce)

Darnes de Saumon Lucullus
(Salmon Steaks Braised in Champagne and
Garnished with Crayfish and Puréed Oysters)

Aiguillettes de Caneton Rôti Duxelles
(Sliced Roast Duck with Mushroom Purée)

Pommes Allumettes
(Matchstick Potatoes)

Soufflé au Fromage
(Cheese Soufflé)

Fraises Romanoff
(Strawberries in Orange Liqueur)

Petits Fours

Café

The following wines were served:

Krug (en Magnum)

Kaseler Herrenberg, 1953
Estate-bottled—Von Kesselstatt

Bâtard-Montrachet, 1947
Estate-bottled—Louis Poirier

Château Canon, 1953
Château-bottled

Château Gris/Nuits St.-Georges, 1928
Estate-bottled

Château Coutet, 1953
Château-bottled

The Krug champagne was not a vintage one, but it seemed no less good for that. As I have said before, I count champagne as the best of all apéritifs, and the fact that it came from the huge magnum bottle added to its appeal. Somehow wine is better in a magnum. One of Ernest Hemingway's characters in *The Sun Also Rises* makes this reflection, adding regretfully, "Yes, but it takes longer to cool."

The light, fresh Kaseler Herrenberg, a Moselle from the Von Kesselstatt family vineyards in Kasel on the Ruwer, accompanied the calf's brains. For the fish course, Louis Poirier's Bâtard-Montrachet was exceptional, a rich, full-bodied white wine. It is too powerful for fish simply poached or broiled, but a fine accompaniment to the more complex *saumon Lucullus.*

Châteaux Canon is a St.-Émilion, which is the most robust of Bordeaux red wines, excellent with roast duck and fine preparation for the red Burgundy that followed.

The Nuits St.-Georges/Château Gris was terrific. We were all astonished that a Burgundy should not have faded after 30 years. It was an exception to my experience with Burgundies; 13 years earlier on my return to England from service in the Middle East, I had found that the Richebourg 1923 that I had hopefully laid down in 1935 had died. But this Nuits St.-Georges was at its peak.

The conclusion of the dinner was celebrated with the Château Coutet, a first-growth Barsac, a slightly drier wine than most Sauternes are, and therefore it was my preference as partner to the strawberries in liqueur.

Regions of France where wine is produced are relatively small. Yet they put forth a variety of excellent wines; detailed maps of five of the greatest districts—Bordeaux, Cognac, Champagne, Burgundy and Alsace— appear on the pages indicated under their names on this map.

France

The menu described the dinner as being offered to nine wine-conscious friends. Its cost per head was 20 dollars.

There are two kinds of dinners at which the main object is the enjoyment of wine—a dinner such as I have just described in which you gradually lead up to a great wine, and one in which you compare different wines tasting one against the other. This latter kind of tasting party was a specialty of my late friend Vyvyan Holland, one of England's premier wine scholars. He would open three or four different wines, preferably red Bordeaux, and all of about the same quality. The glasses were numbered, so that we could keep the wines distinct. Sipping and savoring each glass, just before the main course of the dinner, we would assign our individual ratings to the wines and then compare notes. It was an intellectual as well as epicurean exercise, and I can recall happily many such an evening in his house at Carlyle Square.

In recent years I have enjoyed somewhat similar evening tastings in Washington, D.C., with a group of men interested in wine, of whom Fred Burka, the wine merchant, is the pivot. A dozen of us sit around a long table, with nothing to eat except bread and cheese to clean our palates and act as blotting paper. The session begins at 8 p.m. and the host insists upon punctuality; the wiser ones have probably taken a dish of soup earlier in the evening. (A winetasting is described on pages 196 and 197 in the Appendix.)

The bread, the butter and the cheese are excellent. They blend admirably with the different wines. The bottles are sampled; they are not drained. There is a patrician disregard of waste. We sip and talk, debating the merits —and faults—of this or that glassful, for 90 minutes or so, then the cheese plates and the glasses are cleared away and the kind of cake that would make the mouth of any schoolboy water is set upon the table, and tall tapered glasses are brought out to accommodate a white dessert wine, usually a Rhine wine. After half an hour or so the party will break up.

They are very pleasant evenings and very instructive as well. It is only by tasting one wine against another that one can learn how to discriminate between them. And the layman has so few opportunities of doing that. It is easy for one of a group of wine merchants, sitting around their board room, to say, "I wonder how the '57s are coming along. Let's have a bottle of the Margaux up and see." But you and I can do that only rarely. We cannot afford to often, nor are we often enough in the right company to make such experiments. It is impossible to recall in October 1967 how a Château Margaux 1959 tasted in July 1965. We can never become experts, so we have to rely upon the professionals who spend all their time with wine. But though we cannot become experts in that sense, we can have a great deal of fun for ourselves, and we can immeasurably enlarge our knowledge of wine, and what is more, increase our appreciation of it by experimenting as far as lies within our powers: to set, for example, a California red wine made from the Pinot noir grape against one made in Burgundy itself, and see if we can sense the difference. The more we are able to discriminate, the more shall we be able to appreciate the finer points of what is set before us. Wine has been sent to us for our enjoyment. It is certainly one of God's greatest gifts to man. Let us learn therefore how to make the most of it.

VI

Wines of Italy and America

The whole world makes, drinks, and cooks with nearly seven and a half billion gallons of wine every year, and from what one hears it sometimes seems that the French make and drink most of it. But this is not so. Although France does account for nearly a quarter of the whole, there are many lovely, wonderfully potable wines made in great quantities in Germany, Italy, Spain and Portugal, of course, but also in many other places: in Israel and Algiers; on the plains of Hungary and through the Balkans; in South Africa, Australia, China and Japan; in Argentina and Chile; and in Mexico, Canada—and the U.S., where total production soars higher every year.

I am a great believer in drinking the wines of the country. For one thing they are cheaper at home, and also many local wines do not travel well, so that you may be disappointed in New York by the taste of a French rosé wine that had delighted you after a long morning's tramp in the Provence hills. Local tradesmen want to push their own wares, but they know what to recommend. You can be certain, too, of the provenance of the wine. It has come straight from the local vineyards, and as it is a commodity that turns over quickly, it should be in good condition.

I spend a great deal of time in Tangier, and I invariably drink Moroccan wines there. The cheaper ones are sour and have an acid taste. But the Rosé du Cabernet and the Cabernet du President are very pleasant. I am not tempted by the French and Spanish wines that appear on the menu, not only because they are expensive, but because I cannot be sure that they will be good. There is so little demand for imported wines in Tan-

Ripe grapes frame the church of the village of Marano, in northeastern Italy. From the district around Marano comes a light, red wine known the world over as Valpolicella.

Rolling and braiding straw by hand, dexterous women fashion coverings for Chianti wine flasks on a public terrace in Certaldo, Italy. In an eight-hour day a worker can complete around 50 of the coverings; she is paid about seven cents for each.

gier that I wonder how the bottle came to reach the wine list. Was it bought at an auction sale, after a bankruptcy or a death? May it not have been frozen in an unheated shed in winter or left in a boiler room in summer? It may also, when at last it has found a home for itself in a restaurant's cellar, have been moved repeatedly from one bin to another because there was so little demand for it. Better not run the risk.

If you are in a Paris restaurant, you are less likely to be offered a wide variety of Rhine and Moselle wines than you would be in Cologne. If I were staying at the Hôtel de la Poste in Beaune, I would order a Burgundy rather than a Bordeaux. In Madeira, I would not ask for vintage port. In fact, I would say that you get the best variety of great wines in areas that owe no loyalty to a local vested interest. The four cities where I have sampled a variety of the greatest wines are Chicago, London, New York and Washington, D.C., where a discriminating clientele knows what is the best and insists on having it. Perhaps San Francisco should be included, but it is the center of the California wine trade, and as you can find the best California wines there, I am always tempted to try them.

The best reason for drinking local wine is that it is likely to be good. Dining in any of the wine-producing countries, you can probably find native wines to suit even so elaborate a meal as the one we have been following through this book.

120

Italian wines.   Of all the world's wine-making countries, Italy is in terms of production the most important. France produces over one and a half billion gallons of wine every year, but Italy produced nearly two billion gallons in 1967. The vine virtually covers Italy, growing in exuberant profusion from one end of the peninsula to the other, and covering the offshore islands of Capri, Ischia, Sardinia and Sicily. The warm climate encourages the vines to yield abundantly, and quantity rather than quality has been the first consideration. But in recent years attempts have been made, through the efforts of cooperatives and government agencies, to maintain a consistent standard by blending, in the same way that champagne shippers standardize their nonvintage wines. The I.N.E. (Istituto Nazionale per l'Esportazione) stickers that you will see on Italian bottles are a government guarantee that the wine at least came from the place it claims for its origin. Italian labels do not give the detailed information that German and French labels give. Most show only the name of the wine—and the name of either the maker or shipper.

Italy's wines cover a wide range of tastes, from sweet to dry, from sparkling to still. They can be rough and hearty, with an earthy flavor, or they can be soft and ripe, disarmingly light and delicate. They do not all travel well, and Italians keep many of their better wines to drink themselves. Some very good ones do, however, reach the United States.

There is no doubt that the finest Italian wines are produced in a few tiny villages in the mountains of the Piedmont just south of Switzerland. They earn their acclaim with two heavy red wines, Barolo and Barbaresco (of which Barolo is much the richer in body and in color), and the sparkling white *Asti spumante*. Some wine lovers, accustomed to the drier French champagnes, consider *Asti spumante* oversweet, but it is delicious at the end of a meal, with dessert and fruit. It is made from the muscat grape, which gives it a rich, room-filling fragrance.

The countryside west of Venice is the source of both red and white still wines of very high quality. Its gentle white Soave, along with Orvieto from the Umbrian hills, has gained wide popularity in the U.S. And its red wines from Lake Garda, Bardolino and Valpolicella, are so light and smooth and fresh that it is traditional there to drink one of them, rather than a white wine, with the famous trout from the lake. Valpolicella is a little lighter than Bardolino; it is often allowed to mature in the bottle, but in my opinion it is best drunk young and slightly cooled, like Beaujolais.

Tuscany, the fabled home of the Etruscans in central Italy, is also the home of Chianti and the straw-covered flask that contains a liter of it. But only the wine that is meant to be drunk young is put in flasks, since a round-bellied flask obviously cannot be binned to age the wine. The young Chianti in flasks can be very good. The Italians themselves like it that way—*frizzante,* as they say, prickly on the tongue, but not sparkling. It loses its quality, however, after about two years, and much of what is sold, particularly abroad, is too old. It was intended to be drunk young and has not been. This fact has harmed the reputation of the good Chianti as well as the poor, of which there is a great amount.

The best of this vigorous red wine is called *Chianti classico* and is identified by a special trademark on the label—a black cockerel on a gold ground. It comes from one particular area, specified by government regulations, between the ancient cities of Florence and Siena, and its production is carefully supervised. The result is a smooth, well-balanced wine that ages well. The larger estates in this circumscribed area, such as Ricasoli, Serristore and Antinori, produce a *Chianti classico* called *riserva* which can be excellent. It is aged in oak casks from four to six years before it is bottled—not in round flasks but in tall bottles with short necks.

In the other regions of Italy, each local wine has its special characteristics and native proponents. In Rome, for instance, the invariable *vin de table* is Frascati, a sturdy white wine perfect for washing down big meals. In Campania they tell us that Vesuvius gives the agreeable red wine Vesuvio a volcanic flavor. In Sicily they make the same claim for Mt. Etna. From Naples comes the well-known white Lacrima Christi (bottled in both sparkling and still forms), whose name means "tears of Christ." Legend has it that our Lord looked down on the beautiful paradise that had once been Naples and wept to see it filled with wickedness. Where His tears touched the earth, green vines sprang forth, the vines of Lacrima Christi. Some of

From Lombardy to Sicily, there are few stretches of Italian soil where the wine grape does not flourish. The country's abundant wine production is matched by a diversity that is not widely known; where the French concentrate on a few varieties of grapes for their wines, the Italians grow almost every type in the world.

Italy

122

the wine is excellent, but no steps have been taken to supervise production, which is inconsistent, typically Neapolitan, in fact.

From Lombardy comes one of Italy's few estate-bottled wines, Frecciarossa—"the red arrow"—whose owner proudly employs French vines and methods to produce red, white and rosé wines. Lombardy also prizes its Valtellina reds, Sassella, Inferno and Grumello, and the lovely Lake Garda rosé, Chiaretto. Orvieto, a white wine from Umbria, is a great favorite with Italians who prefer the traditional semisweet version over the dry Orvieto that is exported. From the Marches, on the Adriatic coast, comes the dry white Verdicchio dei Castelli di Jesi, whose high alcoholic content enables it to withstand the test of travel. Its amphora-shaped bottle is often seen on tables in the United States.

Italian wines have played a large role in literature as well as in legend. Several of Hemingway's characters were committed absorbers of them. In *Across the River and into the Trees* the colonel and his lady took Valpolicella with them in their gondola. In *A Farewell to Arms* Frederick Henry and Catherine smuggled vermouth into their hospital. They also consumed more than their share of dry white Capri.

American Wines.   There are not one but two separate wine industries in the U.S. Each produces wine so different from the other's that they cannot be compared. Each has its legions of devoted wine drinkers and each group contains many who cannot abide the wines of the other. But both, I am assured, for I have my own strong preferences in the matter, produce good wines delightful to the tastes of their own fanciers. One, called eastern, is centered in New York State but has vineyards in Ohio and as far away as the Puget Sound area of Washington State as well as others in the South and Midwest. The other, called Californian, is centered in five growing regions of that state but also has vineyards in Washington State's Yakima Valley and in Oregon and Arizona.

The difference between them, say the true lovers of New York's sparkling and still wines, results from choice. The difference, say Californians, results not from choice but was imposed on the East by its weather. In the land of rugged winters such hardy native American vines as Catawbas and Concords must be used. In the mild climate of California, which equals the best winegrowing regions of the world, *Vitis vinifera*, the traditional wine grapes of Europe, are grown.

Now all lovers of European-type wines owe a great debt of gratitude to the eastern American vines. In the 1870s the phylloxera pest threatened the destruction of every vineyard in the world except those of Chile, which was protected by its geographic isolation. But the vines of Europe were saved only by grafting them onto phylloxera-resistant eastern American roots. And the post-graft grapes, for reasons beyond my ken, retained their original European flavor.

Gratitude, however, will not get us past the fact that wine made from the native American grapes has a taste and aroma that lovers of European-style wine, I among them, do not expect when they drink wine. We call it "foxy." This has nothing to do with the little animals that are pursued around the fields of England by mounted men in pink coats. The word probably came from the fox grape, an early American type that was, indeed, pretty foxy. Some eastern wine companies try to blend the foxiness out of their wine by mingling it with California wine. Others are seeking a hardier European-type wine by crossing European and American vines. Dr. Konstantin Frank, of the Gold Seal Vineyards in the Finger Lakes region, has had notable success with his Johannisberg Riesling and Pinot Chardonnay wines. And tribute should be paid to Philip Wagner's experiments in Maryland in the Boordy vineyards. I have drunk a white wine of his, labeled Boordyblümchen, that was clean and fresh, reminiscent of a light Hungarian wine. Everett Crosby's High Tor Vineyard, nestling in the foothills of the Catskills north of New York City, also does extensive experiments with European hybrids. He makes a very pleasant white wine, resembling a young Moselle; a delicious rosé, and a Beaujolais-like red.

There is much to be said for these wines, but it is in California, I feel sure, that the real future of American wine growing rests. There conditions are just right for the traditional *Vitis vinifera*.

California.   The vine was introduced to California by Spanish missionaries in the middle of the 17th Century, many years before the state was populated by a torrent of immigrants, who quickly realized that their thirst for wine need not go unassuaged. The men who launched the wine industry knew their business, many of them through previous European training. They imported their vines from France and Germany: for their red wines, the Pinot noir and Gamay from Burgundy and the Cabernet Sauvignon from Bordeaux; for white wines the Pinot blanc and Pinot Chardonnay from Burgundy, the Sémillon and Sauvignon blanc from Bordeaux, the Sylvaner, the Traminer and the white Riesling from Alsace, the Johannisberg Riesling from the Rhine.

The father of California wine making was the dashing Colonel Agoston Haraszthy, a Hungarian nobleman who brought his family to California in 1849. Haraszthy came from a long line of wine makers in Hungary. He was a bold and vigorous fellow who made and lost several fortunes during a long and colorful career. At one point, when his vineyard in Sonoma Valley was at the peak of its success, he was commissioned by the state government to ransack Europe for the best vine cuttings for California vineyards. But when he returned after many months and asked to be reimbursed for the $12,000 he had spent, there was great fumbling in the state legislature, and he never got the money. Undaunted at being stuck with 200,000 vines, he distributed them up and down the state at his own expense—a generous act for which he will be long remembered.

Haraszthy was probably responsible for developing the mysterious zinfandel grape, which is grown almost exclusively in California. It is believed that he had wanted to acquire the German Zierfandler, but the vine when it arrived bore little resemblance to the vine that he had ordered. It produced, however, a unique wine, full and fruity, that has proved very popular with Californians; and it is so plentiful that it is blended into some of the Burgundy-type wines available in gallon jugs.

The wine industry was progressing very favorably in California until the nation launched the unfortunate experiment of Prohibition. That grimly dry period lasted for 14 years, and its baleful influence is only now being dissipated, some 35 years after Repeal. For not only was it with rusty machinery that the industry had to set itself to the restoration of its fortunes; it had to re-educate a country that had got attuned to a regimen of bathtub gin and home-brewed "Scotch."

Much of this output comes from the south around Los Angeles—mainly in the San Bernardino Valley—and is sold in large glass jugs. The wines are inexpensive and a vast solace to those—and I am one of them—who feel that a day is incomplete that has not included the consumption of a liter of table wine. The rich soil of the Los Angeles area is particularly well suited to the production of sweet dessert wines that pass as sherries, ports, muscatels and vermouths. Commercially they are a great success: half of California's production, which accounts for 70 per cent of all the wine drunk in America. But the best California wines come from the northern part of the state around San Francisco.

There are two main geographical divisions in the important vineyards of Northern California, those that lie north of San Francisco Bay in the Sonoma and Napa Valleys and those that lie to the southeast and south in Santa Clara County. When you consider the distance between Buena Vista in the north and Almadén in the south, about 100 miles, you would expect there to be as much difference between their wines as there is between those of the Loire Valley and Bordeaux, but this is not the case. The climate is so consistent and the soil and terrain generally are so similar that the wines produced from the Riesling grape by Buena Vista are very much like those that are produced from it by Almadén.

By and large the California wine industry has done everything to make things easy for the neophyte. It does not confuse him with technicalities. The labels on California wines are accordingly simple but informative. In early days the wines were given what are known as generic names—chablis, burgundy or claret (meaning red wine of Bordeaux)—that usually indicate a family resemblance to a European wine of the same name. The principal exception is California sauterne; it is not at all like French Sauternes (with an "s" on the end). Both are white, it is true, but the California version is usually dry whereas the French one is always very sweet. Many of the popular but minor wines are called "mountain" red or white, burgundy or chablis. The better wines, however, do not trade on Old World traditions, but are simply named according to the variety of grapes from which each was made. The customer is left to make his own choice, in the belief he will soon discover that red wines made from the Pinot noir are better than those made from the Gamay—as they are in France. Many of the wineries also paste on the bottle an explanatory description of the kind of wine that it contains. It has been my experience with American wines that by and large you get what you pay for, and that a wine costing two dollars is usually better by 60 cents than one costing a dollar and 40 cents.

The traditional styles of bottle are used. The bottles for Burgundy-type wines have sloping shoulders as they do in France, those for Bordeaux types have high shoulders and those for Moselle-like whites, the tapering German wine shape.

Until recently the wineries did not bother to date their wines, but now many of them have begun to do so, to protect customers against a wine

Overleaf: In an illustration from *Harpers Weekly* of 1878, Chinese laborers trample grapes in great redwood tanks at a California vineyard. Cheap Chinese labor, originally imported to work on transcontinental railroad building in the mid-19th Century, later was widely used in the wine regions.

Continued on page 128

that is too old. If the label is not dated, sometimes the age of the wine can be checked by turning up the bottle and reading the date on the bottom. This is the date of bottling. The wine will not have been kept in wood longer than two years prior to that.

Not many California wines are allowed to mature in the bottle. For this there is a sound business reason. The vintners have to pay a tax on their entire warehouse inventory every year. To keep a large stock of wine on their premises is expensive and sends up the price to the consumer. Since the wine must usually be marketed as soon as it is bottled, it could be argued that the amateur of wine would be wise to change his buying habits. Instead of living from hand to mouth, ordering just as much as required for each week's needs, he should take the same care of his California wines as of his French and German wines and lay away a case or so at a time. The other day I tasted a 1957 Pinot Noir by Louis Martini that was excellent and proved to me that California wines are capable of a far greater measure of improvement than most of us suspect.

The worth of California wines is only now beginning to be recognized. A while ago President Johnson expressed the wish that his diplomats abroad should offer American wines at their luncheon and dinner parties. I have only once been honored with an invitation to dine at a U.S. embassy since then. The ambassador in question ignored the President's fiat, and a worthy Bordeaux followed a delicate Moselle; greatly though I enjoyed them, I was disappointed, for I had been curious to see which American wines a discerning and generous host would give his guests.

Unfortunately, some of the best California wines are not available at wine stores outside their home state, since they come from wineries that are so small the shippers cannot distribute their product widely. In André Simon's *Wines of the World*, John N. Hutchinson writes of California wines, "The best standard wines of the state can hold their own with the best standard wines of the world," but he adds, "California wines which can truly compete with the great wines of France and Germany can be found only in small quantities in private cellars or for virtually private sale." When you are in California, look for such names as Hallcrest, Heitz, Stony Hill, Mirassou, Sebastiani and Souverain; you will be agreeably surprised.

The markedly local characteristics of California wines have been noted by a number of connoisseurs. Cyril Ray, one of the best of the English writers about wine, ranks California as being, after France and Germany, the winegrowing region with the highest proportion of very carefully made serious wines among its total output. But he also reminds us that "in different soils and under different suns, the same grapes will produce wines of markedly different character." Consequently, a California Pinot or Cabernet will not smell or taste or age in bottle in the same way as a French Burgundy or Bordeaux, though it may be pressed from the same kind of grapes, made with similar care and drunk with similar seriousness. Such differences need not detract from excellence. Ray especially picked out for praise Paul Masson's Emerald Dry—a Riesling, pale in color with a slight background sweetness, to which I was introduced to my great delight a few weeks ago. Another California wine that stirs my memories was among those served at a cheese-tasting party in New York City. The white wine that went with the Norwegian Tilsit was a Pinot Chardonnay

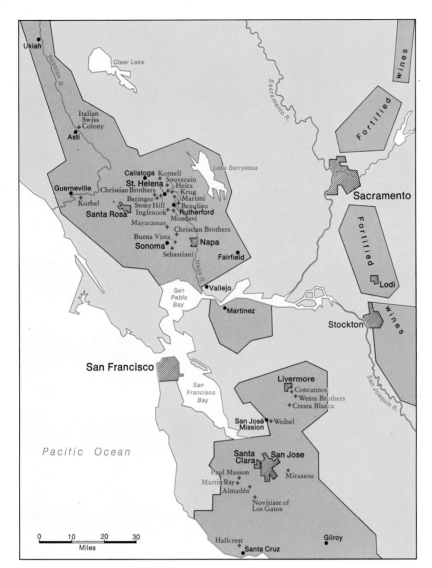

+ Wineries

Wine regions:
1 Northern Coastal
2 Central Coastal
3 Sacramento Valley
4 Great Central Valley
5 San Joaquin Valley
6 South Coast

Northern
California

from the Beaulieu vineyards in the Napa Valley, and it was excellent.

Those who know wines and want the best from California will usually turn to a Cabernet Sauvignon, and with good reason. This grape produces the great Bordeaux wines of France, and California growers make a wine as well-balanced as the French counterpart. Americans do it an injustice by drinking it much too soon. At maturity it is rich, smooth and generous. The best ones are made by Charles Krug, Louis Martini and Beaulieu.

Excellent as such wines are—comparable in some instances to the fine wines of Europe—they do not yet appear to be great in the sense that a vintage Bordeaux is great. Still there is no reason why they should not become so. In the past mankind has come by chance upon those fate-favored folds of soil where great wine can be produced, and such places may well exist in California.

Inevitably, any discussion of the future of California's wine must finish with a question mark. The industry has been aided by a great deal of research by the Oenological Station at the University of California at

California's best wines come from the regions included in the enlarged map at left. The northern and central coastal regions produce mostly table wines; the other California regions make mostly fortified dessert wines.

Continued on page 132

Brother Timothy, cellar master for the Christian Brothers, inspects the vineyards of the wine-making religious order.

"Drink Thy Wine with a Merry Heart"

In the Book of Ecclesiastes the Bible says, "Eat thy bread with joy, and drink thy wine with a merry heart. . . ." No one takes the injunction more literally than the Christian Brothers, a worldwide religious teaching order with schools and vineyards in California. The brothers have been producing wines there since 1882. They began with sacramental wines, but today they make vermouths, apéritifs, table and dessert wines, champagnes and brandy. When the brothers gather for a meal *(opposite)*, they drink their own wine—with a merry heart.

The great variety of table wines produced in America includes a number of excellent reds, whites and rosés. The wines displayed here are stored as they should be, on their sides. Unlike French and German wines, the best American ones are known by the names of the grape varieties from which they are made: such as Cabernet Sauvignon, Pinot noir and Zinfandel for reds; Pinot Chardonnay for whites; and Grenache for rosés. This sampling is stored in an accordion wine rack of wood. Other ways of keeping wine at home are shown on page 198.

Davis. They have at their disposal the most up-to-date machinery; they have excellent chemists; they want to create, and to create a steady demand for, a sound standardized commodity, which will not vary from one year to another. Is there any sound business reason why they should hunt for that one place that can produce exceptional vintages? Everything is going so well the way it is. Yet at the same time I did draw hope from the White House's concern over California wines. Could it not go one step further and add the search for a truly great wine to its many other projects? There is great need for it. The population is increasing at an alarming rate. More and more people capable of enjoying the amenities of living are anxious to enjoy great wines. The supply of the current great wines cannot be increased. Bordeaux and Burgundy, the Rhine and Épernay can only produce just so much. In 50 years time their price may well put them out of reach of all but a few. It is sad for me to reflect that my grandchildren will be able to afford only on occasion the third- and fourth-growth Bordeaux that in the 1930s I drank three or four times a week, reserving Chambertin and Château Margaux for the special dinners—unless some new source of excellence is discovered. Why should not such a miracle be accorded us? The legions of Crassus when they assailed Bordeaux did not suspect that soon there would be stored within its cellars wines finer than their own Falernian. Why should not some California valley, tilted at a certain angle to the sun, prove capable of producing wines as great as Europe's but different from them, as Bordeaux is from Burgundy and Chablis is from Moselle, some new supremacy of bouquet that will permanently enrich mankind?

Other Wines of the World

Argentina

Argentina produces more wine than any other country in the Western Hemisphere—more than 500 million gallons a year—yet little of it is seen in the U.S. This is because the Argentines themselves drink most of it—23 gallons per person per year, not far behind the French, who at present hold the world's record for per capita consumption, 32 gallons a year.

It was the Italians, in fact, who were largely responsible for building up Argentina's wine industry. Following two waves of immigration, late in the 19th Century and again after World War II, Italian settlers introduced their new countrymen to the wines and wine-making techniques of Europe. In due course, a variety of creditable local wines—red, white and rosé—were developed along with several popular sparkling wines. The Mendoza region—due west of Buenos Aires on the Chilean border—produces three quarters of the nation's total.

Australia

Although Australian wines are a rarity in the U.S., they are widely sold in England, where preferential tariff rates make up for the cost of shipping them halfway around the world. But these exported wines lack the exceptional character of the wines Australians drink at home. The reds have a powerful and surprising flavor that seems to reflect the tang of the country's air and sunlight.

Australia's coolest wine-producing zones, those nearest the South Pole, yield the best varieties. These include fine red and white table beverages labeled with the names of such growing areas as Magill, McLaren Vale and Barossa Valley.

Austria

Austrian wines closely resemble German wines. They come, in fact, from some of the same grapes: Riesling, Sylvaner and Traminer. Austrian labels may also use German descriptive terms, such as *Auslese* and *Spätlese*, but even the finest of such wines do not quite match Germany's.

The vineyards ringing Vienna yield reputable white wines. Probably the most famous is Grinzinger (from the town of Grinzing). Another is the full and fruity Kremser, from the Wachau district to the north, near the city of Krems. But Austria's so-called "wine quarter" south of Vienna in Burgenland produces the Austrian wine most frequently seen in America, a fresh, spicy white called Gumpoldskirchner.

Chile

The wines of Chile have a special interest because its vines escaped the devastation of mildew and phylloxera that in the 19th Century destroyed most of the world's vineyards, leading some to believe that Chile's finest white wines, made from the Riesling grape, may one day challenge those from the Moselle.

Not surprisingly, in view of Chile's geographic disposition—a long, thin line stretching 2,600 miles along the Pacific Ocean—the country provides a considerable variety of wines. Fortified wines come from the north, good table wines from the center and *vins ordinaires* from the south. In the middle region the Cabernet grapes make a red wine of the Bordeaux type, and the Pinot noir yields a Burgundian type.

All told, there are more than 30,000 vineyards in Chile, but more than half of these are less than three acres in size. Vintners find it difficult to expand because the government strictly regulates the industry and limits output in an effort to prevent alcoholism. Four government-controlled classes of wine are exported: *courant* is aged for a year; *special*, two years; *reserve*, four years; and *gran vino*, six years.

Greece

Wine has always played a significant role in Greek life. The ancients believed it was a divine gift from the god Dionysus, whose symbols were a vine leaf and drinking goblet. Greek artists and poets throughout the ages have included references to wine in their creations, extolling its salutary effects, and Homer chose "wine-dark" as the most fitting description for the Aegean Sea, from which ancient Athens drew her prosperity and power.

The most Greek of Greek wines is retsina, a white wine developed in antiquity. It contains sandarac, a pine resin used elsewhere as an ingredient of varnish. Some say the custom of adding resin originated in an effort to disguise the flavor of the goatskins that were once used to store and transport the beverage. Others think it was used as a preservative. However the practice arose, the Greeks liked the raw, earthy taste of the resin and added it to many types of white wines.

Unresinated reds, whites and rosés are also made in Greece. One of the driest and most delicate of these is a white known as Pallini, which comes from the vineyards around Athens. Dozens of sweet wines also flourish, mostly from the muscat grape. The best is a luscious, heavy red from the Peloponnese called Mavrodaphne.

Hungary

The most famous Hungarian wine is the rich white dessert wine called Tokay, or *Tokaji* as it appears on some labels. It was known for centuries as the wine of royalty, and Catherine the Great, who ruled Russia during the 18th Century, so prized the beverage that she detailed a special troop of Cossacks to guard her private stock. There are two kinds of Tokay, dry and sweet. The bone-dry variety, usually called Szamarodni, is the type most often found outside Hungary. But sweet Tokay, either Eszencia or Aszú, is costlier. It is made by blending the honey-sweet juices of dry, selected grapes with the wine of ordinary grapes. The greater the proportion of syrupy liquid in the mixture, the sweeter and more expensive the Tokay. This ratio is expressed on the label by means of little pictures of wine baskets, called *puttonyos*.

Hungary makes excellent dry wines, too. Some of the best come from vineyards covering an extinct volcano known as Somló Hill, which rises steeply from a wide plain of wheat farms in central Hungary. Somló wines have a sharp flavor and are usually brilliant green in color. A glass of this wine, the local lore insists, has great medicinal properties and, when drunk at a wedding, guarantees male offspring. The fine Badacsony wines come from the shores of Lake Balaton in southwest Hungary.

Hungary's best red wine is Egri Bikavér, meaning the "blood of the bull," an apt name for this strong, dark robust wine.

The table wines of Hungary were once consumed all over Europe and widely appreciated for their excellence. Since the

In many lands the pause that refreshes is a "wine break." These Italian grape pickers share a flask of Bardolino.

Iron Curtain descended over Eastern Europe, Hungary's wine exports have decreased in quantity and quality; some are still good, but none reaches greatness.

Japan

The national drinks of Japan are sake and beer, and sake is similar to beer in that it is fermented from a grain—white rice—rather than from grapes, like orthodox wine. However, as a finished product sake resembles a white wine; it is colorless in appearance, slightly sweet and winelike in flavor.

Like the rest of the Orient, Japan produces little grape wine. What is made comes from imported French vines, such as the Merlot or Pinot blanc. Much of the production is sweet fortified wine.

Middle East

In the countries of the Middle East—Turkey, Iran, Lebanon, Syria, Israel and Jordan—the story of the grape is a paradoxical one. It was here, many centuries before vineyards were planted in the West, that man first discovered the pleasures of wine, but today the grapes are harvested almost solely for eating as fruit, and very little wine is produced. The reason for this is religious. Most of the inhabitants of the region are Arab Muslims, and the Koran forbids alcohol to the followers of Islam. As a result, although all of these countries make a few table and dessert wines—mostly for export—the only nation in the group with a thriving wine industry is Israel.

In the 1880s, Baron Edmond de Rothschild introduced French vines and viticultural methods to Israel and financed the vineyards planted by the earliest Zionist settlers. Ultimately Israel's vintners merged to form a cooperative that today produces the majority of Israel's wines.

North Africa

The dry, warm climate of North Africa, in Algeria, Morocco and Tunisia, is well suited to the growth of the *Vitis vinifera*, and when Carthage ruled the region in the Fifth Century B.C., it produced wine in quantity. This era ended after Carthage fell and the conquering Romans decided to make North Africa their empire's breadbasket. The vineyards were plowed under and grain planted. Then came the Moorish invasion and Muhammad's edict against alcohol. It was not until France began its colonization of North Africa in the early years of the 20th Century that grapes once again began to flourish on the southern flank of the Mediterranean.

Most of the wines produced in North Africa are common table varieties that are seldom rated by connoisseurs. Algeria makes hardy, rough red wine, much of which is exported to France to be blended with the lighter wines of the Midi. The Moroccan vineyards located around Casablanca, Marrakesh and Meknes make similar reds, and Tunisia produces reds, whites and sweet fortified wines.

Portugal

Portugal produces some of the world's great wines under conditions that appear hopelessly primitive. The famed Madeira, a host of distinguished ports *(Chapter 7)* and some excellent

rosés are somehow wrested from a land where primitive ox-carts with wooden wheels still haul wine over unpaved roads, and many Portuguese wines are still pressed with human feet. Stems and stalks, which in other countries are usually removed by machine in order to make lighter and faster-maturing wines, wind up in the fermenting vats. Only within the last three decades has the Portuguese government begun to set standards for the wine industry or established educational programs for vintners. The result is that most Portuguese wine destined for local consumption reaches the marketplace prematurely, and the young wine is likely to be rough and distasteful. The one happy result of Portugal's industrial lag is that properly aged wines—as much as 10 years for a red wine from Colares—are likely to be quite good.

The aging process works against one group of Portuguese wines called the *vinhos verdes*, literally "green wines." In trade terms this most often refers to wine that is raw or harsh, but in this case it simply means young and fresh. It is usually bottled very early in the spring while still fermenting, which makes it mildly sparkling during the brief period when it should be consumed. Grown in the northwestern corner of Portugal, *vinho verde* comes in all forms—red, white and rosé. The white variety, particularly, can be very delicate; it is suitable only with lightly flavored foods.

The choice Portuguese wines are labeled *reserva* or *garrafeira,* meaning specially selected. The rosés are excellent—young and fresh, ready to drink as soon as bottled. The best rosés are Mateus and another, made in both still and sparkling versions, that is called Faisca in Portugal but is exported as Lancers. It is a familiar wine in the U.S.—very visible on liquor-store shelves because, unlike other Portuguese rosés, it comes in a pottery crock instead of a glass bottle.

South Africa

South Africa was making wine a century before the Declaration of Independence was signed in America and in the 18th Century was producing a highly prized dessert wine known as Constantia, which rivaled similar wines made by the greatest European vineyards. Unfortunately, the techniques for making it were lost when unscrupulous vintners, bent on greater export profits, fortified Constantia beyond the point intended by nature. Years later, when wiser heads began to prevail, it was too late. Nobody could recall the secrets of the original process.

Today, the principal wines produced are port and muscatel, although some full-bodied dry reds and whites are also made, the best coming from the winehouses of the Wynberg, Stellenbosch and Paarl districts in the southwest.

Spain

Spanish wines—except the sherries, which are made for Anglo-Saxon rather than Spanish tastes—are among the most unpredictable in the world. Some of them vary enormously but many of the table wines have an excellent future because of increasingly high quality and quantity at low cost. Only nominal regulations exist to control quality, and the industry itself suffers, as in Portugal, from outmoded techniques. Experts consider the government's official designation of quality, *Denominación de Origen,* is all but worthless, and search instead for a label that reads *Garantia de Origen,* a reliable indication

A perfect blending of food and drink matches a hot cheese fondue with a cool, delicate Swiss Neuchâtel wine.

that the wine was made by a member of Spain's elite, self-regulating corps of vintners in the Rioja, or northeast section of the country just south of the Pyrenees.

With the exception of the sherries from Jerez *(Chapter 7)*, Rioja wines—red *(tinto)*, white *(blanco)* and rosé—are indisputably the nation's best. Specially aged varieties are labeled "Reserva" and carry a date. Among the best Riojan reds and whites are the *reservas* and *reservas especial* of the finest wine companies, Marqués de Murrieta, Bilbainas, Marqués de Riscal and Compañia Vinícola del Norte. These wines have an intriguing flavor, earthy and quite distinct from other European ones. Among the rosés, those from the winehouses of López de Heredia or the Marqués de Murrieta are highly regarded.

Switzerland

Swiss wines, both red and white, often have a quality of crispness that distinguishes them from the wines of nearby vineyards in France, Germany, Italy and Austria. They resemble the wines of these countries and come from many of the same grapes, but their sprightliness sets them apart.

Switzerland specializes in making white wine. One of the most popular is called Fendant de Sion—referring to the capital of the canton Valais on the upper Rhône, where it is grown. The vineyards of this region and those around Lake Neuchâtel are Switzerland's best, and the Swiss claim their famous fondue *(opposite)* is at its most delicious with a crisp Neuchâtel wine. The most familiar reds, Dôle and Cortaillod, are produced in these areas, as is Oeil de Perdrix, a lovely rosé. It is rich and fruity, as might be expected from its burnished red color, but it is also pleasantly dry.

U.S.S.R.

The southern republics of the Soviet Union—Georgia, Moldavia, the Ukraine, the Crimea, Azerbaidzhan and Turkestan—produce the major portion of that nation's wine. Reds and whites, both sweet and dry, are made and exported to Western Europe, but not, as yet, to the U.S. Russia is increasing its output of wine at a rapid rate and may one day outrank both Italy and France (now neck and neck) as the leader in world production. The Russians are particularly proud of their sparkling wines—Kaffia, from the Crimea, is said to be the best—but their interest in wine, including even champagne, which they import in great quantities from France, does not hold a candle to their love for vodka.

Yugoslavia

The wines of Yugoslavia, enjoyed for years by tourists, are making their way both to the U.S. and to Western Europe in increasing quantities. They tend to be light-bodied but high in alcoholic content (14 to 15 per cent), and their relatively low cost makes them good value as everyday table wines. The white wines tend to be better than the reds; they are named after their grapes—the Rieslings, Sylvaners and Traminers of Germany and Alsace. The best of these wines come from Slovenia and are identified by the town name of Ljutomer preceding the grape name. The choicest reds, including a sweet one known as Prošek, come from Dalmatia, and they are generally robust and very full-bodied.

The World's Top Wine Producers

Country	Annual production, in millions of gallons
1 ITALY	1,694
2 FRANCE	1,619
3 SPAIN	842
4 ARGENTINA	570
*5 ALGERIA	423
6 U.S.S.R.	412
7 UNITED STATES	312
8 PORTUGAL	232
9 YUGOSLAVIA	148
10 WEST GERMANY	115
*11 RUMANIA	112
12 BULGARIA	111
13 UKRAINE	111
14 SOUTH AFRICA	109
*15 CHILE	94
16 GREECE	91
17 HUNGARY	86
18 MOROCCO	52
*19 BRAZIL	50
20 AUSTRALIA	40
21 AUSTRIA	34
22 TUNISIA	33
23 SWITZERLAND	20
*24 TURKEY	12
25 ISRAEL	9

These are 1966 production figures with the exception of those starred (*), which are for 1965. All figures were provided by the Food and Agricultural Organization of the United Nations.

VII

Dessert Wines: Sherry, Port, Madeira

B y now our fictional dinner party will have progressed to the dessert, and it is time for the appraisal of such delights as sherry, port and Madeira, those noble beverages from Spain, Portugal and Madeira that come under the heading of fortified wines.

We call "fortified" those wines to which alcohol has been added—either to check the fermentation as in the case of port, or simply to raise the alcoholic content, as with sherry and Madeira. There are other fortified wines, among them the Sicilian Marsala, but those from Portugal, Spain and the Portuguese island of Madeira are the most important. Each of these wines was originally developed to suit English tastes, as a bracing antidote to the damp English climate, and a large part of the trade is still in English hands.

Sherry. This was the first of the fortified wines to become popular in England. In Shakespeare's day it was known as "sack," or "sherris sack," the word sack deriving from the Spanish *sacar,* meaning "export," and sherris being an Anglicization of Jerez, the town in Spain where sherry is made. (Sherry is made elsewhere in the world too, notably in California; but we are here concerned with the original product from Jerez.)

Spanish sherry is made only from grapes grown in the triangle formed by three Spanish towns that lie north of Cádiz in Andalusia: Jerez, properly known as Jerez de la Frontera; Sanlúcar de Barrameda; and Puerto de Santa Maria. The Spaniards are very strict about such limitations. For in-

In the mountainous southern part of Madeira, three farmers carry wine-filled goatskin containers called *borrachos* along a precipitous path from vineyard to wine lodges. The terrain is so difficult it is necessary to press the grapes where they grow and transport their juice, rather than carry them down to the wine lodges for pressing.

stance, they deny to the wine makers of nearby Montilla the right to call their product sherry because the grapes are grown outside the triangle, although at one time some of its wines were sent to Jerez and bottled as sherry. (Montilla, a pale, dry white wine, is never fortified, but its alcoholic content is naturally high, 15 to 16 per cent. Because it is extremely dry it is very popular in southern Spain, and it has also contributed at least to the nomenclature of sherry. The famous amontillado takes its name from the dry Montilla wines—the word means "in the style of Montilla.")

There are two main types of sherry: fino and oloroso. The finos, which include manzanilla and amontillado, are pale in color, rich and dry in flavor and bouquet. The olorosos are heavier and dark, with the exception of amorosa, which is medium dry, and are sweetened before they are sold. "Brown" and "cream" sherries are olorosos; their flavor is more full-bodied and they are slightly less fragrant then finos. The Spaniards describe them as having *gordura,* stoutness. Golden sherry is almost exactly like cream sherry, sometimes a little lighter. Finos can be drunk with soup and they can also be taken as an apéritif; olorosos are better as an after-dinner drink. Dr. Abernethy, a well-known surgeon of 19th Century England, when asked by a lady what was the best time to drink a glass of sherry, replied, "Whenever you can get it, madam, whenever you can get it." There is always a right moment for a glass of sherry.

Among the best-known finos are Tio Pepe and La Ina. They are the driest of the sherries, and it is essential that they be served cold, since all finos are better chilled. Tio Pepe is made by one of the largest shippers

Grapes of the Iberian Peninsula and Madeira yield six major fortified wines (areas indicated in red): sherry, port, Madeira and the less well-known Málaga, Moscatel and Tarragona. The map also shows areas producing unfortified red and white wines, mostly for local consumption.

Spain and Portugal

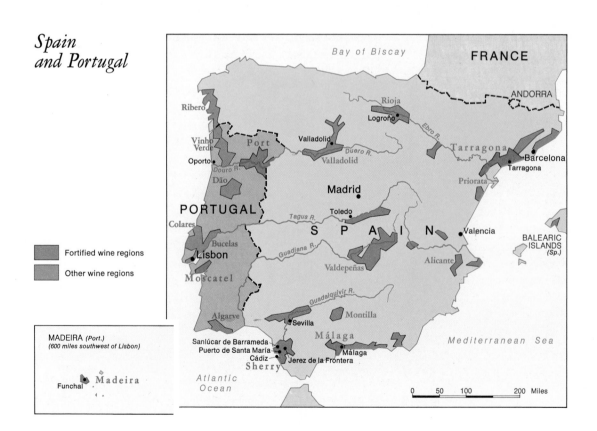

Fortified wine regions

Other wine regions

MADEIRA *(Port.)*
(600 miles southwest of Lisbon)

Funchal ⚓ Madeira

in Jerez, Gonzalez Byass, and its origin is entertaining. *Tio* is Spanish for uncle, and Pepe is an abbreviated Christian name much like Joe. Nobody seems to remember very much about this Gonzalez who was known as Uncle Joe, except that he was a man who delighted in manzanilla, and who asked a forebear of the present Manuel Gonzalez if he could not produce a similar fino for him. And so Señor Gonzalez set aside a special corner of the cellar for him, and there the old gentleman would entertain his friends with his own dry wine and the slices cut from a ham that hung overhead. The name Tio Pepe caught on, and it has been skillfully publicized.

Spanish wine merchants do not have a monopoly on the name sherry (as the Portuguese do on the name port) and there are many imitations of the product. During the Spanish Civil War, a great many English and American Loyalists declined to drink sherry while Jerez was in Franco's hands, making do with such substitutes as were available. In England, a dry South African sherry was in active demand, and it was pleasant enough, though I did not feel it had the essential quality of Spanish sherry. In the United States, however, I recently drank an Almadén cream sherry from California that I thought was Spanish. Perhaps the distinctive quality of Spain is more marked in the fino than in the oloroso; the fino is a more natural wine, being unsweetened, and therefore its special quality is harder to imitate.

Sherry is so very much a manufactured and blended wine that one would scarcely say of it, as one does of Burgundy and Bordeaux, that this particular wine could have been made only in this particular place under these particular conditions. Yet the whole technique of producing sherry is so unusual, in fact, so mysterious, that one may well wonder if anywhere but in that triangle a fino could be produced.

A visit to one of the bodegas, or warehouses, of Jerez is an experience that no wine lover should deny himself. Jerez itself is a charming, long-storied city. For 500 years it was part of the Moorish Empire, and architecturally the Moorish influence is very marked. Though there are references to the town in Classical times—the Greeks in the Fourth Century B.C. called it Zera, the Romans changed the name to Ceret, and the Visigoths called it Serit—its real history begins when the Moors captured it in 711 A.D. and Serit became Saris. It is to the Moors that Jerez owes its city walls and its turreted *alcázar,* or palace, but Spain is responsible for its gracious squares, its white houses with ironwork balconies, and its unexpected anglings of light and sudden long vistas down narrow streets with a church spire at the end.

The Moors did a great deal for Andalusia. They were good husbandmen; they irrigated the countryside; they not only built palaces but they planted vines. They brought with them the art of distillation, and though they themselves as Muslims could not drink wine, they saw no reason why they should not make a profit out of selling it to the infidels. The tourist can easily and pleasantly spend two days in Jerez, but he will need to spend two more days at least in the bodegas.

The obvious time to go to Jerez, of course, is during the harvest in September, a gay time of song and dance and the ceremonial trampling of the grapes. Yet this is when the winegrowers have the least time to de-

Many Casks to Blend One Sherry

Blending sherry so the product will be consistent in
character, a worker in Jerez draws off new wine to add
to older ones in the lower casks of this stack, called a
Solera. To select wines for blending, tasters classify
each new cask with one of the chalk marks at left—the
Y-shaped symbol, for example, is for fino, a dry sherry.
Added to other finos already aging in one Solera, such
a young wine acquires the taste of the older blend.

vote to visitors. If you go out of season, as I did, in April, you can be given more attention, and my real reason for going there was to see how the Solera system works.

The sherry grapes, Palominos, are not hurried to the vats to be pressed, but are laid outside the *lagar,* or pressing house, on rush mats for 24 hours so that some of their moisture can evaporate. After the pressing, gypsum is added to the must to increase acidity. Purists have objected to this habit—"plastering" is the technical term for it—but gypsum is only the calcinized essence of the white soil in which the grapes are grown, and in the days when the grapes were taken along the road by cart, the dust from the road settled on them. The dust, therefore, has been accepted as an integral part of wine making in Andalusia. After plastering, the wine is left to ferment in casks. No brandy is mixed into the must to halt fermentation, as in the making of port, nor are the casks themselves completely filled; the wine is left open to the air.

As a result of this peculiar treatment, the fermentation lasts a long time, usually three months. Also—and this is the most surprising feature about sherry—the vintner cannot tell until the fermentation is complete what kind of wine the cask will contain. The contents of one cask may be completely different from the contents of another that was filled with wine produced from the same vineyard on the same day. You could ask the vintner in November whether either cask contained a fino or an oloroso and he would not know. It seems unbelievable, yet it is so.

That is the first highly curious feature about sherry; the second is a development that occurs in December, after the young wine has been racked, or drawn, into new casks in order to leave the sediment behind. At this time a white film or soft crust known as *flor* (flower) appears on the suface of the wine. The formation of the *flor*—actually a fungus, *Mycoderma vini*—is essential in making fine dry sherries and is the phenomenon that gives them their unique character. One of the first objects of my visit was to see this "flower." It is quite easy to do so. The barrels are not filled to the brim and the two bungholes are not yet stopped. If the guide lifts one cover and flashes a torch on the surface, you can see the *flor* through the other hole. To me it looked much like the scum one sees on a brackish pool. Wines that develop a thick, heavy *flor* will become finos; those with no *flor,* or only a scanty one, will be olorosos.

In South Africa you will also find this *flor* as part of the wine-making process, but it occurs only in one other place in Europe, in the village of Château-Chalon in the Jura, where Pasteur studied it as part of his experiments with fermentation. The village wine belongs to the family of *vin-jaune,* yellow wines. "Through some vinish freak" (I quote Hugh Johnson), "*flor* gives Château-Chalon the ability to age for seven or eight years in cask . . . . It also gives it the strange, yeasty, soft freshness that is found in a good fino." It is interesting to note that the Jura was Spanish until the end of the 17th Century. Can there be some strange, mystical communion between Château-Chalon and the vineyards of its former landlords? There are still mysteries in the world of wine. May they long stay mysteries.

It is at this point of production, around December, that the winegrower can judge the quality of his sherry, his ratings being based on evaluations by skilled tasters. He marks the barrels with white chalk, one stroke for

Under the hot Andalusian sun, two laborers in a Spanish vineyard refresh themselves with lunchtime bottles of the local sherry. Also resting is a mule that carries the grapes from vineyard to bodega.

the best, two for those of medium quality, three for the least good, which will be distilled into brandy.

The graded wines are then drawn into fresh casks and fortified with Spanish brandy, a further distillation of sherry. Those wines to be designated as finos will be brought to 15 per cent alcohol, the olorosos to 18 per cent. The extra quantity of brandy in olorosos kills the *flor,* which continues for 18 months or more with the finos. The wines are tasted and graded again and left to develop for a year or two.

The wines are then subjected to the Solera process of maturing and blending. The system is one in which a series of casks are replenished from one another. There are many Soleras in a shipper's bodega. The casks are stacked one on top of the other in a pyramid. Usually the rows are three casks high, but there can be as many as four. The youngest wine is in the top cask, the oldest in the bottom ones. A Solera continually renews itself as the young wine is transferred from the top barrels, blending with older wines as it descends, and finally entering the bottom casks, from which the wine is drawn for bottling or further blending. The evaporation is great and the replenishment is constant, as each cask is refilled with wine from the ones above it.

There can, of course, be no vintage years in sherry, and the Solera may continue indefinitely. In a Solera that was started in 1908 there will remain hardly any wine made from grapes that were pressed in 1908. But

144

the fact of age has a significance: It means that the maturing wines have been constantly blended, that there is a residue, an inherited maturity about the older Soleras that improves and gives character to the younger wines. If one was told that a sherry came from a Solera 1908, he might expect it to come from grapes gathered and pressed in 1908. But that is not the case. It would mean that the Solera had been *begun* in 1908, which is a very different thing.

When the sherry is drawn from its final cask, it is completely free of sugar. It is then fined, or clarified, with egg whites, which gather the sediment and sink to the bottom of the vat. Following this, in the case of oloroso sherries, the wine is sweetened with a heavy, sweet wine made from Pedro Ximenez grapes, which have been left in the sun on rush mats till they have achieved a *pourriture noble*.

Since sherry is a blended wine, the winegrowers are able to maintain a consistency of flavor. The wines that have matured in as many as 15 Soleras may go into the composition of a single shipment. Some of the sherry that is drunk in the United States has been bottled in England by Harvey. It is shipped to Avonmouth in casks made out of New Orleans oak, and since there is a shortage of that oak, foreign merchants have to return the empty casks to Spain.

The bodegas of Jerez are always ready to welcome visitors. Their owners hold, with justice, that the more one knows about sherry the more one will want to drink it. On his arrival, the visitor is usually given a glass of sherry brandy; it is considered that this will be a mellowing influence and prepare him for the treasures that are in attendance. He will then be conducted through the bodega, and the Solera system will be explained to him. Then, as a reward for his industry, he will be taken into a long room, decorated with bullfighting posters, in which he may sample the wines he has seen maturing in the Soleras. It is a very special experience. The wine is handed to him by an expert. It is taken from the cask in a *venencia*, a narrow silver container attached to the end of a long, springy whalebone handle. The cellarman, in a single motion, skillfully draws and pours the wine into a glass in a cascade from a distance of 18 inches. It is a delightful addition to the unique pleasure of taking a glass of sherry in the bodega where it was made.

Port.   This is the potation with which the Englishman is universally connected. An Englishman and his port! What Galsworthian associations those five words contain. Though port comes from the town of Oporto at the mouth of the Douro River in Portugal, it was the Englishman's invention, created to suit the peculiarities of his climate at a time when, because of the Methuen Treaty, the wines of Portugal were the only ones available to him.

There are essentially two kinds of port, vintage port and wood port. Vintage port matures in bottle, whereas wood port matures in cask. When the wine of a certain year promises high distinction, as in 1927, almost all the shippers decide to declare a vintage. They select a certain proportion of their wine and keep it in wood, in Oporto; then after two or three years the casks are shipped to England, their contents are refortified, then bottled and left to mature for 10, 20, even 40 years, as long as their owners can afford. For eight years the wine is raw, for the harsh, fiery spirits have not yet mellowed. But after 10 years it is invariably palatable, and with each passing year it gains in character and distinction.

There is nothing really like vintage port, but "crusted" port bears a strong resemblance to it. This is a blended wine, though sometimes from a single vintage, that matures in bottle after it has spent four or five years in wood, then forms, or "throws," a crust and has to be decanted with care. It is usually excellent; it is cheaper than vintage port and makes an adequate substitute.

The other ports, ruby and tawny, mature in wood, and it is only these wood ports that are found in the United States and continental Europe. They do not improve in bottle; they should be drunk within six months of being bottled. They can be left in a decanter for a week or so without deteriorating, whereas vintage port should be finished within three days. Some wood port is superb, some is pleasantly casual. The color of wood port varies from bright red to ruby to tawny, depending on age. It takes 12 years for a wine to become tawny, and a good tawny is as good as anything one is likely to meet this side of the Elysian fields. It is essentially a dessert wine. It is excellent with cheese or cake at the end of a meal, but it is too heavy to be drunk as an apéritif, except for white port, from white grapes, which tastes the same as red but is drier. There is a great deal of excellent tawny port now being sold in the United States.

Ruby port should have spent eight years in wood, and the best ruby has. Some of it is supremely good, only slightly inferior to the best tawny. But there is also a great deal of very ordinary wine sold as ruby, and it can taste a bit harsh.

Actually, a very small proportion of the wine that is sold in the United States under the name of port comes from Portugal; most of it is California-made. The word port, however, has always been given legal protection. If a label on a bottle says "port" without any qualification, then it must come from Portugal. Otherwise the name of the producing country has to be shown on the label, as California or Australian or South African port. I have never tasted an alien port that bore any resemblance to that which had come from the Douro, although some claim that a very small portion of California port is worthy of the name.

It is always well worth while to visit a vineyard at harvest time, but a visit to the Douro, I think, is more rewarding than any other. When I went, it was exciting to watch the men treading the grapes in the late evening, to a special music, with the girls coming down to dance till midnight, and the music getting keener as the marching men were refreshed with tots of the powerful local brandy. (I sipped it once but could not swallow it; it was too fiery.)

But the actual treading of the grapes was only a part of the three-week festival. At the particular vineyard I visited, some 40 men and women were gathered from the neighboring villages. Year after year they are assembled by the same foreman, and as nearly as possible he brings the same team each year. They arrive like schoolchildren back home for the holidays. Some of them have traveled on foot as far as 30 miles over a rough road. They come in two separate files, men and women, led by musicians playing an accordion, a whistle or a flute. The women carry their personal possessions on their heads, in wicker baskets under a black shawl. The men carry hoes over their shoulders and move at a quick jog, shouting, singing and waving.

The same festive air continues right through the harvest. Everything goes to music. It is a very strenuous period. The women spend all day in the vineyard, picking the grapes under a hot sun. As they carry their baskets to the pressing vaults, the men move in line at a jog trot, as Africans do, to keep the weight off their feet. At their head is a musician, blowing time for them on a whistle.

For the people of the Douro, these are the three big weeks of the year. They are comfortably housed and better fed than at home, and they have their liter of wine with every meal. They meet old friends and make new ones. The men and women occupy different quarters, even if they are married; but even so it is a time of courtship, and there are local jokes about "June babies."

Right through the harvest the spirit is maintained. The departure is as vivid as the arrival. The girls parade before the *quinta*, or vineyard, in single file. Their spokeswoman carries a *rama*, a symbolic wand decorated with grapes and paper flowers, which she brandishes with a flourish of "Vivos": "Long live Portugal! Long live England! Long live the Quinta da Roeda!" There is a whole litany of "Vivos"; then finally she shouts "Long live myself!"

It is in the classic tradition that wine should be made with revelry, yet one reflects a little wistfully that by the time the fruit of the grapes that have been gathered has finally been set upon the dinner table, the feet that jogged so briskly between the vineyards and the presses will be aged and weary. One's appreciation of the ritual that attends a sampling of port is considerably heightened by the memory of the ritual that graced its birth. And one can then appreciate the care that must be taken—especially with vintage port.

This noble wine cannot be moved with impunity. All red wines throw a sediment, but port, because it has so much brandy to absorb, throws not only a sediment, but also a crust inside the bottle. A bottle of vintage port is always marked with a splash of white paint on the top, so that if the bottle has to be moved to another cellar, the same side will lie uppermost in its new bin. It takes a long time to throw a crust and when the crust is broken it takes a long time to re-form. The longer a wine lies still, the better. The shipper hopes that his wine will be moved only twice in its life, from his cellars where it was bottled to the wine merchant who will store it, and finally to the private customer or hotel or club where it will be consumed.

The decanting of vintage port is an operation that needs a great deal of care. As in the case of all old red wines, the bottle should be taken from its bin to the decanting table in a cradle. The extraction of the cork presents a problem. It is very likely to break or to disintegrate; when it does, there is really no alternative to breaking up the cork, and forcing it back into the bottle. It is possible to strike off the top of the bottle, cork and all, with a single sharp stroke from a carving knife. It needs a special knack, which I never have acquired. My late friend Vyvyan Holland was a master of it. One day he deployed his skill in the presence of my two

Continued on page 154

147

On a rocky hillside in the upper Douro, the village of São Cristovão lies among vineyards that climb the slope like stairs.

The Port Harvest in Portugal: A Time for Celebration

With their baskets precisely balanced, a double file of workers swings along a road beside the Douro River in Portugal, marching to terraced vineyards like those above. This group is lead by finger-snapping Luciano Silva, who has brought his villagers to the same farm every year for 50 vintages of port-making grapes. The musicians are paid time and a half at the farm for their special skills. Besides helping with the harvest, they play for the villagers' nightly dances and provide music for the traditional treading of the grapes *(overleaf)*.

Thigh-deep in grapes, the villagers march rhythmically around in a trough for four hours at a stretch.

When the harvest and the pressing are over, the Douro villagers and the wine go their separate ways. The port is transported downriver to waterside wine lodges in casks, known as pipes. It used to travel aboard picturesque *rabelo* boats like the one at left, shown in front of ancient Oporto. The boat trip took up to five days. Today the port is shipped in trucks that make the trip in four hours. The vintners of Oporto produce several different types of port, three of which are shown above: ruby, white and tawny. Resting on an old wine press, the glasses are set against the background of the Douro Valley as seen from the home of a leading port producer and shipper, Manuel da Silva Reis.

elder children, then in their middle teens. They were delighted. I was leaving the country the following week. When I returned two months later it was to find the floor of the cellar covered with tops of bottles. Whenever the children had to decant a bottle of my red wine for their mother, they employed, for the hell of it, the Holland technique!

Even when the cork has come out cleanly, it is likely that there will be particles of cork dust left in the wine. The decanting should be done with a candle or electric bulb behind it so that the sediment can be seen, and through a filter. The filter will catch the pieces of broken cork and any filaments of the crust that may have broken off. (Forty years ago it was held that port should in addition be decanted through muslin. I question now if this is really necessary. If the mesh of the filter is small, only the smallest particle of dust can get through, and the dregs, apart from the crust, do not reach the neck of the bottle till the very end.)

When my two elder children were four and five, I used to take them down to the cellar to watch me decant vintage port for the weekend guests. I wanted to imprint in their minds that wine is something to be attended with pomp and ceremony—an affair of ritual, not to be taken as a matter of course, but still a normal part of civilized family life. I did not want them to think of it as something "dashing and wicked."

I hope that I succeeded. Certainly, in their early thirties now, they are reasonable and temperate drinkers, but I cannot pretend that as children they did not approach the ceremony with the spirit of mischief that is appropriate to childhood. As I twisted the corkscrew home, they would exclaim "Oh, I do hope that the cork does not break," but in fact that is precisely what they hoped for. When I explained to them that the last half inch of wine was muddy, they would not be convinced of this, until they had seen the dregs poured out.

The serving of the port is the big moment of the dinner to which this book is striving to pay tribute. The dinner plates and glasses are cleared away; fruit is set upon the table and perhaps a few dry crackers, if it is not the season for walnuts. The decanter is placed before the host. He fills the glass of the guest on his right, then, after filling his own glass, he passes the decanter to his left. Port must go clockwise, the way of the sun. No one knows quite why; it may have some nautical significance. But it is certainly a grave solecism not to follow it. And it is the duty of each guest to keep the decanter moving, once the host has started a second or third round. Port should go around twice, at least.

In England, at public dinners, it is when the port is served that the sovereign's health is drunk; when the company has resumed their seats, the chairman says, "Ladies and Gentlemen, you may smoke." It is a permission of which many will not avail themselves. There are many who consider it an insult to the wine to smoke a cigarette when port is on the table. As for myself, a nonsmoker, I do not particularly like the smell of smoke, yet I do not believe that it spoils the palate. If it did, why should so many winetasters smoke cigarettes? Nor do I believe that one's own enjoyment of wine is spoiled because the man or woman next to one is smoking a cigarette—provided the smoke is not blown across one's face, or one's neighbor, when turning to talk to the guest on his other side, does not leave his hand dangling a smoldering cigarette under one's nose.

When I was in Oporto, our party was honored by an invitation to dine at the Factory House, the home of a 150-year-old club formed by the member firms of the British Association of Port Shippers. It is a large, unpretentious building, in staid and sober contrast to the convoluted Rococo architecture that surrounds it. It was intended to typify the British way of life—sound, solid, unostentatious—and inside it has the opulent dignity of a London club.

Forty of us sat down to an admirable, straightforward dinner. As an apéritif we had a dry white port; with our fish we had a white Graves; then a Pontet-Canet 1929. Cheese straws cleaned the palate for a tawny port. According to the menu we were then to weigh the respective merits of two vintage ports, a 1917 and a 1927. The names of the shippers were not given; it might have led to invidious comparisons. The chairman rose to his feet. We could not, he told us, appreciate the bouquet of vintage port in an atmosphere tainted with the fumes of food. We were invited to move into an adjoining room, taking our napkins with us. In that room, a second table awaited us, again set with 40 places.

It was a lovely sight: a gleaming stretch of mahogany, a cluster of chandeliers, high piles of fruit, bowls of red roses, cut-glass decanters. There was a Doulton dessert service, and a cherry-colored carpet to match. It was a delight to the eye, but that pleasure was slight in comparison with the enchanting assault upon one's nostrils of a cool, fresh room, scented with fruit and flowers. It was one of the most acute physical sensations of my life, but I am not sure that the port tasted any better.

Madeira. There is a close kinship among port, sherry and Madeira. All have been exploited by British merchants. Madeira, like sherry, can be drunk both as an apéritif and a dessert wine. There are four types of Madeira: sercial, verdelho, bual and malmsey, named after the different kinds of grape from which they are made. Sercial and verdelho are light and dry and can be drunk as an apéritif, or with soup. Bual (sometimes called boal) and malmsey (the English name for the *malvoise* grape) are rich, full and heavy, and are incontestably dessert wines, though there are those who do like to take bual with turtle soup. Experts consider bual the best balanced of the four. Malmsey is a much heavier wine. Its grapes are gathered late as in Sauternes and are cultivated only on the sunnier southern shores. It is as rich as liqueur. Its production requires more time and trouble, so it is more expensive than the other three. It is my favorite; it rounds off a meal as perfectly as a vintage port.

All these wines come from the small volcanic island 500 miles southeast of Portugal that was uninhabited when the Portuguese discovered it early in the 15th Century. Madeira has been always a lucky island. Its summer is mild and it has no winter. It has been spared dissension. One of its greatest pieces of good fortune is that it was not included in the marriage dowry that Portugal's Catherine of Braganza brought to the impecunious and volatile Charles II of England. He got Bombay and Tangier; Madeira was the card that the Portuguese had up their sleeve, if Charles proved obdurate. But luckily for Madeira, Charles took the cash in hand, and so that charming island was spared involvement in Britain's 18th Century wars with France under Napoleon. Portugal was a nonbelligerent,

trading with both sides, profiting from the quarrels of both houses, and Madeira was admirably placed to take advantage of the Thirteen Colonies' trade with Africa and the West Indies. It was also very soon discovered that Madeira was one of those few places where could be grown a wine, unique and personal to itself; no one has successfully imitated it.

In its early days, fruit and sugar cane were the chief products of the island, but the vine soon supplanted the sugar cane, and before long Madeira was helping to supply the drinking needs of the American Colonies. Its wines were known at that time by the names of the New World families who imported them—the Pinckneys and the Rutledges in Charleston, the Aspinalls and Howlands in New York, the Cadwalladers in Philadelphia. After the Jacobite rebellions of 1715 and 1745, a number of Scots settled in Madeira and names like Blandy, Leacock and Cossart-Gordon appeared on the shipping lists.

Madeira is a delightful island, rich in flower and foliage. I was there in early May, when the sea was warm enough to bathe in; the jacaranda was out and, though the skies were often overcast, the landscape was ablaze with color. The hills are very steep. Until comparatively recent times there were no motor roads, and the roads are too steep for wheels anyway so that one used to be transported on an iron-runnered *caro,* a sledge that had an awning and sun curtains and could seat four passengers. This sledge, originally used for carrying grapes, was drawn by a couple of oxen, and managed by two grooms who wore wide-brimmed straw hats, bound with light-blue ribbon rather like a Venetian gondolier's. One of the grooms, often a boy, would go in front, pulling on a cord that was attached to the oxen's horns. The other walked behind, prodding the animals with a long pike and yelling at them. The *caro* moved at a rate of a mile and a half an hour, and though it is no longer in active use, it provides a splendid tourist attraction.

In addition to the *caro,* Madeirans used a *carinhos,* a kind of toboggan, for downhill journeys. It is a wicker basket, large enough to accommodate two people, set on runners and guided by a man from the back. The conductor gives it a push to start it off, then jumps onto a narrow foot ledge to go along for the ride.

The automobile has rendered these devices obsolete, but the necessity for them—and I have seen no equivalent for them in any other place—indicates how very great are the difficulties with which the Madeira vigneron is faced. The tightly terraced hills provide far more arduous work for the grape than do those of the Rhine and the Moselle.

Land is scarce and valuable in Madeira. It is for the most part divided up among small peasant proprietors who are resolved to exploit their inheritance to the full and make double use of the ground. They arrange their vines on pergolas, six feet high, very much as the ancient Egyptians did, and they plant their potatoes underneath. This may be peasant economy, or it may be that the sun is stronger than in other vineyards, and the vigneron wants to protect his grapes from the heat reflected from the earth. Be that as it may, the potato is planted in October after the harvest, when the vines are leafless, and pulled up in April, when the leaves have begun to bud. I visited Madeira in late May, and this pergola arrangement gave the impression that the hillside was covered with the awnings of

Opposite: Madeira Islanders serve their dessert wine, bual, with fruit and sweet cakes and biscuits like the dark treacle cake called *bolo de mel,* the circular biscuits called *rosquilhas,* cream-filled horns and meringues.

Continued on page 160

Magnificent Madeira: Still a Man-made Wine

Proprietors of small vineyards on the island of Madeira
follow the old, unmechanized ways in producing their
unusual dessert wine with its subtle, smoky taste. The
men in the picture opposite carry grapes in splay-topped
baskets along narrow mountain paths, often for long
distances, to crushing troughs like the one shown above.
After the grower marks down the number of baskets of
grapes he has dumped into the crusher, he jumps in
barefoot to help tread the grapes. Further pressing occurs
when a weight is lowered into the trough by a man
turning a screw outside. The rich red, frothy juice runs
into barrels through a basket strainer stained blood-red.

bright-green tents dotted with white flowers. It was lovely beyond words.

Owing to the steepness of the hillside, pack animals cannot be taken up for the picking of the grapes, and so the proprietors press the grapes on the spot. Madeira, like the Douro, is a place where most of the pressing is still done by the human foot. After the treading, the mash is further compressed by means of a huge stone, which is forced down by a wooden screw. The *mosto*, or juice, is then brought down to the main town of Funchal by *borracheiros*, runners who carry 12-gallon goatskins slung over their shoulders. In the wine lodges the juice is fermented, usually for two to four weeks. It is then known as clear wine, *vinho claro*. After it is fortified with brandy distilled from Madeira wine, it is moved to a hot room called an estufa, where it is literally cooked for three to six months. The temperature of this hot room depends on the length of time that it is intended to keep the wine there: the shorter the time, the higher the heat. The wine is heated as a means of aging and maturing it. In very early days it was found that Madeira reaching America after having traveled in the holds of ships through tropical heat for many months was at its peak of excellence. Whether this was due to the extreme heat of the tropics or the pitching action of the ship, or both, no one knows, but the estufas produce the same result.

In the estufa that I saw, there was a thermostatic seal set by the government at 130°. The government is insistent upon this seal. If it is broken by overheating, then the wine is confiscated, because overheated wine appears older than it is. In Madeira, as in Oporto, the Portuguese government is jealous of the reputation of its wines.

When the heating is over, the wine is allowed to rest for 18 months to two years. Then it is blended and racked into fresh casks, and at last the wine is additionally fortified, to 20 per cent. Now it is *vinho generoso*, "generous wine," and the time has come for it to mature. Maturing is a long process, taking several years, and inevitably an expensive one. Yet it must not be forgotten that the price of the wine depends mostly on the tax that governments choose to impose on it. Wine would be as cheap as it was in Shakespeare's day if we were allowed to enjoy at liberty "the kindly fruits of the earth."

Madeira is the longest-lived of any wine. During my visit to the island I drank wines over a century and a half old: a malmsey of 1795 and a sercial of 1802. If they had lost any of their quality in the course of years, then indeed they must have been terrific in their prime. In Funchal the Solera system does exist, in that wines of different vintages are blended in the final stage. In Spain you would never see the date of a Solera on a wine list, although in the bodega you will see a date. But on a list of Portuguese wines you might see a Solera date—the date of its oldest wine— and if you did, there would be a definite guarantee of longevity.

No one seems to know how long Madeira can last. Eighteenth Century bottles still turn up every now and then, and there appears to be no loss of quality. I have never heard anyone say, "I am afraid that this Madeira has begun to fade." I question if any Madeira has been allowed to live long enough to "go off."

Not very much Madeira is drunk now in the United States, but there may be a vogue for it again. I hope so.

The freshly pressed juice of Madeira grapes is sloshed over a young boy of the island in the belief it will promote health.

VIII

After-Dinner Drinks: Brandy and Liqueurs

When the last glass of port has been consumed, the dinner itself may be said to be at an end. Now is the time for the ladies to leave the gentlemen, and for the gentlemen to converse at the table or retire to the library. At any rate, it is the time for coffee, cigars and liqueurs—for what was, and among some still is, called the pousse-café. There are many kinds of drinks with which to bring to an end an evening, and our fictional host will presumably have a number of diversely shaped bottles to which the company can address themselves. There may be five or six kinds of drinks, but one there certainly will be—brandy in some form or other. And if the meal is being held in France, Britain or the United States, the brandy will probably be cognac.

Spirits from Wine.   "Brandy" is a shortened form of the word brandywine, from the Dutch *brandewijn,* and that is what it is, burned (or distilled) wine. The greatest of such spirits come from the region around the town of Cognac in southwestern France, from the thin new wine made on the River Charente, which is a little north of the Gironde River and the city of Bordeaux.

In medieval days a great deal of table wine was shipped from this area to England, Denmark and the Low Countries. As duty was then levied on bulk, the winegrowers decided to lower the volume of their produce by distilling the actual liquid into what was then known as *eau de vie,* or water of life, a clear spirit for which there was a good export market. Be that as it may, the winegrowers of Charente were soon to discover that

It takes a steady hand to pour these rainbow cordials, called pousse-cafés, for the colorful layers are individual liqueurs. *Left:* Crème Yvette rests on parfait amour. *Center:* Cognac floats on Cherry Heering, yellow Chartreuse and green crème de menthe. *Right:* The gold of Grand Marnier tops white crème de menthe and crème d'amande. Complete recipes for these cordials are in the Recipe Booklet.

163

their spirits had a quality to be found nowhere else. There is no reason that we know of why this should be so. It is just one of those miracles of the world of wine.

Cognac, by definition and by law, can be distilled only from wines made from grapes grown within a legally defined area in the Charente district. There are seven geographical divisions within this area and seven grades of cognac. These are (in descending order of quality): Grande Champagne, Petite Champagne, Borderies, Fins Bois, Bons Bois, Bois Ordinaires and Bois Communs. Only the first two, which are the best, will appear on a cognac label (Grand Fine Champagne, which the Frenchman orders simply as Fine from the waiter at his café, is a blend of cognac from these two areas). The word champagne appears simply because it refers to an open field area (*champagne* is the French word for countryside), as opposed to the less desirable *bois*, or forest part, of the Charente district. The effect of the lime in the soil on the thin, acid wine of the Charente is such that wine from Grande Champagne and Petite Champagne, which have the most lime, invariably makes a better cognac than wine from the other places.

The vineyards in the seven Charente divisions are split up among numerous small proprietors, and they distill most of the grape crop themselves; the remainder goes to professional distillers and cooperatives organized by small growers. The small proprietor takes samples of his brandy into the town of Cognac, where he sells all of his product to one of the big shippers. The date of such a sale depends on the grower's own finances. He may sell the brandy when it is young and white, or he may let it mature in his own cellars if he can afford to wait. The Frenchman is supposed to keep his money in a stocking under his bed—not so the prudent grape grower in Charente; he keeps his money in his cellars. It is liquid gold.

There is no mystery about the making of cognac. It is distilled from wine that is made chiefly from the St.-Émilion grape, although the Folle-Blanche and Colombard are also used. Distillation takes place when the fermentation of the wine is finished at the beginning of the year, and continues for several months thereafter, depending on the size of the crop. The traditional copper pot stills produce brandy for 24 hours a day during the distilling season.

An important aspect of the production of cognac is that it is, in fact, doubly distilled. The first distillation, which is called the *brouillis,* comes out at about 50 proof. The *brouillis* is then redistilled, going through the still to produce *la bonne chauffe,* which is the raw cognac, about 135 proof. It is this colorless brandy, or *eau de vie,* which is then put into barrels made from Limousin oak, a species of tree that grows only in the forests of nearby Limoges.

The double distillation in pot stills is one reason for the special flavor of cognac in its raw state, and long aging in the Limousin oak gives mature cognac special characteristics. Color and flavor are picked up from the oak, and the oxidation that takes place through the porous wood develops the bouquet and taste. As the brandy mellows in the barrels, it also loses some of its alcoholic strength. Since it will be reduced to the desired strength in any case, this does not matter.

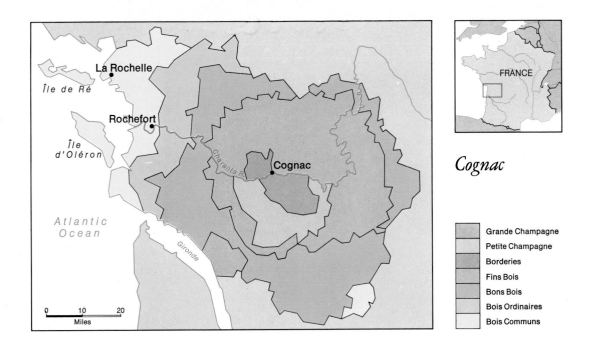

Cognac

Grande Champagne
Petite Champagne
Borderies
Fins Bois
Bons Bois
Bois Ordinaires
Bois Communs

Blending Cognac.   Since cognac is a blend, there can be no vintage years declared. Some months before the blends are to be bottled, the firms' tasters choose brandies that conform to the house style. As in the champagne houses of Rheims and Épernay, the famous firms of Cognac must match a particular style year after year to provide their established customers with a continuity of taste. When they have been thoroughly tested, the chosen lots of brandies are put into huge oak vats where they are turned with giant paddles until the flavors are completely married. After several months of maturing in the vats, the brandy is bottled.

Most firms indicate the relative quality of their cognac with stars and letters. There symbols are not prescribed by law but by each firm's custom. They can be confusing. Three stars on a label usually indicate that the cognac has spent five years in cask; four stars, six years; five stars, seven years. The law does not permit any other indication of an age beyond five years. As for the letters, V.O. means very old, V.S.O. very superior old, V.S.O.P. very superior old pale; E means extra or especial, F means fine, Q means quality, and X also stands for extra. The fact that the letters refer to English, not French adjectives indicates the importance of the English-speaking market to the cognac trade. Various firms use various combinations of letters to describe their products, but the best guide for a buyer is to go by price, a firm's general reputation, and his own trial-and-error experience.

There is a great deal of chichi about brandy. Wine waiters like to bring up from the cellar a bottle impressively covered with cobwebs. But this is pointless, as a distillate does not improve in bottle. Brandy is held to be at its best when it is between 25 and 50 years old, and those years should have been spent in wood, not glass. There are those who like to drink their brandy out of lagoon-sized goblets, which they have heated first over a flame, or they will hold the glass between both hands and swirl

The color key above identifies the zones of the Cognac region and ranks them in descending order of quality, starting with Grande Champagne, finest of the seven grades of brandy.

Continued on page 168

From Steaming Pot Stills
Comes the Brandy Called Cognac

Watched by an attentive French workman, the copper pot still in the picture at left is distilling wine that will become the very special brandy entitled to be called cognac. Only the brandy from an explicitly defined area around the town of Cognac in western France may bear the town's name. During the season, which lasts from three to eight months, the region's pot stills operate round the clock, first vaporizing the alcohol in the wine, then condensing it at a temperature that is the distiller's secret. The liquid drawn from the still is colorless, as in the left-hand glass above, but it darkens gradually by absorbing tannic acid from the oaken casks in which it matures. The other glasses contain, from left to right, cognac that has aged for one, four, six and more than 20 years.

the cognac around in it. The use of a flame or a special brandy warmer is considered pretentious now; you can warm it just as well between your hands, and the object of doing so—to release the bouquet more fully—is just as effectively achieved. And, really, one hand is enough, particularly if you are smoking a cigar. The whole performance is rather ostentatious; moreover, if the glass is very large, it is difficult to tell how much you are drinking and most of the bouquet evaporates into the air.

Apart from the pleasures of tasting cognac, a visit to the city where the brandy is made is a reward in itself. Cognac is a charming, tranquil town, with a statue of François I in its rounded *place*. Cognac scents the air—they say that the equivalent of the contents of 25,000 bottles is lost in evaporation from the casks every day. It is called "angels' drink" and the walls of the city carry a dark patina from the fumes.

Nobody seems in any hurry in Cognac. The folk of the city describe themselves as "slow but wise." "Time is our friend, not our enemy," they say. Why should not human beings mature slowly, in the way that cognac does? Yet, for all that, there is a pervading air of industrious application. The young lady who showed me around the Hennessy distilleries pointed out to me how the women took out their knitting during the 15-minute break in the afternoon. No time is wasted. She also showed me a picture of the long, narrow projecting hat that the local women used to wear. It was devised in Plantagenet days to repel the amorous advances of the British soldiers during various wars. It was known as a *kichenot* (kiss-not).

I spent much of my time in Cognac as the guest of Maurice Hennessy, director general of his company. There was a lot for him to show me. A great deal of his production was destined for the export trade. And it interested me that each country wanted its consignments packaged in a different way. The Venezuelans, for example, insist that bottles destined for their market be packed in wicker baskets. The British want their brandy sent in wooden casks, although the shippers are trying to persuade them that the individual cartons that the Americans demand are just as safe and are easier to handle. I was in Cognac in May, and it was somehow strange to see the stacks of gift cartons ready for America, with the bottles inside already wrapped for Christmas.

But what fascinated me most in the distillery was the atmosphere of bulk. I had never pictured brandy as a river splashing through pipes from one vast container to another. I had seen it as an amber thimbleful in a capacious goblet, not as a seething torrent.

Famous Names.   Hennessy is one of the world-famous names in Cognac; others are Martell, Hine, Otard, Bisquit, Delamain, Courvoisier and Remy Martin. But there are also a number of excellent and honored houses of which most of us have never heard, and certainly my own impression of Cognac would have been incomplete had I not spent 90 minutes in the company of Henri Martin, the director of Barnett & Elichigaray, who produce a high-grade cognac for a small but loyal and increasing clientele. Their factory had the atmosphere of one of those solid family businesses that you find in provincial towns. Typical of this kind of business was a room that contained a large quantity of demijohns filled with old brandy. The wine would not improve in a demijohn, of course, but the firm had not enough capital to afford the loss caused through evaporation, which would occur if it was kept in casks. They called this fragrant room Le Paradis.

Monsieur Martin opened his showcase. He grinned conspiratorially as he handed me a bottle labeled Napoleon. It was ridiculous, he agreed; Napoleon had nothing to do with the so-called "Napoleon brandies," but then, if people asked for this kind of nonsense they had to be given it. M. Martin also had a bottle labeled "chef's cooking cognac." It was a promotion idea of his, of which he was very proud. The brandy, he explained, was just as good as three quarters of what was sold as a liqueur, but because its purchasers thought it of small account, they scattered it freely in their chafing dishes, to the great improvement of their sauces and at considerable profit to himself.

Other Brandies.   Only a small part of the brandy produced in France is entitled to the name of cognac. There are many other brandies, of course, even though they are not as well known. One other district in particular produces something that can approach cognac. The noble liquid, armagnac, comes from vineyards south of Bordeaux, in Gascony. The sandy soil of this region produces a different wine than does the Charente, and the preparation of armagnac is somewhat different from that of cognac: it is distilled in one operation. Yet there are many people who prefer a good armagnac to all but the best cognacs. They find it has a harder, more individual taste, because less of the raw product has been distilled out of it. Since production of this brandy is not dominated by a few houses, as is the case with cognac, there are more small firms that are able to produce armagnacs, their flavor developed with time spent in barrels made of the special black oak of Gascony. Inevitably there is a great range of quality among armagnacs.

Another brandy that you will come across occasionally is marc (pronounced "mar"). It is a spirit that is distilled from the pulp, or marc, that remains after the grapes have been pressed and the juice run off. Most vineyard districts in France and Italy produce a marc, but Burgundy produces the best-known one. Marc de Bourgogne is a rather pungent brandy, not as fine as cognac, but with a very distinctive character of its own; it is consumed in quantity in Burgundy. In Hemingway novels, there is much postprandial consumption of *grappa*. This is the Italian version of marc, and tends to taste less rich and less mellow.

In Normandy, apple cider is distilled to make Calvados, and a well-aged example of this apple brandy can be delicious. Calvados is the finest apple brandy in the world. The best comes from Vallée d'Auge. The American equivalent, popular in parts of the South, is applejack. In World War II, Calvados was highly favored by American GIs in northern France.

Alcools Blancs.   The fruit brandies of Alsace, Germany and Switzerland are widely known under the name *alcools blancs*, which means white alcohols. These *eaux de vie* are clear as water because they are aged in crockery rather than in wooden casks, which would color them. Each *alcool blanc* has its own distinct fruit flavor. Kirsch, for instance, is the

Continued on page 172

All the dry plants shown above are
used in the recipe for Benedictine:

1 Melissa
2 Arnica
3 Hyssop
4 Maidenhair Fern
5 Vanilla
6 Cinnamon
7 Myrrh
8 Coriander
9 Nutmeg
10 Cardamom
11 Artemisia
12 Pine Cone
13 Angelica Root
14 Aloe
15 Mace
16 Saffron
17 Grain Seeds

Two Renowned Liqueurs That Began as Monastery Medicines

The collection of plants shown above includes some—not all—of the flavoring
agents in Benedictine, a liqueur that, like its companion-in-mystery, Chartreuse, is
made by secret formula. Originally a medicinal elixir evolved in the 16th Century
by a Benedictine monk, Brother Bernardo Vincelli, Benedictine is now produced
on a secular and commercial basis—but still in its birthplace of Fécamp in
Normandy, where the flavor of plants seems to be enriched by the seaside air. It
is claimed that no more than three people at a time know the complete formula.
Also most secret are the proportions and preparation used for Chartreuse, a
liqueur perfected in the 18th Century by a Carthusian monk, Brother Jérôme
Maubec, and still made by his order. The formula is known by only five monks,
four of whom manage a distillery near Grenoble, in the French Alps, and
another in Tarragona, Spain, that they operate about six weeks each year.

Even though the formula for Benedictine is secret, it is known that 27 plants, some of them herbs, go into this amber-colored liqueur. At the left, pot stills have been opened to remove spent herbs that have been soaked in alcohol for 18 to 24 months and then distilled. The herbs' distillates will be blended, mixed with other ingredients, including more alcohol, and then aged in casks for at least four years.

Frère Laurent, the Carthusian brother in charge of all production of Chartreuse at Grenoble, makes a last analysis of green and yellow Chartreuse liqueurs before they are put into oak casks for aging. The instrument in his hand is a hydrometer, which measures the alcoholic strength of the liqueur.

distilled essence of wild cherries, including the essence of their stones. It is a superb addition to a fruit dessert, and of course it is a fine drink in itself. *Alcools blancs,* which are sweet, are generally more favored by the ladies than by the gentlemen, but their admirers of both sexes are certain that they have the most distinctive and extraordinary bouquet of any brandy, and the ripe fruit aroma from a glass of *framboise* (raspberry) or *poire* (pear) brandy can fill a room.

Fruit and Plant Liqueurs.

I have written at some length about brandy, but there is a diversity of liqueurs and cordials on which man has for several centuries exercised his ingenious talents. André Simon wrote of them in his *Wines and Spirits:*"Man is here at liberty to give to his liqueurs practically any shade or color he thinks best to attract the attention, raise the curiosity, and charm the eye; he also has at his command all the fruits of the earth from which to extract an almost unlimited variety of aromas and flavors, wherewith to please the most fastidious taste and flatter the most jaded palate."

There are a number of ways to blend flavoring into alcohol, but the two principal methods are by infusion and percolation. By the infusion method, the flavoring elements—fruits, plants or herbs—are steeped or soaked in alcohol until the flavors are completely absorbed. The flavored spirit is then distilled to intensify it.

The percolation method is similar to the making of coffee. Leaves or herbs are placed in the upper part of an apparatus that resembles a coffee percolator. A spirit, such as brandy, is placed in the lower part. Through the agency of heat, either the alcohol vapors are passed through the flavoring and are recondensed or the liquid spirit itself is popped up over the substances and allowed to percolate through.

Whatever blending method is used, the flavored spirit is sweetened—with either sugar, syrup or honey. Coloring is added if desired, and the mixture is again finely filtered. Some liqueurs are aged in wooden casks; others are bottled right away.

A number of houses have produced their own special brands of fruit and plant liqueurs. There are, for instance, pineapple liqueurs, as well as banana, cocoa, plum, pear, peach, strawberry, raspberry and rose liqueurs. Flavorings such as caraway seed give kümmel its special taste. Peppermint is the chief flavoring in crème de menthe.

There are also certain proprietary brands that are internationally famous, three or four of which have romantic and centuries-long histories. Of these the two most famous, and in many ways the most excellent, are Benedictine, and yellow and green Chartreuse.

Benedictine and Chartreuse.

On Benedictine bottles appear the letters D.O.M., for *Deo Optimo Maximo* (to God most good, most great). Benedictine is amber in color; its base is cognac brandy and it is flavored with a variety of herbs and plants. It is claimed that only three people at any given time know the exact formula for Benedictine, and it is also claimed that it was first made in 1510 at the Benedictine monastery in Fécamp, in France, by Bernardo Vincelli.

The monks found Benedictine an excellent medicinal and a welcome re-

storative after their daily labors, and in 1534 François I, King of France, conferred on it the honor of his approval. Unfortunately, the monastery was destroyed during the French Revolution, and for some 70 years Benedictine completely vanished from the market. The formula, however, was not lost and eventually it came into the hands of a Monsieur Alexandre Le Grand, a scholar who found a copy of it in a collection of manuscripts and records. That was in 1863, and Le Grand set himself the task of launching the manufacture of Benedictine on a secular and commercial basis. The industry is now housed in sumptuous buildings and there is a museum in Fécamp that well repays a visit.

The liqueur is rather sweet, and a few years ago the directors of the company discovered that many of their customers were mixing it with brandy to give it a drier taste. As a consequence, they decided to manufacture their own mixture of Benedictine and brandy, which they call B & B and which has proved very popular.

Benedictine no longer has any connection with a religious order, but Chartreuse still has. There are two types of Chartreuse: yellow, which is 86 proof, and green, which is 110 proof. Chartreuse, too, is made from a secret formula, which was given to the Carthusian Fathers of the convent of the Grande Chartreuse at Grenoble in 1605 by the Maréchal d'Estrées.

As richly toned as a medieval stained-glass window, these variously shaped bottles of liqueurs and cordials please the eye while their contents beguile the palate. Since most liqueurs are colorless when they are first distilled, producers can add attention-getting hues, such as the familiar mint green of the crème de menthe.

173

This formula was modified a century and a half later by one of the monks, Brother Jérôme Maubec. The liqueur was at first reserved for the enjoyment of the holy brethren, but its fame quietly spread to the outside world by word of mouth.

It quickly caught the popular favor, but it was to know various vicissitudes of fortune. Although the monastery had been spared the worst effects of the French Revolution, the formula for the liqueur was requisitioned by the civil authorities and turned up in 1810, in an office actually called the Ministry of Secret Remedies. The minister, however, did not recognize its possibilities, and returned it to the holy fathers. (The parchment contains, in addition to his seal and signature, the word "refused.") But the elixir, as it was called, was to suffer a major setback at the start of the 20th Century. After a law was passed in France outlawing religious orders, the fathers were expelled from their monastery and sought sanctuary in Tarragona, in Spain. Their property in France was sold by auction and their trademarks passed into alien hands. Luckily, the fathers had taken with them their secret formula. The French owners of the trademark continued to put on the market liqueurs that bore the name Chartreuse, but the quality was very different from that of the original. The fathers in their new home in Tarragona resumed the manufacture of Chartreuse, but as they no longer held the rights to their trademark, the bottles were labeled *Liqueur Fabriquée à Tarragone par les Père Chartreux*. I can well recall in the 1920s and 1930s how carefully one examined a bottle to see whether it had come from Spain or France. Today, Chartreuse is made by the fathers both in Tarragona and in Voiron, France.

Other Liqueurs.   Since the 16th Century the Dutch have produced an excellent liqueur from the dried peel of the green oranges of the West Indian island of Curaçao. They called it curaçao, and long ago it became so popular that many distillers sold it under a variety of names. Grand Marnier, whose spirit base is cognac, is a type of curaçao. So is Cointreau, which is made in Angers, France, and in the U.S.; it used to be known as Triple Sec White Curaçao. Cordial Médoc, which is made in Bordeaux, combines brandy and crème de cacao with curaçao. Spain also produces a superb liqueur, Crema de Lima, made from citrus fruit.

For those who might find Scotland's straight malt whisky too strong on the palate and yet wish to savor something of old Scotland other than the blended whiskies, there is the delightful Drambuie, which is made from Scotch malt whisky and heather honey. It is claimed that Drambuie is based on a formula brought to Scotland in 1745 by one of Bonnie Prince Charlie's French attendants, and it has conferred on itself the title, Prince Charles Edward's Liqueur. Irish Mist also uses heather honey, with a base of fine Irish whiskey.

Everyone has a favorite liqueur, usually for sentimental reasons. I am not sure if I really like the taste of the ultrasweet yellow Italian Strega, which is flavored with more than 10 herbs and barks. I sometimes feel when I sip it as though I was pouring varnish over my tongue, yet I always order it when I am in Italy. It recalls my first trips to that charming land, when I stayed in Florence and Pisa in the early 1920s with Scott-Moncrieff while he was translating Proust. The weeks I spent there, when I

met men like Norman Douglas, Reginald Turner and Orioli, the publisher of Joyce, added a dimension to my world. I remember the excitement, after the train had passed the frontier at Ventimiglia, of going down to a restaurant and seeing the menu written in Italian, and I decided that I would celebrate my being there with Strega. That yellow liquid was the proof to me that I really was in Italy.

It is for sentimental reasons, too, that I am attached to Cherry Heering; I drank it almost daily during a romantic winter in Copenhagen. But I am also an aficionado of its richness, its warmth, its glamor. There are a number of cherry brandies and they are good enough, but Cherry Heering —it is named after the firm of Peter Heering—is something altogether

A potent drink from Colonial times, the rum and peach brandy Fish House punch originated in the mid-18th Century at the fishing and social club called "State in Schuylkill," in Pennsylvania. It contains rum, peach-flavored brandy, lemon juice and water, chilled with an ice block. The full recipe is in the Recipe Booklet.

175

different from all the rest. Because of the number of cherry stones used in the distillation, it is not oversweet.

When I left Copenhagen, Peter Heering gave me a charming decanter made of Danish porcelain. It was full of Cherry Heering. I vowed to myself that I would keep it constantly replenished. I did for several months, then one evening I returned to find empty the decanter I had refilled only three days before. I learned that my sailor son, then in his 19th year, had poured it over a dessert that was based on rice. It tasted marvelous, he said. I am sure it did, but I did not again expose him to temptation and the decanter now functions as an ornament.

Valediction.   As Shakespeare wrote in *The Tempest,* "Our revels now are ended." It should be in a spirit of warm and responsive well-being that hosts and departing guests bid one another au revoir on the porch or in the hallway, and it should be in a continuing state of euphoria that they wake the next morning. Good wine taken in moderation is a good digestive, and as was said in the opening pages of this book, wine and distilled spirits are among the Almighty's greatest gifts to man, and it has been the purpose of the book to help the reader to get the maximum enjoyment and profit out of them, even if he has no present desire to become a connoisseur.

I sincerely hope that nothing I have written here will have made the reader feel that wine is an abstruse and awkward subject. Nothing is more tiresome than the wine snob. May I recommend the reading or rereading of Roald Dahl's story "Taste," the first story in his collection *Someone like You.* It pillories forever the kind of person whose assumption of superiority discourages so many from taking their first hesitant steps toward a knowledge of this subject.

For 35 years wine has been my hobby. I first began to enjoy it in November 1918 when I was released from servitude as a prisoner of war in Germany. I was 20 years old and I spent much of my new-found freedom in the restaurants of Mainz, Nancy and Boulogne, sampling the best of the food and drinks that the restaurants of those gracious cities had to offer. From then on I have drunk wine every day for dinner whenever possible and as often as not at lunch as well; but it was not until the Wine and Food Society was founded in 1932 under the aegis of André Simon that I began to read about wine and to pay attention to what my elders and betters had to say about it. I soon found that my enjoyment of wines was immeasurably increased. I had a cellar in a small house in the country, and I would show my friends the wines that were maturing there with as much pride as I showed them the first and autographed editions in my library.

That is what I would wish for the readers of this book. You do not need to have a great collection of books to be a bibliophile, and you do not need to have acquired many bottles to be an amateur of wines and spirits. Books are one's friends and so are bottles; and one needs to have in one's home the friends that lie close to one's heart. If this book manages to give its readers a new, warm and intimate outlook upon wines and spirits, then I shall feel that the pains that I have given to its compilation have been repaid in ample measure.

Opposite: These elegant servings of Irish coffee get their distinctive flavor from Irish whiskey that has been poured over clove-studded orange and lemon peel, cinnamon stick and sugar *(foreground),* and then set aflame. Both this dramatic version and a simpler one *(Recipe Booklet)* are topped with whipped cream.

A Guide to Using Wines and Spirits

What makes a wine "good on the nose"? The cellar master on the opposite page, sniffing a glass of fine Bordeaux, might have difficulty explaining it, but his nose certainly knows. In taste, bouquet and other qualities, wines and spirits exhibit a wide range of personalities—and inspire an equally wide range of personal tastes and preferences. Over the centuries, however, there has grown a body of information and opinion, on which most scholars and connoisseurs are in general—if not always precise—agreement, that can constitute a good working guide for anybody.

The elements of such a guide are contained in this Appendix. It is a special section prepared by the editors with invaluable assistance from three major advisers whose credentials and likenesses appear on page 4. Consultant Sam Aaron was chiefly responsible for the up-to-date vintage guide and wine classification charts on the next six pages. His in-depth approach to vintages is based on one pioneered by Frank Schoonmaker, the famed author of *Frank Schoonmaker's Encyclopedia of Wines*.

Following this material are illustrations of bottle and glass shapes properly used for various wines, a section on how to read and interpret wine labels, a discussion of techniques and equipment for opening wine and for decanting it before use. The following guidelines for selecting suitable wines to go with various foods were provided by consultant Alexis Bespaloff. They are followed by suggestions for the educated tasting of wine, a program for your own winetasting party at home, a section on the proper storage of wines, and selections for "cellars" to fit budgets of $100, $250 and $500. Finally, there is a discussion of bar equipment and techniques for making mixed drinks, prepared with the help of consultant André Gros-Daillon, and a glossary. In all of this there is both food for thought and room for argument; the Appendix is designed for enjoyable present reading and useful future reference. To your good health!

Anticipation lights the face of M. Olivier Penigaud (*pages 94-95*) as he prepares to taste a wine professionally. At the moment, he is savoring the wine's bouquet. For expert and novice alike, this is an important step, one that is explained on pages 196-197.

A Guide to Recent Vintage Years

The following guide has been prepared by Sam Aaron, consultant on this volume, with assistance from other authorities in the United States and Europe.

The vintage year of a wine is the year in which its grapes were harvested. Like any crop, grapes may vary in quality from year to year. A great vintage year is one producing wines that can remain at peak quality for a long time in the bottle. A poor vintage year is one in which the crop was inferior to begin with and the wine is poor and doomed to a relatively short life.

The evaluation of wines by vintage year is a relatively recent innovation. It sometimes can prove misleading because, in the very worst of years, when vintage charts rate everything with a contemptuous "zero" and when most winegrowers are cursing their lot, there are still exceptions favored by some accident of soil or climate.

It is in the château-bottled and estate-bottled wines that vintages have the most meaning (the more commercial regional wines represent blending skill rather than nature's influence). But even in these elevated categories, soil is generally more important than weather. For instance, a Château Haut-Brion of an unfashionable year such as 1960 will prove more of a thoroughbred than a lesser red Bordeaux of a great year like 1959.

Because there is good in every bad year and bad in every good, we have avoided the quick rating system of the movie critic such as "2 star," or "3 star"; this kind of skimpy information can only mislead. What follows is a more discursive rating system that will give a clearer understanding of the complexities and meaning of a "vintage year." It is based on daily wine tastings over three decades, and constant interchange of views with the men who tend the vines. We have rated each vintage from 1 to 20, based on the relative merits of the wines as they stood in the late 1960s, and not by the rating they enjoyed after the harvest. Thus, the superb 1961 Red Bordeaux vintage is rated 20, while the poor 1965s are put at 10.

The ratings are:

VERY GREAT—18, 19 and 20
GREAT—16, 17
VERY GOOD—15
GOOD—14
FAIR—12, 13
POOR—11
VERY POOR—10 and under

Red Bordeaux

1967. The crop was most beneficial to the wine drinker because it was exceptionally large, above average in quality, and produced a soft, quick-maturing, fruity wine with a fine bouquet. This most useful, satisfying vintage can be consumed joyously while we wait for the slower maturing '61s and '66s to come to their full fruition. 16.
1966. The château owners were happy as they gathered this great vintage; they were able to obtain the highest prices for claret in Bordeaux wine history. A bit less body than the '64s, but compensated for by unusual bouquet, better balance, and a remarkable similarity to the extraordinary '53s, as well as sufficient tannin to provide

the backbone for exceptional longevity. Recommended for laying down in private wine cellars. 18.
1965. Basically a year to forget. Some châteaux bottled a small portion of their crops, which will provide light, pleasant wines at bargain prices. 12.
1964. Rich in fruitiness and charm. Wines from the lesser vineyards are showing attractiveness for present drinking but more time will be required to bring out the ultimate virtues of the "first growths." Some vineyards of the Médoc fared badly because of the rain during the latter part of the picking season—an ill fortune that spared St.-Émilion, Pomerol and Graves. A year eminently worthy of laying down. 17.
1963. Bad weather struck and nothing worthwhile was produced in St.-Émilion or Pomerol. Although generally poor in the Médoc, there are exceptions of extraordinary value—specifically, the vineyards that generally produce heavy-bodied wines: Latour (Médoc), Château Haut-Brion and La Mission Haut-Brion (both Graves). 12.
1962. Quietly, and with a minimum of publicity, the neglected 1962 clarets have finally won deserved recognition among the world's wine lovers. In their own way, they have something to offer us. Uniformly, they are excellent, early-maturing, soft, fruity, of fine bouquet and can be enjoyed for present drinking. Undoubtedly, the best claret values available today. 16.
1961. One of the best years of this century, the equal of 1945. Unfortunately, the crop was about half the normal size. The grapes were well nourished, resulting in concentrated wines, rich in every quality including color, body, bouquet and fruit. They are the most long-lived wines of our generation—in the classic tradition. 20.
1960. Sandwiched between two great years, the 1960 vintage has suffered from being unfashionable. In fact, the '60s are better than average wines, soft with a pronounced bouquet—among the best values in good claret on the market today. Buy them for drinking during the next three or four years, not for laying down. 15.
1959. Acclaimed at the time as the "Vintage of the Century," '59 enjoyed the advantage of early charm and pleasant fruit. Beautiful wines, rich in many elements but lacking the staying power of the '61s. They can be enjoyed today; the great vineyards still possess a life expectancy of at least 20 years. 19.
OLDER CLARETS. The '58s are not a good bet; the '57s are hard, unattractive and may never come around; the '56s are mostly no longer drinkable; the '55s are near perfect and provide a dramatic taste experience for present drinking; forget the '54s, some of the '53s can highlight the great dinner, but try a bottle before you buy a case; the '52s are truly great in St.-Émilion and excellent in Médoc; forget the '51s; the '50s have been ignored but can be remarkable when originating from a great vineyard such as Lafite, Haut-Brion or Pétrus; the '49s provide glorious experiences if you stay with the "first growths"; some '48s, especially Pomerol and Médoc, are proving excellent; the '47s promise noble heights in wine drinking if properly stored; the '46s are tired; the '45s are dramatically great and can live many more years. There are older claret vintages that still remain excellent, among

White Bordeaux

Here it is important to differentiate between the dry white wine produced in the Graves district and the rich, sweet wine produced in Barsac and Sauternes. The same weather conditions may provide opposite results because the sweet wines are picked a month later.
1967. In Sauternes, this is the best year since 1962 and can be pronounced great. 18. In Graves, particularly in such wines as Château Haut-Brion Blanc, the whites are fresh, well-balanced, vigorous and dry. 17.
1966. Sauternes and Barsac completely failed here. 10. The dry white wines of Graves fared much better. They are rich in flavor, balance and finesse (defined as a quality of subtle refinement and distinction). 16.
1965. Poor in both Sauternes and Graves. 9.
1964. Excellent in Graves but somewhat heavy. Lacks finesse. 15. Sauternes performed poorly. 10.
1963. Should be ignored. 8.
1962. The Sauternes, including Château d'Yquem, are glorious. 18. Be careful about the dry whites of Graves—they are getting too old. 15.
1961. Great in Sauternes and Barsac. Will last many more years. 19. Only a few of the dry whites have survived.
1960. Of no interest. 8.
1959. Great heights achieved in Sauternes. Will last for decades. 20. The dry whites are now too old. 8.
OLDER VINTAGES. The great vineyards of Sauternes can be enjoyed today in classic vintage years: '55, '53, '49, '45, '34, '24, '21, '18, '14 and '08. The dry whites should be ignored completely.

Red Burgundy

1967. Although this was an excellent vintage in southern Burgundy, there was ill fortune along the Côte d'Or. There was frost in the spring, then considerable loss due to summer hail—followed by cold and rainy days just before the harvest. Most '67 Burgundies proved much too light, lacking in balance and color. 10.
1966. Outstanding year. Great fragrance, fruit and superb balance. Will prove to be a better year than '64 or '59. Shows remarkable promise of longevity. 19.
1965. Skip this year completely. 8.
1964. Rich in fruit, well-balanced, big and sturdy. Sufficient depth and staying power to indicate many glorious years ahead. A worthy successor to the '61s. 18.
1963. To be ignored, a dismal failure. 9.
1962. Following so soon after the great '61s, the '62s did not receive their proper recognition. The wine is not simply good but can be considered great. Red Burgundies ideally suited for present drinking. 17.
1961. Here, we must shout "Bravo!" and salute. The production in 1961 was half of normal and the wines are of exceptional quality and longevity. The better vineyards will still be great 20 years from now. 20.
1960. A year to forget. 8.
1959. If you seek great red Burgundy vibrantly alive with fruit and charm, drink the '59s for the next few years. 18.

OLDER YEARS. Since a decade is the usual life span of a red Burgundy, it is hard to talk about the older years. If you are lucky, you will still find some outstanding '52s and '49s.

Beaujolais (Southern Burgundy)

The rule is simple—if the label reads "Beaujolais" or "Beaujolais-Villages," choose the youngest possible year, preferably to be consumed within two years of its birth. However, the *grands crus*, such as Fleurie, Morgon, Moulin-à-Vent, may be at their best three to six years after the harvest.

1967. A small crop, but the best Beaujolais produced in many years. The simpler Beaujolais is fresh, rich in fruit, and with a disarming, arborlike bouquet. The better ones, from the renowned villages, will be well-balanced and have six or seven years of good life ahead. *19.*

1966. A record-breaking production of all the fine Beaujolais. Softer and less firm than the '67s. *18.*

1965. Never mind these. *10.*

1964. The simple, less expensive ones are now too old, for the fragrance and flavor of the grape are gone. Any of the nine village appellations *(page 183)* will provide joyous drinking for another three years. *16.*

OLDER YEARS. Beaujolais does not live long. Do not get involved with anything older than 1964.

White Burgundy

1967. A variable year. A May frost destroyed over half of Mâcon's and Pouilly-Fuissé's crop, leaving Chablis untouched; a July hailstorm inflicted added damage to the hopes of many growers, often leaving a next-door neighbor unscathed. The result was that very bad and extraordinarily fine white wines were produced simultaneously. Thus, white Burgundies range from *10* to *19* depending upon nature's kindness or malice.

1966. Better than '64 and in the exalted class of '61, wines of airy lightness and extraordinary bouquet. The wines of Chablis and Pouilly-Fuissé are outstanding. *18.*

1965. Relatively good in Chablis but generally not acceptable elsewhere. *12.*

1964. Fruity, full-bodied, but somewhat uneven. Similar to 1959 in weight and ripeness. *17.*

1963. Showed early promise but can be forgotten now. *10.*

1962. Beautifully balanced, relatively light, much finesse, good for present drinking but not for laying down. *16.*

1961. The most long-lived of all white Burgundies since 1952, these are just demonstrating their stature now and many of the great ones like Montrachet, Meursault and Corton-Charlemagne have a decade of glorious life ahead of them. *19.*

OLDER VINTAGES. Generally, white Burgundies, with the exception of remarkable years such as '66, '61 and '52, do not have a life expectancy of more than 10 years.

Côtes du Rhône

1967. The reds are full-bodied and well worth drinking. *16.* The whites and rosés did not fare as well. *12.*

1966. Excellent everywhere. The red Hermitage and Châteauneuf-du-Pape are well-balanced, long-lived, and charming. *18.* The white Châteauneuf-du-Pape, Hermitage, Condrieu and Château Grillet are also superb. *18.* The rosés, in-

cluding Tavel, are the best in many years. *19.*

1965. The reds are fruity but light. *15.*

1964. The reds are big, of great weight, but relatively hard and somewhat unbalanced. *14.*

1963. To be ignored. *8.*

1962. A very good year—followed the pattern of Burgundy. *17.*

1961. Best year in the Rhône since World War II. Great depth, beautiful balance, much fruitiness and great longevity. *19.*

OLDER VINTAGES. If you can find any, you are lucky. These wines can be long-lived. Look for '57, '52, '49 and '45. You will find a lot of sediment in the bottle, so decanting is in order.

Loire Valley

1967. A great year everywhere in the Loire, whether it be Vouvray, Muscadet, Pouilly-Fumé, Sancerre, Anjou or Chinon. All are fresh, glowing with fruit, vigorous, and well-balanced. *19.*

1966. On a relatively high level throughout. *16.*

1965. Uniformly poor. *8.*

1964. The reds are still thriving. *17.* The dry whites and rosés are now too old. *10.*

1963. Alas. *8.*

OLDER VINTAGES. The Loire wines, on the whole, should be drunk when young. But there are exceptions such as the sweeter white wines of Anjou, Vouvrays of great vintage, and, of course, the reds such as Bourgueil and Chinon.

Alsace

1967. Yielded a quantity below the norm, some failures in the lesser wines, but in summation, we can consider this the best year in Alsace in the last decade. Rieslings and Gewürztraminers have extraordinary bouquet and balance. *19.*

1966. A great year. It shares neither the failures nor the heights achieved in '67 but the average is superb. *17.*

1965. A failure. *9.*

1964. The distinguishing characteristics of this vintage are great weight and much power, but the wine lacks subtlety and can often be dull. *14.*

1963. Was acceptable when young, now over the hill. *10.*

1961. The good Rieslings and Gewürztraminers are surprisingly excellent and actually taste young. Superb bottles can be found in the United States. *16.*

1960. Over the hill. *8.*

1959. They were always too heavy and rich in alcohol. Now they are completely gone. *10.*

OLDER VINTAGES. Forget them. Few have survived.

Champagne

Champagne shippers declare a vintage only periodically, and most of the wine they sell bears no vintage at all. Unless the storage conditions have been perfect, these declared vintage years are now too old for present drinking: '52, '55 and, in some instances, '59. These years represent excellence for current consumption: '61, '62 and presently '64. As for the future, the vintage years of 1966 and 1967 are reported to be outstanding.

Rhine and Moselle

1967. Greatness and failures exist side by side. You will find truly great wines from the Rhine

and the Moselle—especially among the dramatically rich *Auslese, Beerenauslese* and *Trockenbeerenauslese,* the best of our generation. But alas, some of the lesser wines are poorly balanced. Overall, the equal of 1964. *17.*

1966. Although rain prevented the production of *Beerenauslese* and *Trockenbeerenauslese,* all of the Rhines and Moselles below this exalted level achieved outstandingly high quality. Just showing their greatness now with at least five good years ahead. *18.*

1965. Slightly below average. Drinkable but not outstanding. *12.*

1964. The Rhines are a bit too fat in body but most pleasant for present drinking. *16.* The Moselles turned out fresh, of good constitution. *17.*

1963. Should be overlooked. *10.*

1962. Relatively dry, fresh, light but never dramatically big. Still good. *14.*

1961. Sound, useful wines without distinction. *12.*

1960. Very poor. *8.*

1959. The greatest year since 1921. The inexpensive wines are either gone or are too old, but the great *Spätlese* and *Auslese* are the best German wines we can possibly drink today or even five years hence. True dramatic glories, they deserve the highest award. If you can acquire them, you are lucky. *20.*

OLDER VINTAGES. Do not touch any German wines older than 1959 unless they are *Beerenauslese* or *Trockenbeerenauslese.* These are expensive but will provide an extraordinary wine experience.

Italy

The cheerful wines of Italy are generally made to be consumed when very young. The vintage on the label, in many instances, does not mean much because these dates are controlled not by the government but by the whim of the wine shipper. However, there are some fine Chiantis (not in wicker-covered flasks but in ordinary claret bottles), as well as Barolos and Valpolicellas that improve with age and generally show the true vintage year. There is no point in providing vintage advice here; but in general, "the younger the better."

California

The weather in California is relatively constant from year to year, but nevertheless there are differences in the quality of the wine produced in one year as opposed to another. Most California producers do not put the year's date on the bottle because they prefer to maintain continuity without vintage problems in restaurants and stores. This trend is now changing. Many of the best growers of Northern California are putting a vintage year on their finer wines, particularly when a superior grape variety such as Cabernet Sauvignon, Pinot noir, Pinot Chardonnay, and Johannisberg Riesling is involved. When buying any of these four classic wine varieties look for a vintage on the label; and you will probably be experiencing one of California's best.

Our advice is: buy the best red wine produced in California—particularly when the best grape, Cabernet Sauvignon, appears on the label. Put it away for two or more years and you will be enjoying America's best wine, favored with sufficient bottle age to give it the all-important roundness and bouquet—the sure sign of a distinguished red wine.

Bordeaux

The Médoc

Official Classification of 1855

This classification was made in 1855 by a group of wine brokers in Bordeaux, who divided the 62 leading vineyards into five ranks, and rated the vineyards in descending order within each rank. Numbers in parentheses represent an updating of the list based on the best modern opinion of authorities in Bordeaux; each number corresponds to the division of the classification to which, it is now felt, the vineyard would belong if reclassified today. For example, Château Palmer would move from third growth to second; Château Kirwan would move from third to fifth. The symbol (X) means the vineyard no longer exists; the symbol (*) means the wine is no longer château-bottled; (B) indicates that the vineyard should be reduced to *crus bourgeois*, below the fifth rank but a highly honorable classification in itself.

FIRST GROWTHS—*Premiers Crus Classé*

Vineyard	*Commune*
Château Lafite	Pauillac
Château Margaux	Margaux
Château Latour	Pauillac
Château Haut-Brion	Pessac (district of Graves)

SECOND GROWTHS—*Deuxièmes Crus*

Château Mouton-Rothschild (1)	Pauillac
Château Rausan-Ségla	Margaux
Château Rauzan Gassies (3)	Margaux
Château Léoville-Las-Cases	St.-Julien
Château Léoville-Poyferré	St.-Julien
Château Léoville-Barton	St.-Julien
Château Durfort-Vivens (4)	Margaux
Château Gruaud-Larose	St.-Julien
Château Lascombes	Margaux
Château Brane-Cantenac	Cantenac-Margaux
Château Pichon-Longueville	Pauillac
Château Pichon-Longueville-Lalande	Pauillac
Château Ducru-Beaucaillou	St.-Julien
Château Cos d'Estournel	St.-Estèphe
Château Montrose	St.-Estèphe

THIRD GROWTHS—*Troisièmes Crus*

Château Kirwan (5)*	Cantenac-Margaux
Château d'Issan (4)	Cantenac-Margaux
Château Lagrange (4)	St.-Julien
Château Langoa (4)*	St.-Julien
Château Giscours	Labarde
Château Malescot-St. Exupéry	Margaux
Château Cantenac-Brown (5)	Cantenac-Margaux
Château Boyd-Cantenac	Margaux
Château Palmer (2)	Cantenac-Margaux
Château La Lagune	Ludon
Château Desmirail (X)	Margaux
Château Calon-Ségur	St.-Estèphe
Château Ferrière	Margaux
Château Marquis d'Alesme-Becker (4)	Margaux

FOURTH GROWTHS—*Quatrièmes Crus*

Château St. Pièrre-Sevaistre†	St.-Julien
Château St. Pièrre-Bontemps†	St.-Julien
Château Talbot (3)	St.-Julien
Château Branaire-Ducru	St.-Julien
Château Duhart-Milon (3)	Pauillac
Château Pouget (5)	Cantenac-Margaux
Château La Tour-Carnet	St.-Laurent
Château Rochet (5)	St.-Estèphe
Château Beychevelle (2)	St.-Julien
Château Prieuré-Lichine	Cantenac-Margaux
Château Marquis de Terme (5)	Margaux

FIFTH GROWTHS—*Cinquièmes Crus*

Château Pontet-Canet (4)*	Pauillac
Château Batailley	Pauillac
Château Haut-Batailley	Pauillac
Château Grand-Puy-Lacoste (4)	Pauillac
Château Grand-Puy-Ducasse	Pauillac
Château Lynch-Bages (4)	Pauillac
Château Lynch-Moussas (B)	Pauillac
Château Dauzac	Labarde
Château Mouton Baron Philippe† (4)	Pauillac
Château du Tertre (B)	Arsac
Château Haut-Bages-Libéral	Pauillac
Château Pédesclaux (B)	Pauillac
Château Belgrave	St.-Laurent
Château Camensac (B)	St.-Laurent
Château Cos Labory (4)	St.-Estèphe
Château Clerc-Milon	Pauillac
Château Croizet Bages	Pauillac
Château Cantemerle (3)	Macau

The following Médoc châteaux, listed in alphabetical order, are selected from among the many vineyards of the *crus bourgeois* because they have proved so outstanding over the past decades that they deserve to be ranked with the fifth growths of the 1855 classification.

Château Angludet	Cantenac-Margaux
Château Bel-Air-Marquis-d'Aligre	Soussans-Margaux
Château Chasse-Spleen	Moulis
Château Fourcas-Dupré	Listrac
Château Fourcas-Hostein	Listrac
Château Gloria	St.-Julien
Château Paveil	Soussans-Margaux
Château de Pez	St.-Estèphe
Château Phélan-Ségur	St.-Estèphe
Château Siran	Labarde-Margaux

Sauternes and Barsac

Classification of district of Sauternes was made in 1855 along with the Médoc.

GREAT FIRST GROWTH—*Grand Premier Cru*

Château d'Yquem	Sauternes

FIRST GROWTHS—*Premiers Crus*

Château Latour-Blanche	Bommes
Château Lafaurie-Peyraguey	Bommes
Château Haut-Peyraguey	Bommes
Château Rayne-Vigneau	Bommes
Château Suduiraut	Preignac
Château Coutet	Barsac
Château Climens	Barsac
Château Guiraud	Sauternes
Château Rieussec	Fargues
Château Rabaud-Promis	Bommes

†Now merged as Château Pièrre   † Called Château Mouton d'Armailhacq until 1956

Château Sigalas-Rabaud . . . . Bommes

SECOND GROWTHS—*Deuxièmes Crus*

Château Myrat . . . . Barsac
Château Doisy-Daëne . . . . Barsac
Château Doisy-Dubroca . . . . Barsac
Château Doisy-Védrines . . . . Barsac
Château d'Arche . . . . Sauternes
Château Filhot . . . . Sauternes
Château Broustet . . . . Barsac
Château Nairac . . . . Barsac
Château Caillou . . . . Barsac
Château Suau . . . . Barsac
Château de Malle . . . . Preignac
Château Romer . . . . Fargues
Château Lamothe . . . . Sauternes

St.-Émilion

Official Classification of 1955

The vineyards surrounding the town of St.-Émilion were not classified in 1855, but they were exactly 100 years later, in 1955, to establish a classification comparable to that of the Médoc. Although Château Ausone and Château Cheval-Blanc are considered the two outstanding vineyards, they share the designation "first great growth" with the 10 other vineyards. The *grands crus* list includes only the vineyards available in world capitals.

FIRST GREAT GROWTHS—*Premiers Grands Crus*

Château Ausone
Château Cheval-Blanc
Château Beauséjour-Duffau-Lagarosse
Château Beauséjour-Fagouet
Château Belair
Château Canon
Château Figeac
Clos Fourtet
Château La Gaffelière Naudes
Château Magdelaine
Château Pavie
Château Trottevieille

GREAT GROWTHS—*Grands Crus*

Château Bellevue
Château Cadet-Bon
Château Canon-la-Gaffelière
Château Corbin
Château Curé-Bon
Château Fonroque
Château Grand-Barrail-Lamarzelle-Figeac
Château Grand-Corbin
Château les Grandes Murailles
Château Grand Pontet
Clos des Jacobins
Château La Clotte
Château La Dominique
Clos La Madeleine
Château l'Angélus
Château Laroze
Château Lasserre
Château La Tour-Figeac
Château La Tour-du-Pin-Figeac

Château Moulin-du-Cadet
Château Pavie-Macquin
Château Ripeau
Château St.-Georges-Côte-Pavie
Château Soutard
Château Trimoulet
Château Trois-Moulins
Château Troplong-Mondot
Château Yon-Figeac

Graves

Official Classification of 1953

The châteaux of the Graves District were officially rated by the Institut National des Appellations d'Origine in 1953, although Château Haut-Brion had been included in the 1855 classification.

CLASSIFIED RED WINES—*Crus Classés (Rouges)*

Château Haut-Brion . . . . Pessac
Château La Mission-Haut-Brion . . . . Pessac
Château Haut-Bailly . . . . Léognan
Domaine de Chevalier . . . . Léognan
Château Carbonnieux . . . . Léognan
Château Malartic-Lagravière . . . . Léognan
Château Latour-Martillac . . . . Martillac
Château Latour-Haut-Brion . . . . Talence
Château Pape-Clément . . . . Pessac
Château Smith-Haut-Lafitte . . . . Martillac
Château Olivier . . . . Léognan
Château Bouscaut . . . . Cadaujac

CLASSIFIED WHITE WINES—*Crus Classés (Blancs)*

Château Carbonnieux . . . . Léognan
Domaine de Chevalier . . . . Léognan
Château Couhins . . . . Villenave d'Ornon
Château Olivier . . . . Léognan
Château Laville-Haut-Brion . . . . Talence
Château Bouscaut . . . . Cadaujac

Pomerol

The district of Pomerol, adjacent to St.-Émilion, has never been officially rated. Nevertheless there are 10 vineyards that are generally ranked in the following order:

FIRST GREAT GROWTHS—*Premiers Grands Crus*

Château Pétrus
Château Certan
Vieux Château Certan
Château La Conseillante
Château Petit-Villages
Château Trotanoy
Château l'Évangile
Château Lafleur
Château Gazin
Château Lafleur-Pétrus

Burgundy

In the following rating of leading vineyards of Burgundy's Côte d'Or (which is divided into the Côte de Nuits and the Côte de Beaune), the vineyards are listed under their communes in geographical order from north to south. The historical *grand cru* vineyards appear in capital letters; most of the other vineyards are *premier cru*. The ratings descend from very great and great to very good and good and reflect current attitudes of outstanding authorities in Burgundy.

Red Wines of the Côte de Nuits

COMMUNE, VINEYARD	RATING

Fixin

Les Hervelets	*Very Good*
Clos du Chapitre	" "
Clos de la Perrière	" "
Les Arvelets	" "
Clos Napoléon	" "

Gevrey-Chambertin

CHAMBERTIN	*Very Great*
CLOS DE BÈZE	" "
LATRICIÈRES-CHAMBERTIN	*Great*
MAZIS-CHAMBERTIN	"
CHARMES-CHAMBERTIN	"
MAZOYÈRES-CHAMBERTIN	"
GRIOTTE-CHAMBERTIN	"
RUCHOTTES-CHAMBERTIN	"
CHAPELLE-CHAMBERTIN	"
Clos St. Jacques	"

Morey-St.-Denis

BONNES MARES	*Very Great*
CLOS DE LA ROCHE	*Great*
CLOS DE TART	*Very Good*
CLOS ST.-DENIS	" "
Clos des Lambrays	" "

Chambolle-Musigny

MUSIGNY	*Very Great*
BONNES MARES	" "
Les Amoureuses	*Great*
Les Charmes	*Very Good*

Vougeot

CLOS DE VOUGEOT	*Very Great*

Flagey-Échézeaux

GRANDS ÉCHÉZEAUX	*Very Great*
ÉCHÉZEAUX	*Very Good*

Vosne-Romanée

ROMANÉE-CONTI	*Very Great*
LA TÂCHE	" "
ROMANÉE-ST.-VIVANT	" "
RICHEBOURG	" "
La Grande Rue	" "
LA ROMANÉE	*Great*

Les Malconsorts	*Great*
Les Suchots	"
Les Beaux-Monts	"

Nuits St.-Georges

Les St.-Georges	*Great*
Les Cailles	"
Clos des Corvées	"
Les Vaucrains	"
Les Pruliers	"
Les Porrets	"
Clos de Thorey	"
Les Boudots	"
Les Cras	"
Les Murgers	"
Les Richemones	"

Red Wines of the Côte de Beaune

Aloxe-Corton

Corton Bressandes	*Very Great*
Corton Clos du Roi	" "
CORTON	" "
Corton Renardes	" "
Corton Perrières	*Great*
Corton-Les Maréchaudes	"

Pernand-Vergelesses

Ile des Vergelesses	*Good*

Savigny-les-Beaune

Vergelesses	*Good*
Lavières	"
Marconnets	"
Jarrons	"
Dominode	"

Beaune

Grèves	*Great*
Fèves	*Very Good*
Les Cras	" "
Champimonts	" "
Marconnets	" "
Bressandes	" "
Clos de la Mousse	" "
Clos des Mouches	" "
Les Avaux	" "
Aigrots	" "
Clos du Roi	" "
Les Theurons	" "
Les Cent-Vignes	*Good*
Les Toussaints	"
En l'Orme	"
À l'Écu	"

Pommard

Rugiens	*Great*
Épenots	"
Pézerolles	*Very Good*
Clos Blanc	" "
Chaponières	" "

Chanlins-Bas — Very Good
Platière — " "
Jarollières — " "

Volnay

Clos des Ducs .... Great
Caillerets — "
Champans — "
Fremiets — Very Good
Chevret — " "
Santenots — " "
Clos des Chênes — " "

Auxey

Les Duresses .... Very Good
Le Val — Good

Chassagne-Montrachet

La Boudriotte .... Very Good
Clos St. Jean — " "
La Maltroie (or Maltroye) — Good
Morgeot — "

White Wines of the Côte de Nuits

Chambolle-Musigny

Musigny Blanc .... Very Great

Vougeot

Clos Blanc de Vougeot .... Great

Nuits St.-Georges

Perrière .... Good

White Wines of the Côte de Beaune

Aloxe-Corton

CORTON-CHARLEMAGNE .... Very Great

Beaune

Clos des Mouches .... Very Good

Meursault

Perrières .... Great
Genevrières — "
Charmes — "
La Pièce-sous-le-Bois — Very Good
Blagny — " "
Santenots — " "
Goutte d'Or — Good

Puligny-Montrachet

MONTRACHET .... Very Great

CHEVALIER-MONTRACHET — Very Great
BÂTARD-MONTRACHET — " "
BIENVENUE-BÂTARD-MONTRACHET — " "
Combettes — Great
Chalumeaux — "
Folatières — "
Claivoillon — Very Good
Pucelles — " "
Cailleret — " "
Champ-Canet — " "
La Garenne — " "

Chassagne-Montrachet

MONTRACHET .... Very Great
BÂTARD-MONTRACHET — " "
CRIOTS-BÂTARD-MONTRACHET — " "
Ruchottes — Great
Cailleret — "
Morgeot — Very Good

The Nine Grands Crus of Beaujolais

Brouilly
Chénas
Chiroubles
Côtes de Brouilly
Fleurie
Juliénas
Morgon
Moulin-à-Vent
St.-Amour

The Grands Crus of Chablis

Blanchots
Les Clos
Valmur
Grenouilles
Vaudésir
Les Preuses
Bougros
La Moutonne (now a part of Vaudésir)

The Best of Chablis Premiers Crus

These vineyards on the right bank of the River Serein get the most sun and produce the best Chablis Premier Cru.

Chapelot
Côte de Fontenay
Fourchaume
Mont-de-Milieu
Montée de Tonnerre
Vaucoupin
Vaulorent

Glasses

Wine experts agree that the best all-purpose glass to buy for table wines is one that makes wine taste, and look, its best. Most recommend one that is: 1) stemmed, to keep hand heat from interfering with proper serving temperature and aroma; 2) clear, to show the wine's true color and clarity; 3) tulip-shaped, to concentrate the bouquet under the nose; and 4) adequately sized, so that an average 4-ounce serving fills the glass halfway or less, leaving space above so that the aroma can be savored. This type and other glasses for special uses are silhouetted on these pages.

ALL-PURPOSE GLASSES
The trend is toward the all-purpose glass, like any of the three above. The first, a 10-ounce size, is best for a household that has only one set of wineglasses. The 9-ounce glass in the center is good for red, rosé or white wine when only one is served. When two are served, the first and third glasses go well together. The former's capacity allows for swirling red wine to develop bouquet; the latter's 8-ounce size is good for white wine.

Bottles

It is often possible to tell a wine's origin and type by the shape and color of its bottle. But beware: Shapes that identify the best-known European wines may also be used for others of lesser quality. For example, the high-shouldered, straight-sided bottle silhouetted at the right was made famous by French shippers in the Bordeaux region. Now the most common bottle shape of all, it is used in almost all wine-producing countries—at times for non-Bordeaux-type wines. Nevertheless, with many wines the shape of the bottle is a rough guide.

BORDEAUX
A true Bordeaux bottle contains 24 ounces and should yield six servings per bottle. Green glass is used for red wine, clear glass for white.

BURGUNDY
This 24-ounce bottle is used for all wines that come from the Burgundy area, for most Rhône wines and for many Italian and U.S. wines.

RHINE AND MOSELLE WINES
Long-stemmed glasses, which are used
for Rhine and Moselle wines, were first
designed and produced in the Rhine
area, long famous for its glassware.

SHERRY
A relatively strong wine, such as sherry,
should be served in 4-to-5-ounce
glasses that are just wide enough at
the top to permit sniffing the aroma.

BRANDY, LIQUEURS
Snifters of 6-to-10-ounce size, used for
brandy, also enhance the aromas of
liqueurs like Benedictine, Grand
Marnier and Chartreuse.

CHAMPAGNE
A narrow goblet holds in, and displays,
the characteristic bubbles of
champagne and sparkling wines better
than the familiar stemmed saucer glass.

RHINE, MOSELLE, ALSATIAN
This tall, slender 24-ounce bottle,
restyled from the Burgundy shape, is
brown for most Rhine wines, but green
for Moselle and Alsatian wines.

FRANCONIA
Similar in contour to ancient Egyptian
flasks, this squat bottle usually
identifies Main wines from Germany
and many Chilean wines.

CHIANTI
Although Italian wine bottles come in
all shapes, the best known is the 32-
ounce rounded straw-covered flask
identified with the Chianti region.

CHAMPAGNE, SPARKLING WINES
Burgundy-shaped and many-sized,
bottles for champagne and sparkling
wine are thick, with corks wired on to
withstand the wines' pressure.

To the novice, the array of foreign and unfamiliar words on wine labels can be bewildering. However, there are patterns of nomenclature common to families of wines that can help you in judging their type and quality. A surprising amount of the information on wine labels is controlled by law. *Appellation contrôlée* (literally, "controlled place name"), which appears in various versions on French labels, is a good example of government supervision, for its appearance guarantees that the wine has met legal standards for its district. Generally, the smaller the area specified as "controlled," the higher the wine's quality. Thus *Appellation Pauillac Contrôlée* on the label below tells us that, since Pauillac is a village, this wine will be superior to a wine bearing simply *Appellation Bordeaux Contrôlée*, which refers to the whole region.

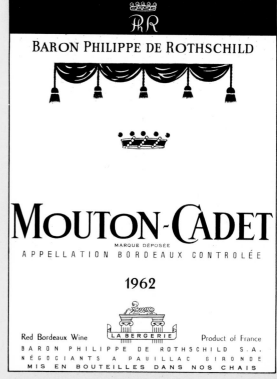

BORDEAUX REGIONAL WINE

This impressive-looking label might easily lead one to think that it identifies a château-bottled wine, but there is nothing on the label to warrant this deduction. The term *appellation Bordeaux contrôlée* signifies that the wine may come from any part of Bordeaux, and can even be a blend of lesser wines. Another clue to the wine's status are the words *dans nos chais* on the bottom line. Meaning "in our cellars," they do not convey the quality that the words *au château* do (*label at left*); the wine is not the product of a single vineyard. However, red Bordeaux wines like this one can be good if the producer is reputable. In this case, he is: Baron Philippe de Rothschild is a highly respected producer of his own fine château wine (Château Mouton-Rothschild), and his lesser regional brand is also popular in England, France and the United States.

BORDEAUX CHÂTEAU-BOTTLED WINE

The name Château Latour proclaims this wine to be one of the best Bordeaux, for the vineyard is in the top division of the 1855 classification, a *premier cru classé* (first growth) (*page 182*). *Mis en bouteilles au château* guarantees that the wine was both made and bottled on the grower's own property. Unlike these terms, which are regulated by law, the words *grand vin* have no legal significance. The small legend at the bottom is simply the owner's company name.

| ESTATE BOTTLED | 1964 | MISE AU DOMAINE |

RICHEBOURG

APPELLATION CONTROLÉE

Société Civile des Domaines LOUIS GROS Frères & Sœur
PROPRIÉTAIRE A VOSNE-ROMANÉE (COTE-D'OR)

ONE OF BURGUNDY'S BEST

Richebourg is the name of a *grand cru* (great growth) vineyard in Burgundy. Vineyards like this one are individually regulated by the government with their own *appellation contrôlée* and are held in such esteem that neither the village name nor the words *grand cru* need appear on the label. (Other vineyards of this caliber include those of Chambertin, Montrachet, Musigny, Clos de Vougeot.) The words *mise au domaine* mean estate-bottled, the equivalent of château-bottling in Bordeaux. It is more difficult to find estate-bottled Burgundy than château-bottled Bordeaux, for the entire Burgundy crop is smaller and relatively few estates do their own bottling.

| ESTATE BOTTLED | MISE AU DOMAINE |

GRAND VIN
DE

Chassagne-Montrachet

« MORGEOT »

APPELLATION CHASSAGNE-MONTRACHET CONTROLÉE

1962	Claude RAMONET
	PROPRIÉTAIRE - RÉCOLTANT
	A CHASSAGNE - MONTRACHET
	(Côte-d'Or)

A BURGUNDY PREMIER CRU

Unlike the *grands crus* of Burgundy, named for vineyards *(left)*, the *premiers crus*, one step down from the great growths as wines are ranked in Burgundy, bear their village names prominently on labels and subordinate the vineyard. In this case Chassagne-Montrachet is the village; it is at the southern end of the Côte de Beaune where the best white Burgundies are produced. Morgeot identifies the vineyard, and although its presence seems secondary, it carries the important assurance that this is indeed a *premier cru* and not a village wine. The latter does not bear a vineyard name at all, only that of the village and sometimes an area name like Côte de Beaune.

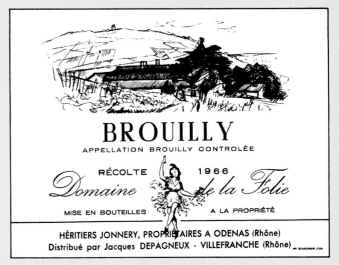

A POPULAR BEAUJOLAIS

Brouilly is one of nine *grands crus* of the Beaujolais district in Burgundy, all designated by specific village names and better wines than Beaujolais-Villages and Beaujolais *(page 185)*. The words *mise en bouteilles à la propriété*, like *mise au domaine*, mean estate-bottled. Domaine de la Folie is the name of the vineyard.

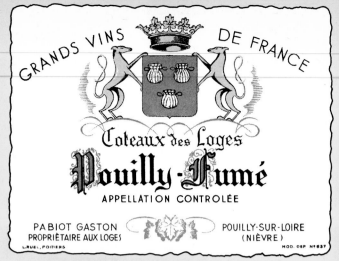

A DRY VINTAGE CHAMPAGNE

This label describes a champagne bottled by St. Marceaux, a shipper in Rheims, and made entirely from 1959's superior grape crop. Vintage years are declared in Champagne only when the quality of the crop is exceptional. The words *blanc de blancs* indicate that only white grapes were used, instead of the usual combination of white and black grapes. *Brut* means that this is the driest of champagnes.

A WHITE WINE FROM THE LOIRE

Pouilly-Fumé derives part of its name from its village of origin, Pouilly-sur-Loire, the other part from the local name for the Sauvignon Blanc grape, *Blanc Fumé* (White Smoke), by which the wine is also known. The vintage date for this Pouilly-Fumé, 1966, appeared on a separate strip above the label. Wines of the Loire Valley are best drunk when they are young.

AN ESTATE-BOTTLED RIESLING

This German wine is from the Moselle-Saar-Ruwer district, the town of Wehlen and the Sonnenuhr vineyard. Although the type of wine does not appear, fine Moselle estates grow only Riesling grapes. *Auslese* (selection) signifies that this Riesling was made from bunches of grapes allowed to become overripe and therefore sweeter. *Original-Kellerabfüllung* (genuine cellar bottling) is one way to say the wine was bottled on the premises—in this case of Joh. Jos. Prüm, from his own growth, or *Wachstum*. By law, any one of the three German terms above guarantees that the wine has not been artificially sweetened.

A GERMAN REGIONAL WINE

A shipper's wine in Germany is often a blend. The town and grape names, Johannisberg and Riesling, are a legal guarantee that at least two thirds of the wine comes from this town and at least two thirds of it has been made from Riesling grapes.

190

A PREMIUM CALIFORNIA WINE

California wines are either "varietals," made from classic grape varieties *(above)*, or generic *(below)*. When the grape type, Pinot noir in this instance, appears on the label, it must by law account for at least 51 per cent of the grapes used in the wine.

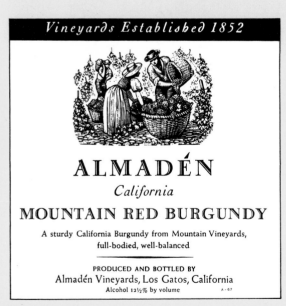

A VIN ORDINAIRE OF THE WEST

Generic, or type-of-product, names such as Burgundy, claret, chablis, sauterne and Rhine appear on the labels of many California wines. No grape variety is mentioned; the wines are blends made from several varieties of grapes similar to those used for the lesser wines of France and Germany. Labels of most generic wines, like this one, usually give the place of origin by state rather than by the locality.

AN ORIGINAL CHIANTI

Of the many wines called Chianti, the original and most reliable is *Chianti classico*, produced in a defined district in Tuscany, Italy. To maintain the reputation of the wine, the local association of vintners tests the quality of members' wine (Nozzole vineyard, in this case) before allowing its seal to be placed on bottles, which are individually numbered. The seal is identified by a black cockerel on a gold background enclosed in a red circle that bears the association's name, Consorzio per la Difesa del Vino Tipico di Chianti.

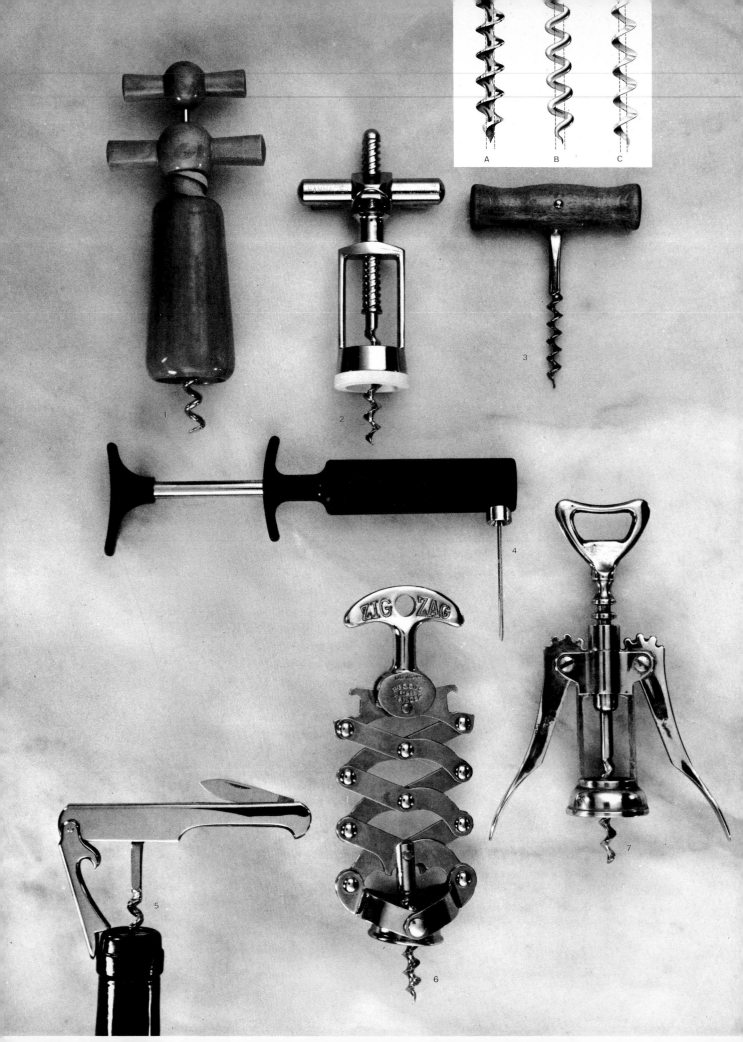

Opening Wine

The appearance of wine at most dinner tables evokes a mellow mood of anticipation. But struggling with an unpredictable cork can quickly turn this mood into one of annoyance for the host, and perhaps one of some amusement for the guests. To avoid such embarrassments, you need a reliable opener—one that meets certain requirements in construction and that is designed for the particular cork you are up against.

The simplest and best-known opener is the old—if not always reliable—corkscrew (*3 in the picture opposite*), a horizontal handle attached to a helical screw, or "worm." Of the three types of worms shown in the inset at top, the one in the center (*B*) is the most efficient. Its open core, as opposed to the solid core in the auger-type worm (*A*), enables each spiral to imbed itself fully in the cork, thus aiding the grip of the worm. At the same time, its outer edges are smooth rather than sharp, as in both *A* and *C*, so they will not cut a new cork or crumble an old one. And finally, there are enough spirals to distribute the force of your pull evenly through the bulk of the cork (there should be at least six spirals, and the worm should be at least 2¼ inches long, preferably 2½, so it can go all the way through the cork and anchor one of its spirals against the cork's under surface).

To make the extraction of cork easier, many corkscrews incorporate the added help of a twisting action, as in (*1*) and (*2*). In (*1*) the worm is twisted in by means of a larger crossbar and the cork pulled by means of the smaller one; in (*2*) one crossbar serves both functions. Dry or relatively new corks are most successfully extracted with this type. Other openers, like (*5*), (*6*) and (*7*), make use of leverage. The opener marked (*5*) is the traditional folding pocket type used by wine waiters; note that it also has a bottle-cap remover, and a knife blade for cutting away foil. The one at (*6*) employs multiple leverage to increase the pulling force, and (*7*) has two side levers that are pushed down to lift out the cork.

Still another type of opener (*4*) has a hollow needle that pierces the cork and projects into the air space below it. When air is fed into this space, by pushing the plunger, the increased pressure inside forces out the cork—often with a champagnelike pop. More automatic types, powered by a replaceable gas cartridge, operate similarly. These pressure extractors are the safest type of opener for expensive wines, whose corks may be 10 or more years old and liable to crumble under direct attack by a corkscrew.

Decanting Wine

Decanting wine—pouring it from the original bottle into another container before serving—is generally recommended for two reasons: 1) to remove natural but muddying sediment that occurs in red wine after six or seven years in the bottle, and 2) to improve both the smell and taste of young red wine. White wine almost never needs decanting, although sediment may be present. This sediment is usually colorless and tasteless and, like that of red wine, always harmless.

Prior to decanting, a bottle should be kept upright for at least two hours, preferably a day, to let the sediment settle (*1 in diagram below*). To decant: first uncork the bottle without disturbing the sediment. Next, peel the foil from the neck, then clean both the inside and the rim of the neck. Now, stand with a light or a white background behind the bottle, so that you can see the sediment clearly. Take firm hold on the bottle, label side up, and pour slowly, in a continuous motion (*2*). As the first streak of sediment nears the neck (*3*), right the bottle. There should be little waste, and your decanted wine will be clear and flavorful.

Which Wine with Which Food?

The question of the proper wines to serve with different foods is one that intrigues many and intimidates some. At one extreme are the organized gourmets who are so concerned with the nuances of food and wine at their gala dinners that a special committee eats and drinks its way through the menu a few days before the actual event, in order to be sure that each wine is *exactly* the right accompaniment for each dish. On the other hand there are those who claim, democratically, that any wine goes with any food—if it suits you. That is fair enough, if your guests share your tastes. But it is a pity not to try the various traditional pairings of food and wine to see why so many people have found them good companions for each other.

Seafood—White with White

Although the longstanding rule of white wine with white meat and red wine with red meat has some notable exceptions, most people seem to find it appropriate most of the time. One exception is any dish that requires fish to be cooked in red wine. In this case, the same red wine should be served with it. Basically, though, the taste of most fish makes a red wine taste slightly odd, while a chilled white wine, with its slight acidity and refreshing taste, sets off a fish dish. Conversely, so most people feel, roast beef or lamb chops have too much flavor to compete with the taste of a white wine but are complemented by a red.

Full Flavor with Rich Food

An excellent guide for choosing which red or white wine to serve is the way a particular dish is prepared. The richer the food is, the fuller flavored the wine should be. A grilled dish, for example, takes a lighter red or white wine than one with a rich sauce. And, properly, you should serve different white wines for sautéed chicken with cream sauce, roast chicken, and a luncheon of cold chicken (*opposite page*).

Regional Pairing

Another useful guide to follow is the pairing of a regional dish with that region's local wine. A *boeuf bourguignon* (Burgundy beef stew) calls for a Pommard or a Nuits St.-Georges, which are the same wines generally used in cooking this dish; an Italian meat dish with a spicy tomato sauce is unerringly served with a Chianti or Valpolicella; a light Spanish Rioja wine goes nicely with *paella*.

Foods to Avoid with Wine

There are some foods with which wine should *not* be served at all. Curries and highly spiced foods are better accompanied by beer. Mint sauce and cocktail sauce, when served with various dishes, will overwhelm the taste of wine. Chocolate tends to throw off the taste of the sweet dessert wines. Egg dishes usually give wine an odd taste (although a cheese omelet would be enhanced by an inexpensive red wine). Salads and antipasto make wine taste vinegarish.

Two Wines at a Meal

If you plan to serve more than one wine at a dinner, there are certain traditional guides that, once you have tried them, will prove to be quite logical. They are: *white before red; dry before sweet; light before full; young before old.* These rules are based on the assumption that a meal should progress from less interesting wines to those with more flavor and complexity, so that dinner does not end with an anticlimax. Thus, a dry white wine is correctly served with a first course, but would be disappointing after the greater richness of a red wine. The exceptions are the sweet white dessert wines, which should always be served at the end of a meal. A sweet wine that is served before dry wines will make the wines that follow, whether red or white, taste bland and perhaps even bitter by comparison.

Assuming that a meal should progress toward the more interesting wines, a Beaujolais would be served before a Pommard or a château-bottled Bordeaux. An assortment of rich, but not strong-tasting, cheeses after the main course and before the dessert is an excellent accompaniment to present along with an exceptionally good bottle of red wine, especially if a lighter red wine has been served with the main course. There is certainly nothing very fancy or difficult about serving two or more wines at the same dinner. It is a simple way of adding an extra note of elegance to a meal. If only two or three persons are dining, they may find two half bottles of different wines more enjoyable than a full bottle of one wine.

Champagne or Rosé

A simple solution to the problem of matching wine with food is to serve champagne or a rosé throughout the meal. Champagne will certainly add gaiety to any dinner party, but it should be noted that it is, after all, a light dry wine. If it were a still wine, it would be comparable to Chablis. Consequently, it is not the ideal accompaniment to all foods. Rosé is excellent with cold foods and there are times when a chilled rosé is a perfect companion to a light meal. But anyone who enjoys food and wine should be more adventuresome when a good deal of effort has gone into a fine meal. In a restaurant, the logical solution to main dishes that include both fish and red meat is to order two half bottles, one white, the other red.

A Menu for Wines

Following is a brief guide to some specific traditional combinations of food and wine. Remember that in cases where a good white Burgundy is suggested, such as a Chassagne-Montrachet or a Meursault, it is equally appropriate to serve a Puligny-Montrachet, a Corton-Charlemagne or a Pouilly-Fuissé. If a Beaujolais-Villages is suggested, a *grand cru* such as a Moulin-à-Vent, Fleurie or Juliénas would be an equally happy choice. If a red Bordeaux is indicated, you can choose one from the various districts of Médoc, St.-Émilion, Graves and Pomerol. If a *grand cru* château would best complement a fine dish, you can choose from more than a hundred in these districts of France.

HORS D'OEUVRE: As we have explained previously, salads and antipasto do not lend themselves to wine, but the flavor of a pâté or bite-sized pieces of a *quiche* is enhanced by a glass of the wine you have chosen for your main course. Pâté also goes nicely with a Riesling, and a *quiche Lorraine*, since it is a regional dish of Alsace-Lorraine, goes well with an Alsatian white wine.

SOUP: No wine is needed, particularly for cream soups. At gourmet dinners, a consommé is often accompanied by an amontillado sherry or Madeira.

FISH: Simply prepared fish calls for a light white wine like a Pinot Chardonnay, Alsatian Riesling, Petit Chablis, Moselle, Pouilly-Fuissé or Pouilly-Fumé. Full-flavored fish and those made with rich sauces call for a full-bodied white wine like a Chassagne-Montrachet, a Meursault, or a German Rheingau (although not an Auslese). Dry sherry is often preferred to a white wine when fish is oily. For shellfish, Chablis is the traditional choice, especially with oysters, but any refreshing white wine—a Muscadet, Soave, Sylvaner or Pinot Chardonnay —will do nicely.

PORK AND VEAL: White wines, such as a Riesling or a Graves, go well with these lighter flavored meats. If you wish you may also serve a light red—a Beaujolais-Villages, a Zinfandel or a Bardolino. A rich pork dish like those served in Alsace and Germany calls for an Alsatian Riesling or a Rheingau.

CHICKEN AND OTHER FOWL: Red or white, light or full wines are all served with poultry, the selection depending on the preparation of the dish and the fattiness of the fowl. For example, *coq au vin* should be served with the same wine that it is cooked with. A goose takes a spicy Alsatian or German wine. A good claret (red Bordeaux) sets off roast chicken or roast duck very well; chicken in a rich sauce calls for a white Burgundy like Corton-Charlemagne or Meursault; a Muscadet, Moselle or chilled rosé are good with cold chicken.

BEEF AND LAMB: When simply cooked, these meats are best accompanied by a fine red Bordeaux or Burgundy; the finer the cut of meat, the more fitting is a classed growth from the Médoc or St.-Émilion or a *grand cru* from Burgundy. Stews not made with wine can be served with a good Beaujolais, a light red Graves or a California Cabernet Sauvignon.

HAM: Some people enjoy a light red wine like a Mâcon or Volnay from Burgundy, particularly if the ham is plainly baked and delicately flavored. A chilled rosé is good with ham that is accompanied by something sweet like pineapple.

GAME: Light-flavored game like pheasant or quail is nicely complemented by a light red wine: a Volnay from Burgundy or a Bordeaux claret (hopefully château-bottled). Strong game like venison or wild duck demands a rich wine—a fine Burgundy such as Pommard, Corton, Bonnes Mares or Musigny. A less expensive but robust wine is Châteauneuf-du-Pape from the Rhône. In Germany, where venison and boar are specialties, these rich dishes are successfully accompanied by a full-flavored Rheinpfalz or Rheingau like Rauenthaler, Schloss Vollrads, Schloss Johannisberger, Marcobrunner or Steinberger.

CHEESES: Among the various flavors of cheeses there are some that lend themselves admirably to almost any wine. If you are using a cheese course to finish off a bottle of white wine from the main course, pick a light cheese such as *fontina* or Havarti. In most cases, cheese is used to accompany red wines because of their full flavor and their position at the end of a meal. Note, though, that pungent cheeses like Roquefort or Liederkranz tend to overwhelm the delicate flavor of a fine Médoc or an aged Burgundy; in fact few people find such strong cheeses compatible with any wine.

DESSERT: With a soufflé, cake or fresh fruit (except highly acid citrus fruits) a sweet wine is the most appropriate. In this category are Sauternes, dessert Madeira (bual or malmsey) and cream sherry, Spätlese and Auslese Rhine wines. You may also serve champagne, but choose one labeled extra dry rather than the bone-dry brut, as the latter may taste slightly sharp in conjunction with a rich dessert. As for port, reserve it for a little later; it is a perfect accompaniment to walnuts or other nuts for nibbling after the meal.

A Winetasting Party

Getting to know wines well enough to have favorites, and relish them, may seem a formidable project if you are a beginner. However, acquiring the necessary expertise has become a pleasant matter since professional winetasting has been domesticated. Winetasting parties, informative gatherings in a friend's living room or patio, are proving an easy way to learn for the novice, as well as enjoyable for the expert.

Evaluating Wine

Like professionals, amateurs should judge wine according to three criteria: 1) appearance, 2) aroma, or bouquet, and 3) taste. First, holding the glass by the stem, raise it to the light to check color and clarity. A Beaujolais, for example, should be a deep purple; an older Bordeaux, brick red. An old Burgundy will be slightly amber at the edges. All wine should be brilliantly clear when held to the light. Any cloudiness present may indicate that the wine is "sick," possibly from a rapid, excessive change in temperature.

Having noted the wine's appearance, swirl it gently for a moment or two. This releases the bouquet, through evaporation. Next, take a hearty sniff. At first you will probably judge the wine simply by how pleasant the aroma is. But you will soon learn to distinguish the flowery fragrance of a Moselle from the rich, more complex bouquet of a fine Burgundy. Learning to appreciate a bouquet is vital, for most of what we think of as taste is part of our sense of smell.

Finally, you are ready to sip the wine. Following the professional winetaster's lead, allow the wine to sit in your mouth for a moment and roll it around your tongue. This enables you to single out the various tastes present in the wine. At this point, the professional spits the wine out, so he can go on with his job; but since a party in the home is a social occasion, the libations are usually happily swallowed.

When you have fully savored the wine, you are ready to enter your comments on your wine program which, besides allowing space for your reaction, lists all the wines served, their vintage and, hopefully, a fact or two about each (*opposite page*).

Wine Terms

Here are a few generally accepted terms to help you describe taste:

Acidity—A pleasant tartness that gives wines a refreshing, lively quality, especially agreeable in white wine. Too much of this, of course, can result in a vinegarish, sour wine, unpleasant to drink.
Astringency—A quality that makes the mouth pucker, especially present in red Bordeaux wine. It is not a flaw; it simply means the wine has been opened for use before it has aged to its full potential.

Bouquet—A combination of all the aromas and fragrances a wine assumes as its alcohol and fruit acids oxidize.
Fresh—Having a lively fragrance and taste, usually found in young white wines, rosés and many light reds. These may lose their charm and fragrance after three or four years and are described then as "tired."
Full-bodied—A fine red or white Burgundy has this quality; it has substance and seems to "fill the mouth." In contrast, a Muscadet is light-bodied.
Harsh—Applied to a rough, immature wine, or an overly astringent one.
Mellow—"Soft," ripe-tasting, often with some sweetness.
Spicy—Used to describe a wine that has a special kind of piquant aroma or taste, most often found in a white Alsatian or Palatinate wine.

Order of Tasting

The usual order of tasting is white before red, and, within each group, from light-bodied to full-bodied. The maximum number of wines that can be comfortably tasted and enjoyed at a home winetasting is eight. These can be from one country, or from several —or from one region of a country if you are a fair expert. We suggest, as a starter, a tasting of eight French wines, like those listed on the opposite page.

How to Prepare

The usual rule of thumb in figuring the total amount of wine to buy for a winetasting party is half a bottle, of all wines combined, per person. The average serving for each sampling is only 1 to 2 ounces; 1 ounce of a dessert or appetizer wine is proper.

White and rosé wines should be chilled; two hours in the refrigerator is ample. (Beware of using the freezer for quick chilling; the bottles may crack.) Red wines should be opened to "breathe" for an hour if they are fairly young, half an hour if fairly old.

In setting up the tasting area (*diagram opposite*), you should provide enough table space so that guests are able to move about freely. Wines should be arranged on the table in the order of tasting. One glass per person is enough. A pitcherful of water and napkins should be conveniently placed for guests to rinse and wipe their glasses between tastings. There should also be two waste collectors—one for water and unwanted wine, one for the soggy napkins.

In addition, it is highly desirable—really necessary in fact—to furnish white bread or bland crackers and a mild cheese, like a Colby or Monterey Jack, for guests to nibble on. These erase the taste of wine and hence pave the way for the next sipping. For an evening tasting, a nice finale is cake and coffee.

196

Table Scheme for a Wine Tasting

White wines

Red wines

Napkins

French bread, cut into cubes

Cheese, cut into cubes

Pitcher of water

Wine glasses, all-purpose type (1 per person)

A Suggested Tasting of French Wines

WHITE

1. A Pouilly-Fumé or a Sancerre from the Loire

2. A Chablis or a Pouilly-Fuissé from Burgundy

3. A Graves from Bordeaux

4. A Chassagne-Montrachet or a Meursault from the Côte de Beaune

RED

1. A *grand cru* Beaujolais, such as a Moulin-à-Vent

2. A Châteauneuf-du-Pape from the Rhône

3. A Bordeaux château wine from Médoc or St.-Émilion

4. A Burgundy, such as a Pommard, Nuits St.-Georges or a Volnay

Winetasting Program

NAME OF WINE

COMMENTS

RATING (1-10)

NAME OF WINE

COMMENTS

RATING (1-10)

NAME OF WINE

COMMENTS

RATING (1-10)

NAME OF WINE

COMMENTS

RATING (1-10)

Starting a Wine Cellar

If you enjoy wine, there are several reasons why you can benefit by having a wine "cellar," or "library," somewhere in your home. A cellar gives you easy access to wine at any time, as well as a better choice of wines to suit different occasions. With a cellar, you can plan toward a broad assortment of wines and buy them at your leisure. Furthermore, you will save money because you can take advantage of sales. Finally, good red wines need to "rest" for a few days at least after being transported, and a cellar allows them to do so. You can start a cellar with as few as 6 to 10 bottles. Just visit a shop with a good selection, pick out bottles at different prices with the help of the wine merchant, and start experimenting.

To do your cellar justice, whatever its size, there are three considerations in providing storage: temperature, light and stability. Ideally, wines should be stored at 45° to 60° F. A temperature over 70° will make wines mature at a faster rate than is good for them. Too much light affects a wine's taste, turning it musty or flat. Vibrations will also damage flavor, since they alter a wine's normal "breathing" pace.

A basement area or an air-conditioned room or adjoining closet should keep wines sufficiently cool. If you are making the best of an ordinary closet, try to choose one that is not hit by sunlight. Arrange the bottles according to type from the floor up, as in the large diagram (5) at right. Because they mature faster than reds, white wines should lie lowest of all, where the cooler temperatures will keep them best. Next come champagne and rosés. Red wines, usually served at room temperature, rest rightfully above.

All table wines must be stored on their sides so that the cork is kept in contact with the wine. Otherwise the cork will dry out and contract, allowing air to enter the bottle, which almost always spoils the wine. (Fortified wines like sherry and port, apéritifs, brandies and spirits are not affected by air—except for evaporation—and may be stored upright, either atop the table wines, as in the diagram, or in a bar area.)

An easily stowed storage rack for the beginning collector is the simple notched design shown at (1) in the illustration at right. The wooden bin next to it (2), which holds two rows of bottles, can be a do-it-yourself project. Its small, multiple compartments separate wines by type, origin and even vintage (experienced collectors demand such separation and often label each compartment). Commercially made units (3,4) are available in many sizes and may be stacked to hold from eight to 100 bottles. In fact, their geometric design often inspires decorative use in a dining room or den, where they may stand free or be stacked as an architectural pattern against a wall.

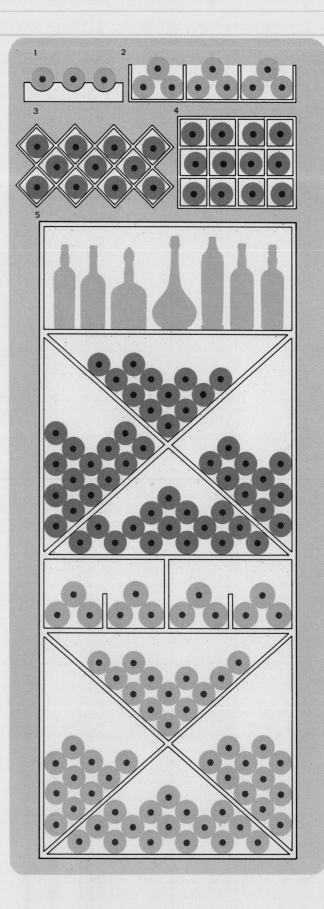

Cellars to Fit Three Budgets

The following recommendations for three wine cellars are based on average costs of wines in the U.S. You will need to adapt suggestions as to numbers of bottles to fit actual costs in your area. Wines specified in the listings were selected on the basis of merit and availability. In the event that certain wines are not available, we suggest you use this guide in conjunction with the vintage and classification charts on pages 180-185, so that any substitutions will be comparable in quality.

A $100 Wine Cellar

(Wines are listed in alphabetical order unless otherwise indicated.)

RED BORDEAUX: Six bottles from the vintages of '61, '62 or '64. Choose wines from the districts of the Médoc, St.-Émilion, Graves and Pomerol. Two should be château-bottled, such as:

Beychevelle	Lynch-Bages
Cos d'Estournel	Léoville-Las-Cases
Gruaud-Larose	Palmer
Lascombes	Pichon-Lalande

WHITE BORDEAUX: Two bottles of château-bottled Graves and one bottle of château-bottled Sauternes or Barsac from the years '62, '64 or '66. Among the names to look for:

Graves	Sauternes or Barsac
Carbonnieux	Climens
Couhins	Latour Blanche
Laville-Haut-Brion	Yquem

RED BURGUNDIES: Four estate-bottlings of the years '61, '62, '64 or '66. Try to buy the wine of such villages as:

Beaune	Pommard
Gevrey-Chambertin	Volnay
Nuits St.-Georges	Vosne-Romanée

WHITE BURGUNDIES: Two bottles from '62, '64 or '66. Ask for estate-bottlings from villages such as:

Aloxe-Corton	Meursault
Chablis	Pouilly-Fuissé
Chassagne-Montrachet	Puligny-Montrachet

VIN ROSÉ: Two bottles from such California vineyards as Almadén, Beaulieu and Louis Martini.

VIN DU PAYS (local wines): Six bottles from '66 or '67. Wines from the following areas are not expensive and are best drunk when they are less than four years old:

French Red	French White
Beaujolais	Alsace
Châteauneuf-du-Pape	Muscadet
Côtes de Provence	Pouilly-Fumé
Côtes de Rhône	Sancerre
Crozes Hermitage	Vouvray
Hermitage	

AMERICAN REDS: Two varietals from these grape types, in order of merit: Cabernet Sauvignon, Pinot noir, Gamay.

AMERICAN WHITES: Two varietals from the following grape types, in order of merit (left column first):

Pinot Chardonnay	Sauvignon Blanc
Johannisberg Riesling	Chenin Blanc
Sémillon	Traminer

RHINES AND MOSELLES: Two estate-bottlings of '66 wine from such villages as:

Rhines	Moselles
Eltville	Bernkastel
Johannisberg	Brauneberg
Nierstein	Graach
Oppenheim	Piesport
Rauenthal	Ürzig
Rüdesheim	Wehlen

CHAMPAGNES: Two bottles of American champagne chosen from the following brands, listed in approximate order of quality (left column first):

Korbel	Paul Masson
Almadén	Christian Brothers
Beaulieu	Gold Seal
Kornell	Great Western
Charles Fournier	Taylor

A $250 Cellar

RED BORDEAUX: Eight bottles of '61, '62 or '64. Choose four bottles from the districts and châteaux listed in the $100 cellar and four château-bottlings from the following eight greatest vineyards of Bordeaux:

Ausone	Latour
Cheval-Blanc	Margaux
Haut-Brion	Mouton-Rothschild
Lafite-Rothschild	Pétrus

WHITE BORDEAUX: Three bottles of '62, '64 or '66 from château-bottlings:

Graves	Sauternes or Barsac
Bouscaut	Climens
Domaine de Chevalier	Latour Blanche
Haut-Brion Blanc	Rayne-Vigneau
Olivier	Yquem

RED BURGUNDIES: Six estate-bottlings of '61, '62, '64 or '66 from among the following great-growth vineyards (arranged geographically from north to south):

Chambertin	Richebourg
Musigny	Corton
Romanée-Conti	Bonnes Mares
La Tâche	Clos de Vougeot
Romanée St.-Vivant	Échézeaux

WHITE BURGUNDIES: Four bottles of '62, '64 or '66 estate-bottlings from villages mentioned in the $100 cellar, including one grand cru Montrachet.

VIN ROSÉ: Four bottles, including two American (Almadén, Beaulieu or Louis Martini) and two French '66 from the vineyards of Anjou, Bourgogne, Provence or Tavel.

VINS DU PAYS: 12 bottles, including '66 and '67 wines listed under the $100 cellar and a selection of non-French wines like:

Reds	Whites
Italian Chianti or Valpolicella	Austrian Gumpold-skirchner
Portuguese Dão	Italian Verdicchio,
Spanish Rioja	Soave or Orvieto
	Swiss Fendant or Neuchâtel

AMERICAN REDS: Four bottles of varietals.

AMERICAN WHITES: Four bottles of superior varietals.

RHINES AND MOSELLES: Four bottles, including a '59 Moselle, the rest '66. Try to buy wines from the following vineyards:

Bernkasteler Doktor
Piesporter Goldtröpfchen
Scharzhofberger
Schloss Johannisberg
Schloss Vollrads
Wehlener Sonnenuhr

CHAMPAGNES: Three bottles, including one nonvintage French and one '61 or '62 vintage French from among the following shippers:

Ayala	Moët et Chandon
Bollinger	Mumm
Charles Heidsieck	Piper-Heidsieck
Clicquot	Pommery
Heidsieck Monopole	Roederer
Krug	St. Marceaux
Lanson	Taittinger

A $500 Cellar

RED BORDEAUX: 14 bottles, including eight of '61, '62, or '64 château-bottled wines and four bottles of '55 and '59 château-bottled wines for consumption while the others mature.

WHITE BORDEAUX: Five bottles of suggested '62, '64 or '66 wines.

RED BURGUNDIES: 12 bottles of suggested '59, '61, '62, '64 or '66 wines.

WHITE BURGUNDIES: Eight bottles of '62, '64 and '66 village and vineyard wines, including one bottle of Montrachet.

VIN ROSÉ: Six bottles, half American and half French, from among those suggested in the $100 and $250 cellars.

VINS DU PAYS: 24 bottles of '66 and '67 wines mentioned in the two earlier listings.

AMERICAN REDS AND WHITES: 24 bottles.

RHINES AND MOSELLES: Six bottles of suggested vineyard wines.

CHAMPAGNES: 10 bottles, including four American, four nonvintage French and two '61 and '62 vintage French champagnes from shippers suggested in the $100 and $250 cellars.

Bar Tips and Tools

As a host or hostess, you will find the role of congenial bartender easier to fill if you use the proper equipment and techniques for preparing mixed drinks. Following are some suggestions (which, for convenience, also appear in the Recipe Booklet):

Glasses

Silhouetted at right are five standard bar glasses; the instructions for mixing drinks in the accompanying Recipe Booklet specify appropriate glasses. Recently there has been a trend toward larger glasses. A larger drink, however, allows more time for the liquid to become warm and the ice to melt. For this reason some hosts still use the smaller sizes, preferring to mix a second drink at full strength and flavor.

Chilling and Frosting Glasses

Many bartenders like to help keep cocktails cold by chilling the glasses beforehand. The simplest way to chill a glass is to place it in the refrigerator for 30 minutes or in the freezer for 5 minutes (10 minutes if you want the glass to frost). Or, you can fill the glasses with ice cubes or cracked ice while you mix the drinks, discarding the ice when you are ready to pour.

To sugar-frost a glass for a Daiquiri, chill it, then rub the inside and top of the rim with a strip of lime peel. Dip the moistened rim into a bowl of superfine sugar, pause a moment, lift the glass out and tap it gently with a finger to shake off the excess sugar. For the tequila-based cocktail called a Margarita, rub the glass rim with lime peel and dip into salt.

Fruit Juices and Peels

Whenever possible, use fresh fruit for drinks that call for fruit flavoring. An orange, lemon or lime may be softened by rolling it on a hard surface like a cutting board, bearing down with your hand. This helps to break down the fibers and makes it easier to extract the juice. In cutting lemon or lime peel, never include the white membrane of the rind; shave off only the colored surface peel, in sections about 1 inch by ½ inch.

Preparing Ice

Use only ice that has been isolated from foods in the refrigerator; if your refrigerator does not have a separate freezer chest, ice may absorb undesirable odors. To rid ice of odors, rinse it quickly under cold water.

Use cubes instead of cracked ice in shaker drinks to minimize dilution. To obtain the cracked ice called for in certain recipes, use one of the several manual or electric ice crushers on the market, or a food blender equipped for the purpose; or simply wrap the cubes in a strong towel or double thickness of plastic wrap and break them up with a mallet or a hammer.

OLD-FASHIONED
6 to 10 ounces

STEM COCKTAIL
3 to 4½ ounces

HIGHBALL
8 to 12 ounces

**WHISKEY SOUR
(DELMONICO)**
5 to 7 ounces

TOM COLLINS
10 to 14 ounces

The items of bar equipment shown opposite and listed below are examples of the man useful gadgets available. A muddler, for instance, is helpfu in crushing lump sugar and mixing it with other flavorings Different types of corkscrews, squeezers, strainers and measuring jiggers are shown; you need only one of each.

1 Muddler
2 Double-lever corkscrew
3 Lemon/lime squeezer
4 Shaker strainer
5 Shaker strainer
6 Shaker and mixing glass
7 Bar spoon
8 Martini pitcher and stirring rod
9 Cutting board and knife
10 Shot glasses
11 Double-ended measure (jigger and pony)
12 Lemon/lime squeezer
13 Funnel
14 Ice chipper
15 Ice shovel
16 Waiter's corkscrew

Also useful but not shown are an ice bucket and tongs, a set of measuring spoons for small amounts of flavorings, an 8-ounce measuring cup for larger amounts, and an electric blender equipped to shave ice and blend frozen drinks.

Equivalents and Servings

1 dash = ⅙ teaspoon
1 teaspoon = ⅛ ounce
1 tablespoon = ½ ounce
1 pony = 1 ounce
1 jigger = 1½ ounces
8 ounces = 1 cup

1 pint = 16 ounces = 8 to 10 servings
1 fifth = 25.6 ounces = 12 to 16 servings
1 quart = 32 ounces = 16 to 20 servings
1 bottle wine = 24 ounces = 6 servings
1 split champagne = 6½ ounces = 2 servings
1 quart champagne = 26 ounces = 6 to 8 servings
1 magnum champagne = 52 ounces = 14 to 16 servings

1

2

4

5

6

8

9

10

11

12

13

14

15

16

Glossary

ABSINTHE: Licorice-flavored liqueur composed of aromatic plants and high-proof spirit, usually brandy. Because it contains dangerous oils of wormwood, its sale is prohibited in most countries

ALCOHOL: Colorless, volatile liquid; the intoxicating ingredient in distilled and fermented beverages

ALCOHOLIC BEVERAGE: Any potable liquid containing any amount of alcohol—from less than 1 per cent up to as much as 80 per cent

ALCOOL BLANC (French): Literally, "white alcohol." Brandies distilled from fruit other than grapes. They are white because they are not aged in casks

ALE: Beverage made from brewed and fermented malt or malt and cereal. Fuller-bodied and more bitter than beer

APÉRITIF (French): Literally, "appetizer." A drink served before a meal to whet the appetite. Vermouth and other aromatic wines are the most common apéritifs

APPELLATION CONTRÔLÉE (French): Literally, "controlled place-name." A guarantee that the wine comes from, and meets the standards of, the vineyard, village, district or region stated on the label

AQUAVIT (Scandinavian): Literally, "water of life." Spirit distilled from grain or potatoes and redistilled with a flavoring agent, usually caraway seed

AROMATIC WINE: Fortified wine that has been flavored with herbs, roots, bark or other plant parts

AUSLESE (German): Literally, "selection." Wine made from specially selected, late harvested *Edelfäule* grapes

BEER: Beverage made from brewed and fermented grain; in Europe and the U.S., from malted barley and cereal flavored with hops

BEERENAUSLESE (German): Literally, "berry selection." Wine made from individually selected *Edelfäule* grapes

BITTERS: Spirits of varying alcoholic content flavored with roots, barks and herbs. They are used in mixing drinks, or as apéritifs, liqueurs or digestives

BLANC DE BLANCS (French): Champagne made from the white Chardonnay grape alone, rather than a combination of white and black grapes

BLANC DE NOIRS (French): Champagne made entirely from the black Pinot noir grape

BLENDED WHISKEY: Whiskey made from at least 20 per cent 100-proof straight whiskey blended either with other whiskey or neutral spirits or both, and bottled at no less than 80 proof

BOCK BEER: Strong, dark, sweet beer, brewed in the spring from the residue left in the vats just before they are cleaned each year

BOCKSBEUTEL (German): The short, flat-sided flask in which some German and Chilean wines are shipped

BONDED or BOTTLED IN BOND: Straight whiskey at least four years old and bottled at 100 proof under the supervision of the U.S. Treasury Department Alcohol Tax Unit

BOUQUET: A wine's fragrance and aroma

BREATHING: The development and release of a wine's bouquet and flavor, afer the cork is removed and the bottle is permitted to stand open

BREED: Term used to describe a wine with delicacy and finesse or distinctive character

BRUT (French): The term used for the driest of the champagnes

CAVE (French): Literally, "cellar." *Mis en bouteilles dans nos caves* ("bottled in our cellars") has no official meaning, but is often seen on shippers' blended wines

CHAMBRER (French): To warm a red wine from the cellar by letting it stand at room temperature for an hour or so

CHAPTALIZATION (French): Process of adding sugar to the must, or grape juice, before it ferments. The purpose is not to make sweet wine, but one with a proper minimum alcoholic content

CHÂTEAU (French): Literally, "castle." The traditional name for a vineyard in Bordeaux—although there are a few vineyards in Bordeaux that do not label themselves châteaux, and a few outside Bordeaux that do

CIDER: Apple juice. Fermented apple juice produces "hard cider" or apple wine. In Spain and England, hard cider is occasionally fermented a second time to produce "champagne cider." In the U.S. and France, cider is fermented and distilled to produce apple brandies known as applejack and Calvados

CLARET: Traditional English term for red Bordeaux wine

CLIMAT (French): Burgundian term for vineyard

CLOS (French): Literally, "enclosure." Used to indicate a specific vineyard

CONSUMO (Spanish and Portuguese): Everyday table wine

CORDIAL: *See Liqueur*

CORKY: Term used to describe wine spoiled by an inferior cork, usually detected by unpleasant odor

CORN WHISKEY: Whiskey distilled from a mash of fermented grain, containing at least 80 per cent corn. It is usually not aged

CORSÉ (French): Term used to describe hearty, full-bodied wine

CRÈME: Sweetened spirit or liqueur

CRESCENZ: *See Wachstum*

CRU (French): Literally, "growth," the produce of a particular plot. In Bordeaux, *cru* is equivalent to vineyard and the *crus classés* of the various main districts represent the best vineyards. In Burgundy, there are *grand cru* and *premier cru* vineyards, representing the best and next-best wines of the region respectively. In Beaujolais, the *crus* are not vineyards, but the nine villages whose wines are best. Other wine districts occasionally use *grand cru* on their labels, but there the phrase has no official standing

CUVÉE (French): Usually, a batch or blend of wine, from *cuve*, meaning a vat or cask in which wine is fermented or blended. The *Tête de Cuvée* ("top of the batch") of a château or estate is the best lot of the vintage. A *Première Cuvée* is one of the best wines of a given commune

DISTILLATION: The process of reducing the water content of alcoholic liquids so that they will contain a greater proportion of alcohol. This is done by heating the liquid until the alcohol boils and vaporizes, then catching and cooling the vapors so they condense again into liquid form

DOUX (French): Literally, "sweet." The term used for the sweetest of the champagnes

DRAFT BEER: Beer drawn from a cask

DRY: Not sweet. A term used to describe wines and other drinks

EAU DE VIE (French): Literally, "water of life." A clear spirit or brandy

EDELFÄULE (German): "Noble rot" in grapes similar to the French *pourriture noble*. The resultant juice is rich in sugar and makes wines of *Auslese, Beerenauslese* and *Trockenbeerenauslese* quality

FASS (German): Cask. Many German vintners keep each day's grape picking in separate barrels, and the cask number occasionally appears on labels

FEINE (German): Fine. Used on Moselle labels to indicate an exceptional lot

FERMENTATION: The process by which sugar is broken down into alcohol plus carbon dioxide and other by-products

FIASCO (Italian): The straw-covered flask used for Chianti and some other Italian wines

FIFTH: Bottle containing one fifth of a gallon, or about 25½ ounces

FINE CHAMPAGNE (French): Cognac brandy that is a blend from the two best districts of Cognac: Grand Champagne and Petite Champagne

FINING: Process of clarifying a wine by adding materials that combine with sediment in it and settle to the bottom, leaving the wine itself clear

FLOR (Spanish): A rare, natural kind of yeast, native to Spain but now used in other countries. It forms a white film, or "flower," on the surface of certain wines, mainly sherries, soon after fermentation, and it gives the flavor and bouquet of fino sherry its dry, nutty character

FORTIFIED WINE: Wine whose natural alcoholic content is increased by adding spirits

FOXY: Term used to describe the pronounced "grapy" flavor of wines produced in the Eastern U.S. from Concord, Isabella, Ives, Elvira, Delaware or Catawba grapes; these grapes are of the species *Vitis labrusca*, sometimes known as fox grape

FRIZZANTE (Italian): Semisparkling wine

FRUITY: Term used to describe a young, soft wine such as Beaujolais or Zinfandel. The bouquet and taste of grape is unmistakable

FUDER (German): Moselle term for cask. *See Fass*

GEWÄCHS: *See Wachstum*

GIN: Spirit distilled from grain and flavored with botanicals

GRAND VIN (French): Literally, "great wine." Used on French wine labels, but essentially meaningless

GRAPPA (Italian): *See Marc*

HOCK: English term for Rhine wine

I.N.E. (Italian): Istituto Nazionale per l'Esportazione, government agency which regulates Italian wine production

KABINETT, CABINET (German): Wine of higher than usual quality from the vineyard on whose label this word appears

KELLER (German): Cellar

KELLERABFÜLLUNG: *See Original-Abfüllung*

KELLERABZUG: *See Original-Abfüllung*

KVASS (Russian): Beer brewed from rye, barley and malt, and flavored with mint or cranberries

LAGER (German): Literally, "to store." Sparkling, clear, light-bodied beer that is aged, or "lagered," and then carbonated

LEES: Sediment left in the bottom of a wine cask, pips, stems, etc.

LIGHT: A term used to describe wine low in alcoholic content; "light-bodied" refers to wines or liquors with relatively delicate flavor

LIQUEUR: Alcoholic beverage produced by combining a spirit (usually brandy) with flavoring and sugar

LIQUOR: American term for spirit or alcoholic spirit

MADERISÉ (French): Descriptive term for white wine that has been kept too long and become dark in color and musty in flavor

MALT: Barley or other grain that has been steeped in water and allowed to germinate so that the insoluble starch becomes soluble sugar

MARC (French): Grape pulp left after the wine or juice has been drawn off; also the brandy distilled from this pulp. *Pomace* and *Grappa* mean the same thing

MARQUE DEPOSÉ (French): Literally, "registered trademark." Used with shippers' brand names. When used on labels of great châteaux, it indicates they have registered their labels to avoid imitations

MASH: In whiskey making, grain steeped in hot water to change its starch to sugar. **SWEET MASH** is produced by adding all or nearly all fresh yeast to the mash. **SOUR MASH** is produced by adding some spent beer (yeast from a previous fermentation) to the fresh mash and fresh yeast

MAY WINE: Light white wine in which the leaves of *Waldmeister* (sweet woodruff) have been steeped

MEAD: Ancient Anglo-Saxon beverage made from fermented honey and flavored with herbs

MEZCAL: *See Tequila*

MIS EN BOUTEILLES À LA PROPRIÉTÉ (French): Bottled at the estate. Used occasionally on both Bordeaux and Burgundy labels, it is a guarantee that the wine was both produced and bottled by the grower

MIS EN BOUTEILLES AU CHÂTEAU (French): Bottled at the château or vineyard—a guarantee of authenticity on Bordeaux labels

MIS EN BOUTEILLES AU DOMAINE or MISE AU DOMAINE (French): Estate-bottled wine—a guarantee of authenticity on Burgundy labels

MISTELLE (French): Grape must whose fermentation is prevented by adding enough brandy to give it an alcoholic content of 15 per cent. Mistelles are usually used as sweetening wines in making vermouths and apéritif wines

MONOPOLE (French): Trademark used on labels of wine from a particular shipping firm, such as Heidsieck Monopole champagne

MOUSSEUX (French): Sparkling

MUST: Grape juice

MUSTY: A moldy, unpleasant smell in wines

NATUR, NATURREIN (German): Wine made without the addition of sugar

NÉGOÇIANT (French): Shipper

NOSE: Aroma or bouquet of a wine or spirit. A wine described as "good on the nose" will have extraordinary bouquet

OENOLOGY: Science or study of wine

ORIGINAL-ABFÜLLUNG or ORIG.-ABFG. (German): Term for estate bottling. *Kellerabfüllung, Kellerabzug* and *Schlossabzug* mean the same thing

PÉTILLANT (French): Semisparkling wine

PILSNER: A light, lager type of beer, which derives its name from the original Bohemian Pilsner Urquell made in Pilsen, Czechoslovakia

PIQUANT (French): Pleasant degree of acidity. Usually applied to dry white wines

POMACE (French): *See Marc*

PORTER (English): Rich, sweet ale with a heavy foam, darker and thicker than stout

POURRITURE NOBLE (French): Literally, "noble rot." The mold or yeast *Botrytis cinerea*, which forms on the skins of ripening grapes in France, intensifying their sweetness and flavor. In Germany, the mold is known as *Edelfäule*

PRESS: Apparatus used to squeeze juice from grapes and other fruits

PROOF: System of measuring the alcoholic content of spirit. In the U.S., proof is double the per cent of alcohol (*e.g.,* a whiskey marked 86 proof is 43 per cent alcohol). In Britain "proof spirits" contain 57.1 per cent alcohol; those with less are "under proof" and those with more are "over proof"

PROPRIÉTAIRE (French): Proprietor of a vineyard

RICH: Term used to describe a full-bodied wine with generous bouquet and flavor

RUM: Spirit distilled from the fermented juice of sugar cane or sugar cane products

SACK: Obsolete English term once used for dry fortified wines, mostly sherries, as opposed to sweet ones

SAKE (Japanese): Winelike beverage fermented from rice

SAUTERNES (French): Sweet white wine from the Sauternes district of Bordeaux. California produces both dry and sweet "sauterne" (spelled without the final "s")

SCHLOSSABZUG: *See Original-Abfüllung*

SCHNAPPS (German): Generic term for distilled liquors. In Scandinavia it is spelled *snaps* and refers to aquavit

SEC (French): Literally, "dry." However, when applied to champagne, *sec* refers to one of the sweeter varieties; *brut* is actually the driest

SEDIMENT: Natural deposit or precipitate of crystals and other solids that many wines develop as they are aged in bottle

SOLERA: System for maturing and blending fortified wines, especially Spanish sherries, to produce wines of consistent flavor and quality

SPÄTLESE (German): Literally, "late picking." Wines made from extra-ripe grapes picked after the normal harvest

SPIRIT: Beverage of high alcoholic content obtained by distillation of fermented grapes or other fruit, grains, potatoes, sugar cane, etc.

SPLIT: Wine bottle containing 6 to 6½ ounces—one fourth the size of a regular bottle

SPRITZIG (German): White wine with a slight effervescence

SPUMANTE (Italian): Sparkling wine

STILL: Apparatus used in distilling spirits. Pot stills are the oldest and simplest, used for making full-bodied rums and whiskeys. An alembic still is a kind of pot still used for brandy. Patent stills are newer "continuous" stills, producing purer spirit at a faster rate and in greater quantity

STOUT (English): Very dark, sweet ale with a strong malt flavor

STRAIGHT WHISKEY: According to United States law, any whiskey distilled at no more than 160 proof and aged in new charred oak barrels for a minimum of two years. Bourbon and rye are often bottled straight

STRAVECCHIO (Italian): Extra old

TEQUILA: Spirit distilled from the fermented juice of the base or heart of the maguey plant. Only that made near Tequila, Mexico, may bear the name. Elsewhere the spirit is known as *mezcal*

TROCKENBEERENAUSLESE (German): Literally, "dried berry selection." The finest examples of *Edelfäule* grapes selected berry by berry to produce dessert wine

V.D.Q.S. (French): Vin Delimité de Qualité Supérieur. Legally just a step below the *appellation contrôlée* wines. A number of country wines are entitled to the V.D.Q.S. stamp but their production is limited and they are seldom seen in the United States

V.S.O.: Very Superior Old, a blend of cognacs usually from 12 to 17 years old

V.S.O.P.: Very Superior Old Pale, a blend of cognacs usually from 18 to 25 years old

V.V.S.O.P.: Very, Very Superior Old Pale, a blend of cognacs usually over 25 years old

VIGNERON (French): Winegrower, wine maker or vineyard worker

VIN DU PAYS (French): Wine made and consumed locally

VIN ORDINAIRE (French): Everyday table wine

VINTAGE: Annual grape harvest and the wine made from it. The year frequently appears on wine labels. Certain wines, such as port and champagne, are blends of various years and bear vintage dates only when the wines have come from a single outstanding crop. Thus the term "vintage wine" is sometimes confused with fine wine, even though in most cases the vintage date is simply the year in which any given crop was harvested and may have been good or poor

VODKA (Russian): Literally, "little water." Spirit distilled from various grains or potatoes. In the U.S. it is not flavored or aged and is nearly tasteless

WACHSTUM (German): Growth of a vineyard. When followed by the grower's name, it indicates that the wine is natural and unsugared, although not necessarily estate-bottled. *Gewächs* and *Crescenz* mean the same thing

WEINGUT (German): Vineyard or estate

WHISKEY: Spirit distilled from barley, rye, corn or other grains that have been fermented. The Scots and Canadians spell the word "whisky"; Irish and U.S. distillers spell it with an "e"

WINE: Beverage made from the fermented juice of grapes, occasionally from the juice of other fruit or even flowers like dandelions

WOODY: Descriptive term for the smell of a wine or spirit that has been too long in the cask, or in a cask made of defective wood

General Index
Numerals in italics indicate a photograph or drawing of the subject mentioned.

Credits and Acknowledgments

The sources for the illustrations in this book are shown below. Credits for the pictures from left to right are separated by commas, from top to bottom by dashes.

All photographs in this book are by Arie deZanger except: 4—Charles Phillips, Donald Miller—Clayton Price, Ronald D'Asaro—Donald Miller. 11—Map by Lothar Roth. 12—Right Almadén Vineyards—University of California—center University of California, Max Yavno. 13—University of California except center Fred Lyon from Rapho Guillumette—center Almadén Vineyards, right University of California—Almadén Vineyards except center. 17—The Metropolitan Museum of Art, Rogers Fund, 1917. 30—Tom Hollyman. 35—Ralph Crane. 49 through 53—Brian Seed. 56—Jerry Cooke. 58—Union Centrale Des Arts Decoratifs. 62, 63—Giraudon, Herbert Orth courtesy The Museum of Modern Art, New York. 67—Map by Lothar Roth. 70, 71—Carlo Bavagnoli. 73—Bottom courtesy Champagne Producers of France. 78, 79— Horst Munzig. 81—Map by Lothar Roth. 82, 83— Horst Munzig. 105—Map by Lothar Roth. 106, 107— Pierre Boulat. 108, 109—Bernard G. Silberstein from Rapho Guillumette. 113, 116—Maps by Lothar Roth. 118, 120—David Lees. 122—Map by Lothar Roth. 126, 127—The Bettmann Archive. 129—Maps by Lothar Roth. 130, 131—Fred Lyon from Rapho Guillumette. 140, 165—Maps by Lothar Roth. 166, 167—Pierre Boulat. 170, 171—Brian Seed. 186—Drawing by Matt Greene. 192—Clayton Price, drawings by George V. Kelvin. 193, 197—Drawings by Matt Greene. 198— Drawing by George V. Kelvin. 200—Drawings by Matt Greene.

For their help in the preparation of this book the editors wish to thank the following: in California, H. Peter Jurgens, president, Almadén Vineyards; H. P. Olmo, Professor of Viticulture, University of California, Davis; in New York City, Edgar Adsit, Twenty One Brands Inc.; Bacardi Imports Inc.; Baccarat Inc.; Brewer's Association Inc.; Henry Brown, Vice President, National Distillers & Chemical Corp.; California Wine Association Inc.; Carillon Importers, Ltd.; Michel Dreyfus of Dreyfus, Ashby & Co.; Frank Feinberg, Monsieur Henri Wines Ltd.; French Government Tourist Office; Fernande Garvin; Robert Haas, Barton Distillers Import Corp.; Italian Consulate General Commercial Office; Jean's Silversmiths Inc.; Georg Jensen Inc.; William Kaduson, Edward Gottlieb Associates; La Vieille Russie Inc.; Mamma Leone's Restaurant, Restaurant Associates; Emil Pavone, Bourbon Institute; RHM International Inc.; Schieffelin & Co.; Donald Sozzi, Fontana-Hollywood Corp.; The Spanish Sherry Institute; H. Gregory Thomas, Chanel Inc.; Clifford Weihman; Julius Wile, Julius Wile Sons & Company, Inc.; in New City, N.Y., Everett Crosby, High Tor Vineyard; Burgess Meredith.

Sources consulted in the production of this book include: *A History of Wine* and *Sherry and Port* by Warner H. Allen; *Wine, an Introduction for Americans* by Maynard A. Amerine and V. L. Singleton; *Social History of Bourbon* by Gerald Carson; *The World of Wines* by Creighton Churchill; *Sherry* by Rupert Croft-Cooke; *Grossman's Guide to Wines, Spirits and Beers* by Harold J. Grossman; *Wine* by Hugh Johnson; *Encyclopedia of Wines and Spirits* and *The Wines of France* by Alexis Lichine; *Scotch* by Robert Bruce Lockhart; *Wines and Spirits* by L. W. Marrison; *The Plain Man's Guide to Wine* by Raymond Postgate; *The Wines of Italy* by Cyril Ray; *Notes on a Cellar Book* by George Saintsbury; four books by André Simon: *A Dictionary of Wines and Spirits, Wines and Spirits, a Connoisseur's Textbook, Wines of the World* and *Champagne; American Wines and Wine-Making* by Philip Wagner; *In Praise of Wine* by Alec Waugh; *Gods, Men and Wine* by William Younger.

✗

PRODUCTION STAFF FOR TIME INCORPORATED

John L. Hallenbeck (Vice President and Director of Production), Robert E. Foy and Caroline Ferri. Text photocomposed under the direction of Albert J. Dunn and Arthur J. Dunn.